Simple as ABC

Gilles LEYDIER (dir.),
Les services publics britanniques, 2004, 304 p.

Renée DICKASON (dir.),
Analyses d'images. Patrimoines visuels dans le monde anglophone, 2003, 304 p.

Françoise CAMUS-BADER,
La population britannique au XXe siècle, 2002, 146 p.

Gilbert MILLAT (dir.),
Approches iconographiques de la civilisation britannique, 2002, 176 p.

Nicole MOULINOUX, Marie-Madeleine MARTINET et Marc PORÉE,
L'épreuve de synthèse aux concours du Capes et de l'agrégation, 2001, 270 p.

Jean-Noël EVANNO,
Le New Labour et l'éducation. La « troisième voie » mise à l'essai, 2001, 146 p.

Jean-Pierre MONTREUIL,
La phonologie de l'anglais, 2001, 172 p.

Étienne GALLE et Jacques RABIN,
Poésie de langue anglaise. Introduction et florilège, 2001, 210 p.

Jean-Christophe MAYER (dir.),
Lectures de Shakespeare. Antony and Cleopatra, 2000, 224 p.

Timothy WHITTON (dir.),
Le New Labour. Rupture ou continuité ?, 2000, 284 p.

André PETTON,
Pratique de la version anglaise pour la préparation au DEUG et aux concours, 2000, 204 p.

Odile LUCIENNE-GAREL,
L'anglais des médias. La version de presse et ses difficultés, 1999, 96 p.

Xavier CERVANTES,
L'Angleterre au XVIIIe siècle, 1998, 176 p.

Renée DICKASON,
Radio et télévision britanniques, 1999, 272 p.

Renée DICKASON et Xavier CERVANTES (dir.),
Enseigner la civilisation des pays anglophones, 1998, 352 p.

Robin M. SPITTAL,
Understanding Sports English, 1997, 192 p.

André PETTON,
Guide de la version anglaise pour la préparation au Capes et à l'agrégation, 1997, 200 p.

Emma RENAUD,
L'Angleterre au XVIIe siècle, 1997, 162 p.

Robin M. SPITTAL,
Thèmes anglais. Communication d'entreprise, 1996, 256 p.

RANNOU
Solène

Robin M. SPITTAL

Simple as ABC

Entraînement au thème anglais par le QCM

PRESSES UNIVERSITAIRES DE RENNES

UHB Rennes 2 – Campus de La Harpe
2, rue du doyen Denis-Leroy – 35044 Rennes cedex

www.pur-editions.fr

Mise en pages : Thomas Van Ruymbeke – PUR

ISBN : 2-7535-0255-2
Dépôt légal : 2e semestre 2006

SOMMAIRE

* Les huit premiers textes sont proposés avec une ébauche de traduction à corriger et à améliorer à l'aide du QCM. Les autres textes sont proposés uniquement avec QCM (sans ébauche de traduction).

AVANT-PROPOS

Le QCM comme exercice de révision grammaticale et lexicale est depuis longtemps un classique dans l'apprentissage des langues étrangères ainsi que dans d'autres domaines d'étude. Et comme le thème est souvent conçu en tant qu'application pratique de cette maîtrise de la grammaire et de l'enrichissement lexical, il est logique de proposer des exercices d'entraînement au thème par l'intermédiaire du QCM, sans retomber pour autant dans le 'thème grammatical'.

Même si cette présentation favorise le travail en auto-formation, elle n'exclut pas une utilisation collective avec un apport complémentaire par un enseignant. Il restera toujours des points de détail pour lesquels l'étudiant curieux demandera des éclaircissements, car tout texte est prétexte à un approfondissement et un enrichissement.

Encore des exercices de thème anglais certes, mais avec une approche nouvelle : au lieu de commencer avec une page blanche, et d'avancer mot par mot, le QCM propose des solutions aux principales difficultés et ainsi se forme l'ébauche d'une traduction que l'étudiant affinera par la suite. L'avantage du QCM est de mettre en évidence, à côté d'une réponse acceptable, jusqu'à trois formulations critiquables pour une raison ou une autre, et d'amener l'étudiant – ou le groupe – à réfléchir avant de faire son choix.

Ce recueil ne prétend pas du tout remplacer l'approche traditionnelle, mais lui propose un complément, car la finalité première n'est pas de trouver systématiquement la bonne réponse – cela aide – mais de se servir de l'ensemble des réponses comme prétexte à des explications. Le but des QCM n'est pas de mettre l'étudiant en difficulté, ni de lui tendre des pièges (autres que ceux qu'il se tend à lui-même), mais de l'amener à des choix raisonnés, en éliminant les propositions qui, pour raisons de grammaire, lexique, structure, faux-sens, style ou autre, sont incorrectes. Tant mieux si la réponse est évidente à certaines questions, car souvent les inexactitudes constatées dans les copies ne sont que de simples maladresses dues à un manque de concentration et non pas des preuves d'incompétence ou de faiblesses. En somme, le but est de faire réfléchir, de faire faire des vérifications, d'apprendre à se servir correctement des dictionnaires et autres outils et, le cas échéant – mais pas uniquement en dernier recours – de se faire expliquer la difficulté.

Les aides et outils modernes, et notamment le libre accès aux services de traduction automatique (T.A.O.) sur certains sites Internet, peuvent tromper la vigilance de l'étudiant linguiste, qui ne doit jamais prendre pour argent comptant ce qui s'affiche sur son écran. Si ces productions instantanées peuvent permettre le déchiffrage approximatif d'une langue peu ou pas connue, elles ne peuvent en aucun cas remplacer le travail d'un linguiste spécialiste ni *a fortiori* servir pour la rédaction dans une langue que l'utilisateur ne maîtrise pas.

D'où le besoin absolu d'une vérification du détail et une attention accrue à la révision d'un texte.

Cependant, du point de vue juridique, l'utilisation de ces aides automatiques doit rester strictement personnelle. Donc les huit ébauches présentées ici en guise de premier jet à corriger sont en fait des compilations d'éléments trouvés dans les copies d'étudiants ou le produit de mon imagination. De la même façon, les propositions dans les QCM proviennent des mêmes sources. Cela n'exclut pas que de temps à autre mon imagination, l'étudiant et la TAO puissent se trouver en harmonie l'un avec l'autre.

Si les conditions de travail le permettent, si l'étudiant dispose d'un laps de temps et de réflexion suffisant pour consulter des sources externes, la recherche de documents anglais sur le même sujet est le plus souvent payante. De même, à côté du dictionnaire bilingue, l'étudiant devrait disposer d'un *thesaurus* ou dictionnaire des synonymes, et d'un dictionnaire unilingue anglais-anglais, qui lui apportera des précisions sur l'utilisation des termes par ceux qui pratiquent la langue. La consultation de sites fiables sur Internet est recommandée, ainsi que même des moteurs de recherche.

À titre d'exemple, en tapant le seul mot « *informatics* » on apprend que cette discipline est très éloignée de l'emploi du terme français « informatique ». *Informatics studies the representation, processing, and communication of information in natural and engineered systems. It has computational, cognitive and social aspects. The central notion is the transformation of information – whether by computation or communication, whether by organisms or artifacts. (Edinburgh University School of Informatics, www.inf.ed.ac.uk)*

Il n'y a pas d'ordre privilégié dans ce recueil. On peut travailler aussi bien en fonction de l'intérêt du thème abordé que de l'ordre de présentation, et on peut également mélanger textes avec ébauche de traduction et textes sans ébauche de traduction. De même, il peut être instructif de "panacher" avec l'approche classique d'un texte – sans passer par le QCM – surtout en sous-groupes, où les uns préparent une traduction seuls sans aides, et les autres suivent le déroulement du QCM, pour ensuite mettre ensemble les résultats et en discuter.

Les sources utilisées et les thèmes socio-économiques abordés correspondent aux objectifs de cours tels que anglais des médias ou traduction générale qui figurent dans la plupart des cursus LLCE et LEA. S'agissant pour moitié de propos concernant la Grande-Bretagne, ils apportent quelques éclaircissements sur la vie et offrent en outre la possibilité de recherches plus poussées sur des sites anglophones.

Tous ces textes ont servi dans des TD avec des étudiants en premier cycle jusqu'en Licence, auxquels, en guise de conclusion à l'étude du texte, je fournis un *fair copy* – terme que le dictionnaire a tendance à traduire par 'corrigé'. Preuve s'il en est qu'il faut parfois s'en méfier, car il n'y a pas, en la matière, de 'corrigé' à proprement parler et la traduction proposée ici reste une production personnelle. Le *fair copy* ne reprend pas systématiquement la bonne réponse du QCM, car parfois une énonciation alternative s'avère préférable. Ces traductions plus travaillées privilégient le sens dans le contexte plutôt que la traduction 'mot-pour-mot', s'éloignant ainsi parfois de l'énoncé français dans le but d'enrichir les connaissances de l'apprenant. Elles sont ici accompagnées d'explications détaillées en anglais, selon le même modèle que mon recueil précédent (Thèmes Anglais : Communication d'entreprise, éditions. P.U.R.).

Remerciements

Mes remerciements aux auteurs, éditeurs et ayants droit pour leur aimable autorisation à reproduire les textes à ces fins pédagogiques. Qu'ils trouvent dans l'utilisation faite de leur travail l'expression de ma reconnaissance.

Mes remerciements aussi à mes anciens étudiants qui m'ont servi de cobayes pour ce travail. Que leurs peines et pleurs (quand même pas) puissent faciliter l'apprentissage pour d'autres.

Mes remerciements comme toujours à ma femme pour son soutien et ses encouragements.

Les erreurs éventuelles sont de ma propre responsabilité.

Health Warning

Please keep in mind that the 'right' answer is often simply the best - or the only possible – response from the four alternatives given, and that if other suggestions were put forward, or the sentence were rephrased, or elements from the four suggestions were pieced together, then other, more preferable solutions might surface.

The aim of these exercises is not to trick you the student, but to make you think about the most judicious choices to be made. In the great majority of cases, the choice is logical once you have eliminated common slips in grammar and vocabulary. In other instances, making the right choice involves activating your feel for English and the recognition of words and expressions that are plausible in the context, that 'sound more English', perhaps even the turn of phrase you yourself might have used. And if you can come up with acceptable alternatives, then all the better. Thus a variety of skills are put to use and tested with these exercises. I make no apology if certain points of grammar, structure or vocabulary appear in more than one questionnaire, as experience shows that repetition is sometimes the only way to drum home some important items.

The underlying reasoning behind this collection of texts is that most errors can be avoided if care is taken in re-reading and checking for slips as you write – one eye on what you are writing, the other on what you have written – the 'three Rs' of general translation are 'writing, reading over & re-writing.' Never leave a recognised error in a draft copy, promising that you will correct it later, as often this is the source of false certainties. Correct it immediately, otherwise you will convince yourself that your version is correct English: the *"pourtant-je-l'ai-souvent-vu-écrit-comme ça"* syndrome, to which the reply is systematically –*"you have, in your draft copies"*. Using a word processor with an integrated word-checker, whenever possible, is one simple method of avoiding spelling mistakes.

Use outside sources that you can trust, but never accept blindly what they say. When a bi-lingual dictionary suggests a term that is new to you, then correct usage by native speakers should be checked in an English-English dictionary.

One obvious danger that has recently appeared in student work is recourse to computer-assisted translation, either on commercial software or via the Internet. Although there may have been tremendous improvement, care is needed. A simple term such as '*bureau*' will throw up several possibilities that the software will probably leave the user to choose from. When is a 'bureau' a *desk*, a *study*, an *office*, or a *committee* ... or even on certain occasions a *bureau*? Where software is more trustworthy is in highly-specialised, technical situations where no contextual ambiguity exists. When it comes to grammar and structure, CAT tends to lean in favour of strict adherence to the structure in the original language and this is very often a source of error for the student.

Besides which, if computer-assisted translation was perfect there would be less need for language specialists. As future graduates either in English Studies or in Modern Languages with Business, you should be more capable than machines.

All this is easier said than done, perhaps, as it requires a certain self-confidence and mastery of the language. But by working on the multiple-choice questions, you will form the outline of an acceptable translation, which you should then complete, introducing minor alterations where necessary in order to improve the flow and readability of the final rendering.

The fair copy which is provided later is intended simply as such a final piece of work, and the footnotes which accompany each text are designed to elucidate points which may or may not have come up in the multiple-choice, but which certainly have come up in dealing with the text in class with undergraduate students.

Finally, as said earlier, do not hesitate to seek advice from competent sources.

1

Textes et QCM

Ever since the London-Birmingham M1 was opened in the 1960s, motorways in Britain have been toll-free and 'gridlocked', with the highest levels of traffic flow of all western European countries. Then in 2003 the first toll road – the M6 Toll – around Birmingham came into service.

Alongside the French text there is a draft translation containing several difficulties and errors in English. With the aid of the multiple-choice questions, decide whether the draft suggestion is correct (indicated by 'text') or choose the best suggestion available. Only the more blatant points are covered by the multiple-choice questions. A more polished translation with explanatory footnotes is provided later.

La route payante

1. Les automobilistes britanniques pourraient se voir imposer un « mouchard » dans leur voiture qui permettrait au gouvernement de les taxer en fonction du nombre de kilomètres parcourus et des routes empruntées, selon un projet d'un organisme gouvernemental rendu public dimanche.

The British motorists could see themselves imposing an "informer" in their car which would enable the government to tax them according to the number of traversed kilometres and the borrowed roads, according to a project of a government agency returned public Sunday.

2. Cette proposition figure dans un plan destiné à réduire le trafic routier et les interminables embouteillages aux heures de pointe, en particulier à Londres, selon la Commission for Integrated Transport (CFIT). Ce plan devrait être présenté au gouvernement lundi.

This proposal appears in a plan intended to reduce the road traffic and the interminable congestions at peak hours, in particular in London, according to the Commission for Integrated Transport (CFIT). This plan should be presented to the government Monday.

3. Selon cette proposition, les automobilistes recevrait une facture mensuelle calculée par le système GPS (*Global positioning System*) via des « boîtes noires » fixées sur le tableau de bord des véhicules.

According to this proposal, motorists would receive a month's invoice calculated by GPS (*Global positioning System*) via "black boxes" fixed on the dashboard of the vehicles.

4. La facture pour ceux qui empruntent les axes les plus embouteillés aux heures de pointes pourraient s'élever à des centaines de livres. La taxe serait au minimum de 3,5 pence (6 centimes d'euros) par mile (1,6 kilomètre) et pourrait atteindre 45 p (57 centimes d'euros) par mile à Londres.

The invoice for those which borrow the axes most bottled from the peak hours could rise to hundreds of pounds. The tax would be at least 3,5 pence (6 centimes of euros) by mile (1,6 kilometer) and could reach 45p (57 centimes of euros) by mile in London.

5. « Les routes constituent le seul service public qui est gratuit d'utilisation », a affirmé le président de la CFIT David Begg. « En conséquence, tout le monde veut uti-

"The roads constitute the only public utility which is free of use," the president of the CFIT David Begg asserted. "Consequently, everyone wants to use the same

liser les mêmes routes au même moment. Résultat : des bouchons. Il doit y avoir une meilleure façon de procéder », a-t-il ajouté.

roads at the same time. Result: stoppers. It has to have a better way of proceeding," it added.

6. « Nous en sommes arrivés au point où les embouteillages menacent la santé de plus en plus de personnes. Nous devons en tenir compte », a-t-il ajouté.

"We arrived from there at the point where the congestions menace more and more health of people. We must hold account of it," it added.

7. La responsable des transports au sein de l'opposition conservatrice Theresa May s'est déclarée opposée au projet, affirmant qu'il ne découragerait pas les automobilistes de prendre leur voiture.

The person in charge of transport within the preserving opposition, Theresa May, declared herself opposed to the project, affirming that he would not discourage motorists to take their car.

8. « C'est une fois de plus une tentative d'imposer une taxe déguisée et je ne pense pas que cela marcherait », a-t-elle affirmé à la BBC radio.

"It is once again an attempt to impose a disguised tax and I do not think that that would go," it affirmed with the radio operator BBC.

Agences (279 mots)

1 *Les automobilistes britanniques* (§1)
a – The British motorists *(text)*
b – Britannic motorists
c – Britain's motorists
d – The Britain's motorists

2 *pourraient se voir imposer un « mouchard »* (§1)
a – could see themselves imposing an "informer" in their car *(text)*
b – could find themselves required a "stool pigeon" in their automobile
c – could find themselves with a "spy-in-the-car"
d – could see them obliged to put a "spy-hole" in their vehicle

3 *permettrait au gouvernement* (§1)
a – would enable the government *(text)*
b – would permit the government
c – should make it possible for the government
d – could give leave to the government

4 *(en fonction du) nombre de kilomètres parcourus et des routes empruntées* (§1)
a – the number of traversed kilometres and the borrowed roads *(text)*
b – the number of miles driven and the chosen routes
c – the number of kilometres crossed and the ways taken
d – the number of kilometres clocked up and the routes used

5 *selon un projet d'un organisme gouvernemental rendu public dimanche* (§1)
a – according to a project of a government agency returned public Sunday. *(text)*
b – according to the government's agency's project leaked to the public Sunday.
c – according to a government agency project made public on Sunday.
d – in the opinion of a government agency project published on Sunday.

6 *Ce plan devrait être présenté au gouvernement lundi.* (§2)
a – This plan should be presented to the government Monday. *(text)*
b – This plan ought to be brought forward to the government on Monday.
c – This plan is said to be introduced to the government on Monday.
d – This plan is to be presented to the government on Monday next.

7 *facture mensuelle* (§3)
a – a month's invoice *(text)*
b – a one-month invoice
c – a month's bill
d – a monthly bill

8 *tableau de bord* (§3)
a – dashboard *(text)*
b – instrument panel
c – control panel
d – performance data

9 *ceux qui empruntent les axes les plus embouteillés aux heures de pointes* (§4)
a – those which borrow the axes most bottled from peak hours *(text)*
b – those who use the most congested routes at rush hours
c – these drivers who take the roads the more clogged during peak periods
d – these cars which chose the most blocked throughways at prime time

10 *pourrait atteindre 45p par mile à Londres.* (§4)
a – could reach 45p by mile in London *(text)*
b – could be as high as 45p a mile in London
c – might attain 45p per mile in London
d – could go up to 45p the mile in London

11 *gratuit d'utilisation* (§5)
a – free of use *(text)*
b – freely used
c – free for use
d – free to use

12 *(Résultat) des bouchons* (§5)
a – stoppers *(text)*
b – snarl-ups
c – corks
d – plugs

13 *Il doit y avoir une meilleure façon de procéder* (§5)
a – It has to have a better way of proceeding *(text)*
b – It has to be a better method of moving forward
c – There has to be a best means to carry on
d – There must be a better way of going about things

14 *Nous en sommes arrivés au point où …* (§6)
a – We arrived from there at the point where …*(text)*
b – We have reached the point where…
c – We have arrived just at the right time when…
d – We have come up to scratch where…

15 *menacent la santé de plus en plus de personnes* (§6)
a – menace more and more health of people *(text)*
b – are becoming an ever greater menace to human health
c – more and more threaten the health of peoples
d – represent a health hazard to more and more people

16 *« Nous devons en tenir compte », a-t-il ajouté.* (§6)
a – "We must hold account of it," it added *(text)*
b – "We must keep count of it," he added
c – "We must keep that in mind," he added
d – "We must take account of that," added David Begg

17 *La responsable des transports au sein de l'opposition conservatrice* (§7)
a – The person in charge of transport within the preserving opposition *(text)*
b – The opposition conservative executive manager for transport
c – The group leader for transport in the bosom of the far-right opposition
d – The Conservative shadow transport secretary

18 *il ne découragerait pas les automobilistes de prendre leur voiture* (§7)
a – he would not discourage motorists to take their car *(text)*
b – he would not dishearten motorists who take their car
c – it would not dissuade motorists from using their car
d – it would not put off motorists of driving their car

19 *C'est une fois de plus une tentative d'imposer une taxe déguisée* (§8)
a – It is once again an attempt to impose a disguised tax *(text)*
b – It is yet one more attempt at a sort of stealth tax.
c – It is a further attempt to put up taxes without openly saying so
d – all of the above

20 *je ne pense pas que cela marcherait » a-t-elle affirmé à la BBC radio* (§8)
a – "I do not think that that would go," it affirmed with the radio operator BBC *(text)*
b – "I do not think that would go down well," he asserted to the BBC radio.
c – "I don't think that would operate well," she confirmed to BBC radio
d – "I don't think that that would be effective" she declared on BBC radio.

Although the incident related here dates back a few years now, it was nevertheless a landmark closure, for which the then chairman of M&S, Luc Vandevelde, has only recently been fined (late 2005) by the French courts for non-respect of the normal procedures.

Alongside the French text there is a draft translation containing several difficulties and errors in English. With the aid of the multiple-choice questions, decide whether the draft suggestion is correct (indicated by 'text') or choose the best suggestion available. Only the more blatant points are covered by the multiple-choice questions. A more polished translation with explanatory footnotes is provided later.

Marks & Spencer France

1. Le groupe Galeries Lafayette a fait une offre pour reprendre les 18 grands magasins de Marks & Spencer France et proposer un emploi à chacun de ses 1.500 salariés, à partir du 1er janvier 2002.

The group Galeries Lafayette has made an offer to take again the 18 large stores of Marks & Spencer France and to propose an employment with each of its 1.500 paid, as from January 1 2002.

2. Les 18 magasins français du groupe britannique Marks & Spencer cherchaient un « sauveur » depuis mars, date à laquelle la maison-mère avait annoncé brutalement de fermer 38 magasins en Europe continentale pour se recentrer sur le marché britannique.

The 18 French stores of the British group Marks & Spencer sought a "saver" since March, ever since the house-mother had brutally announced to close 38 stores in continental Europe to recentre itself on the British market.

3. Sans chevalier blanc, les magasins français auraient dû fermer le 31 décembre. « Ce projet est soumis à la condition suspensive d'un avis favorable du Comité central d'entreprise (CCE) et des organisations syndicales de Marks & Spencer », a précisé les Galeries Lafayette, soulignant que son offre « répond au souhait exprimé par Marks & Spencer ».

Without a white knight, the French stores should have closed on December 31st. "This project is subjected to the condition precedent of a favourable opinion of the central committee of company (the CEC) and trade-union organizations of Marks & Spencer", specified Galeries Lafayette, stressing that its offer "answers the wish expressed per Marks & Spencer".

4. L'annonce en a été faite peu auparavant par la direction de Marks & Spencer France à son CCE. Aucune information complémentaire, notamment sur le prix de l'opération et le sort exact des salariés, « ne sera diffusée avant la réunion du CCE de Marks and Spencer », a annoncé mardi la direction des Galeries Lafayette dans un communiqué.

The advertisement of it has been made little before by the direction of Marks & Spencer France with its CEC. No additional information, in particular on the cost of the operation and the exact fate of the em-ployees, "will not be diffused before the meeting of the CEC of Marks & Spencer" Galeries Lafayette announced in an official statement on Tuesday.

5. Pour le groupe français, cet investissement qui s'effectuera à travers un achat

For the French group, this investment, which will be carried out through a pur-

de titres, constitue « un important projet de développement pour le groupe, engagé dans le renouveau des grands magasins et du commerce de centre-ville ».

chase of titles, constitutes "an important development project for the group, engaged in the revival of the stores and commerce of centre city."

6. En Belgique, où aucun repreneur ne s'est présenté, les 4 magasins de l'enseigne, fermeront définitivement le 22 décembre, a annoncé mardi un porte-parole du réseau belge. Les négociations avec les candidats en France avaient débuté en juillet.

In Belgium, where no reprenor presented himself, the 4 stores of the sign, will close definitively on December 22nd, a spokesman of the Belgian network announced on Tuesday. The negotiations with the candidates in France had begun in July.

7. Le nouveau président de Marks & Spencer France, Alain Juillet, nommé début mai pour mener à bien les négociations, avait déclaré qu'il souhaitait une offre globale incluant la reprise de l'ensemble du personnel.

The new president of Marks & Spencer France, Alain Juillet, named beginning May to complete the negotiations, had stated that he wished a total offer including the resumption of the whole of the personnel.

8. Deux candidats français s'étaient intéressés au dossier, Pinault-Printemps-Redoute (PPR) et les Galeries Lafayette, chacun possédant un grand magasin boulevard Haussmann, en face de l'enseigne parisienne de Marks & Spencer. L'offre de PPR était partielle, ne portant que sur 6 à 8 magasins dont certains en Espagne, tandis que les Galeries Lafayette avaient présenté une offre de reprise globale. Mais début octobre, PPR a retiré son offre, jugeant le prix trop élevé, et laissant les Galeries en première ligne.

Two French candidates had been interested in the case file, Pinault-Printemps-Redoute (PPR) and Galeries Lafayette, each one having a large store Haussmann boulevard, opposite the Parisian sign of Marks & Spencer. The offer of PPR was partial, relating only to 6 to 8 stores, whose certain in Spain, while Galeries Lafayette had presented an offer of total recovery. But at the beginning of October, PPR withdrew its bid, considering the price too high, and leaving Galeries Lafayette in first line.

Agences (366 mots)

1 *reprendre les 18 grands magasins de M & S France* (§1)

a – to take again the 18 large stores of Marks and Spencer France *(text)*
b – to buy out the chain of 18 M&S France department stores
c – to win over the 18 major shops of M&S France
d – to buy back the 18 large stores from M&S France

2 *proposer un emploi à chacun de ses 1.500 salariés* (§1)

a – to propose an employment with each of its 1.500 paid *(text)*
b – to offer a work to each of its 1,500 paid workers
c – to suggest jobs to each of its 1 500 employees
d – to safeguard the jobs of the 1,500-strong workforce

3 *cherchaient un « sauveur » depuis mars* (§2)

a – sought a "saver" since March *(text)*
b – had been seeking a "rescuer" since March
c – were looking after a "saver" for March
d – had looked for a "saviour" since March

4 *la maison mère* (§2)

a – the house mother *(text)*
b – the mother house
c – the parent company
d – the mother company

5 *avait annoncé brutalement de fermer 38 magasins en Europe continentale pour se recentrer sur le marché britannique* (§2)

a – had brutally announced to close 38 stores in continental Europe to recentre itself on the British market *(text)*
b – had brutally announced its intention to close down 38 stores in continental Europe to recentre itself on the British market
c – brutally announced the closure of 38 stores in mainland Europe in order to refocus its activities on the British market
d – brutally announced that it would close 38 stores on the mainland of Europe so as to highlight the British market

6 *chevalier blanc* (§3)

a – white knight *(text)*
b – white horseman
c – white rider
d – blank cavalier

7 *auraient dû fermer* (§3)

a – should have closed *(text)*
b – were due to close
c – ought to have been closed
d – might have to be closed

8 *soumis à la condition suspensive d'un avis favorable* (§3)

a – subjected to the condition precedent of a favourable opinion of… *(text)*
b – submitted to the suspensive condition of the favourable notice from…
c – subject to prior approval by…
d – conditioned by the agreement of

9 *le Comité central d'entreprise (CCE)* (§3)

a – the central committee of company (the CCC) *(text)*
b – the company board of directors (the CBD)
c – the central board of control (CBC)
d – the central works committee (CCE)

10 *a précise les Galeries Lafayette* (§3)

a – specified Galeries Lafayette *(text)*
b – Galeries Lafayette precised
c – Galeries Lafayette asserted
d – Galeries Lafayette pointed out

11 *L'annonce en a été faite peu auparavant par la direction à son [CCE]* (§4)

a – The advertisement of it was made little before by the direction with its [CEC] *(text)*
b – The news had been given a short time earlier by the management to the […]
c – A notice had been posted by the directors a little beforehand for the […]
d – The announcement was made little sooner by the executive in front of the […]

12 *ne sera diffusée* (§4)

a – will not be diffused… *(text)*
b – will not be broadcast…
c – is not to be handed out…
d – will be disclosed…

13 *titres* (§5)

a – titles *(text)*
b – royalties
c – shares
d – degrees

14 *engagé dans le renouveau des grands magasins* (§5)

a – engaged in the revival of the stores *(text)*
b – committed to a renewed interest in the department store
c – undertaking the refurbishing of its stores
d – busy with the spring cleaning of its stores

15 *commerce de centre ville* (§5)

a – commerce of centre city *(text)*
b – high street activity
c – town centre business
d – trading city centre

16 *où aucun repreneur ne s'est présenté* (§6)

a – where no reprenor presented himself *(text)*
b – where no buyer introduced himself
c – where no-one has come forward with a rescue package
d – where no purchaser has applied

17 *le nouveau président de M & S France* (§6)

a – the new president of M & S France *(text)*
b – the new managing director of M & S France
c – M & S France's new chairman
d – (b) & (c) but not (a)

18 *nommé début mai pour mener à bien les négociations* (§7)

a – named beginning May to complete the negotiations *(text)*
b – nominated at the beginning of May to lead the negotiations.
c – called in at the beginning of May to confirm the negotiations
d – appointed in early May to conclude the negotiations.

19 *il souhaitait une offre globale incluant la reprise de l'ensemble du personnel* (§7)

a – he wished a total offer including the resumption of the whole of the personnel *(text)*
b – he hoped for a bid from a single buyer which would include keeping on all of the staff.
c – he wanted a global proposal covering hiring the entire personnel
d – he wished for a comprehensive supply enclosing taking back the set of workers.

20 *dossier* (§8)

a – case file *(text)*
b – company record
c – issue
d – venture

21 *en face de l'enseigne parisienne de Marks & Spencer* (§8)

a – opposite the Parisian sign of Marks & Spencer *(text)*
b – face to the Parisian Marks & Spencer shopsign
c – directly opposite the Paris branch of Marks & Spencer
d – opposing the Paris Marks & Spencer trade name

22 *dont certains en Espagne* (§8)

a – whose certain in Spain *(text)*
b – some of which in Spain
c – of which certain Spanish ones
d – whose in Spain are certain

23 *une offre de reprise globale* (§8)

a – an offer of total recovery *(text)*
b – a tender for global takeover
c – an offer of worldwide revival
d – all-inclusive bid for the whole business

24 *PPR a retiré son offre, jugeant le prix trop élevé* (§8)

a – PPR withdrew its bid, considering the price too high *(text)*
b – PPR removed its offer, judging the price too expensive
c – PPR took back its supply, in view of too high costs
d – all of the above

25 *laissant les Galeries Lafayette en première ligne* (§8)

a – leaving Galeries Lafayette in first line. *(text)*
b – leaving Galeries Lafayette in the prime line
c – leaving Galeries Lafayette in the firing line
d – leaving Galeries Lafayette in the front line

Open hunting season once again for the banks ! Whether in Britain, France or elsewhere, the banking world often comes under attack for ripping off customers. This is only one such incident.

Alongside the French text there is a draft translation containing several difficulties and errors in English. With the aid of the multiple-choice questions, decide whether the draft suggestion is correct (indicated by 'text') or choose the best suggestion available. Only the more blatant points are covered by the multiple-choice questions. A more polished translation with explanatory footnotes is provided later.

La BNP

Retraits :
la BNP facture au guichet

1. Les clients de la banque seront désormais facturés 5 euros pour tout retrait inférieur à 150. Les associations de consommateurs sont furieuses.

2. La facturation des retraits au guichet est entrée en vigueur officiellement vendredi à la BNP-Paribas, malgré la colère des associations de consommateurs. Les clients de la banque, qui justifie sa décision par des impératifs de sécurité, seront désormais facturés cinq euros pour tout retrait inférieur à 150 €.

3. Le but de cette facturation controversée est de « disponibiliser nos collaborateurs aux guichets pour qu'ils puissent davantage apporter des conseils à nos clients », a expliqué Yves Martrenchar, directeur marketing du groupe, sur France-3. Il s'agit aussi de «faire en sorte qu'il y ait moins de fonds dans les agences pour dissuader les malfaiteurs», donc « plus de sécurité ».

FRAGILISATION

4. La banque souhaite supprimer dans la pratique la plupart des petits retraits d'espèces au guichet. Les personnes qui ne dis-

Retreats: the BNP
charge to the ticket office

The customers of the bank will henceforth be charged 5 euros for any retreat lower than 150 euros. Consumers' associations are furious.

The invoicing of retreats in the ticket office came into effect officially on Friday in the BNP-Paribas, in spite of the anger of consumers' associations. The customers of the bank, which justifies its decision by imperatives of safety, will henceforth be charged five euros for any retreat lower than 150 €.

The purpose of this controversial invoicing is of "dispose our co-workers in counters so that they can more bring advices to our customers", explained Yves Martrenchar, marketing director of the group, on France-3. It is a question as well "to see to it that there are fewer capital in agencies to dissuade the criminals", thus "more safety".

FRAGILISATION

The bank wishes to abolish in the practice most of the small retreats of sorts in the ticket office. The persons who do not

posent pas de carte bancaire doivent se voir attribuer une carte de retrait gratuite.

arrange a check card should see attributing a free card of retreat.

5. Selon Serge Maitre, secrétaire général de l'Association française des usagers des banques, cette mesure risque de fragiliser les clients auxquels elle va s'appliquer. «C'étaient des populations qui traditionnellement refusaient en raison de leur insécurité, de leur âge, les cartes de débit, de paiement, de retrait et on les force à aller aux distributeurs », a-t-il déploré sur France-3. « La banque met un obstacle à un accès libre à cet argent. »

According to Serge Maitre, General Secretary of the French Association of the users of banks, this measure risks to weaken the customers to whom it is going to apply. "There were populations which traditionally refused because of their insecurity, of their age, the cards of debit, payment, retreat and one forces them to go to the distributors", he regretted on France-3. "The bank puts an obstacle to a free access in this silver."

6. La BNP, qui a annoncé cette mesure au mois d'octobre, avait alors assuré que les retraits demeureraient possibles gratuitement lorsque l'agence ne comporte pas de distributeur, en cas d'appareil indisponible, de retrait demandé supérieur au plafond de la carte, et pour les clients dans l'incapacité d'utiliser le distributeur en raison d'un handicap, de leur état de santé ou de leur âge.

The BNP, who announced this measure in October, had then assured that retreats would remain possible free of charge when the agency does not contain a distributor, in case of inalienable device, if retreat wanted superior to the ceiling of the card, and for the customers in the incapacity to use the distributor because of a handicap, of their state of health or their age.

Le Nouvel Observateur (299 mots)

1 *Retraits : la BNP facture au guichet* (Titre)

a – Retreats: the BNP charge to the ticket office *(text)*
b – BNP charges for withdrawals from teller points
c – BNP makes pay customers charges
d – Retirements : BNP invoices at the counter.

2 *désormais* (§1)

a – henceforth *(text)*
b – from now on in
c – in the hereafter
d – all of the above

3 *inférieur à 150 €* (§1)

a – lower than 150 € *(text)*
b – below € 150
c – beneath 150 €
d – inferior to 150 €

4 *malgré la colère des associations de consommateurs.* (§2)

a – in spite of the anger of consumers' associations. *(text)*
b – despite of the rage of consumer associations.

c – notwithstanding the wrath of consumers' associations.
d – all of the above.

5 *par des impératifs de sécurité* (§2)

a – by imperatives of safety *(text)*
b – on grounds of security.
c – for the necessity of law and order
d – at the demand of safety

6 *disponibiliser nos collaborateurs* (§3)

a – dispose our co-workers *(text)*
b – avail our employees
c – free our counter staff
d – access our collaborators

7 *qu'ils puissant davantage apporter des conseils à nos clients* (§3)

a – so that they can more bring advices to our customers *(text)*
b – so that they can give more advices to our clientele
c – so that they are more available to advise our clients
d – so that they are more disposed to help our consumers

8 *faire en sorte que* (§3)

a – to see to it that *(text)*
b – to take steps so that
c – to ensure that
d – all of the above

9 *moins de fonds* (§3)

a – fewer capital *(text)*
b – less funding
c – fewer currency
d – less cash

10 *FRAGILISATION* (§4)

a – Fragilisation *(text)*
b – Vulnerability
c – Weakening
d – Fragility

11 *la plupart des petits retraits d'espèces* (§4)

a – most of the small retreats of sorts *(text)*
b – the most small retirements of money
c – the smallest kinds of cash
d – the majority of cash withdrawals for small sums

12 *les personnes qui ne disposent pas de carte bancaire* (§4)

a – The persons who do not arrange a check card *(text)*
b – Customers who have no bank card.
c – Those who do not dispose of a bank card
d – The people who do not draw up a cheque card.

13 *doivent se faire attribuer une carte de retraite gratuite* (§4)

a – should see attributing a free card of retreat. *(text)*
b – should make themselves given a free card.
c – must be awarded a retreat card free of charge
d – will be given a cash card free of charge.

14 *cette mesure risque de fragiliser les clients* (§5)

a – this measure risks to weaken the customers *(text)*
b – this measure is likely to embrittle those customers
c – this measure threatens to work against those customers
d – this measure risks injuring the customers

15 *C'étaient des populations* (§5)

a – There were populations *(text)*
b – It was peoples
c – These are civilians
d – It is those sections of the public

16 *distributeurs* (§5)

a – distributors *(text)*
b – retailers
c – automated telling machines
d – vending machines

17 *met un obstacle à un accès libre à cet argent* (§5)

a – puts an obstacle to a free access in this silver (*text*)
b – places a fence to a free access in this money
c – denies them free access to their money
d – hinders a free approach at this cash.

18 *avait alors assuré* (§6)

a – had then assured (text)
b – then insured
c – gave the assurance at the time
d – had so assured

19 *en cas d'appareil indisponible* (§6)

a – in case of inalienable device (text)
b – in the event of an immutable appliance
c – if the apparatus was engaged
d – if the machine was out of order

20 *[en cas] de retrait demandé supérieur au plafond de la carte* (§6)

a – of a retreat wanted superior to the ceiling of the card (*text*)
b – if the amount requested exceeded that allowed
c – if the figure was superior to the card's maximum
d – when greater amounts than permitted were demanded

The years may pass – Blair is now in his 10th year as PM and bird flu has replaced Sydney flu – but the theme of healthcare is still topical and remains for the British electorate one of the principal benchmarks of a government's record.

Alongside the French text there is a draft translation containing several difficulties and errors in English. With the aid of the multiple-choice questions, decide whether the draft suggestion is correct (indicated by 'text') or choose the best suggestion available. Only the more blatant points are covered by the multiple-choice questions. A more polished translation with explanatory footnotes is provided later.

La Méthode Blair grippée

La méthode Blair grippée

1. *Des soins médicaux à l'euro, la grogne des Britanniques grandit. 49 % d'opinions favorables à Tony Blair (contre 62% en avril). Cette baisse s'explique surtout par les défaillances du système de santé.*

2. Il est des manchettes dont le Premier ministre le plus populaire de l'après-guerre se passerait. « *Les problèmes s'accumulent pour les travaillistes* », titrait hier le quotidien *Guardian*, pourtant proche de ce parti. Un sondage, ce week-end, confirmait que l'étoile de Tony pâlissait. En neuf mois, sa popularité jusqu'à présent inoxydable est passée de 62 % d'opinions favorables à 49 %. Un chiffre encore enviable après deux ans et demi de gouvernement, d'autant que la droite reste dans les choux, mais pour la première fois les électeurs se disent mécontents d'un Premier ministre à qui tout paraissait réussir.

3. **Morgues improvisées.** Le méchant virus de la grippe de Sydney qui a mis à nu l'état lamentable des services de santé est la cause principale de ce détachement des Britanniques. Depuis deux semaines, les journaux et télés sont remplis d'histoires désolantes de cancéreux condamnés à attendre des mois une opération salvatrice en raison de la surcharge des hôpitaux, de morgues improvisées et de médecins et infirmières se déclarant incapables de bien

The Blair method seized

Medical care to the euro, the discontent of the British grows. 49% of opinions favourable to Tony Blair (against 62% in April). This fall is explained especially by the failures of the system of health.

It is cuffs whose the most popular Prime Minister for the post-war period would do. "*The problems accumulate for the Labour Party*", titled the daily Guardian yesterday, however near to this party. A survey, this weekend, confirmed that the star of Tony faded. In nine months, his popularity until now stainless passed from 62 % of opinions favourable to 49 %. A figure still enviable after two years and half of government, the more so as the right remains in the cabbages, but for the first time the voters are dissatisfied with a Prime Minister with whom all appeared to succeed.

Impromptu mortuaries. The malicious flu bug of Sydney which exposed the lamentable state health services is the principal cause of this detachment of the British. For two weeks, the newspapers and TVS have been filled with afflicting stories of cancer patients condemned to await months a saving operation because of the overload of the hospitals, of impromptu mortuaries and doctors and nurses declaring them unable to look after well. Last

soigner. Dimanche dernier, le Premier ministre, sentant l'orage, a donné d'urgence une interview à la BBC. Blair est apparu défensif, reconnaissant que le National Health Service (NHS) était malade et promettant de le mettre au niveau des systèmes de santé français ou allemand. Le NHS, créé après la guerre par les travaillistes et supposé offrir des soins gratuits et universels « *du berceau à la tombe* », est l'un des symboles les plus sensibles pour les Britanniques. Ils ne comprennent pas que Blair, après dix-huit ans de thatchérisme, n'ait pas réussi à enrayer son démantèlement quitte à augmenter les impôts. Comme si sur le NHS, la méthode Blair de beaucoup promettre sans vouloir fâcher les éléments les plus conservateurs de l'électorat avait trouvé ses limites.

Sunday, the Prime Minister, feeling the storm, gave urgently an interview to the BBC. Blair appeared defensive, grateful that the National Health Service (NHS) was sick and promising to bring it to the level of the systems of French or German health. The NHS, created after the war by the Labour Party and supposed to offer free and universal care *"cradle to the tomb"*, is one of the most significant symbols for the British. They do not understand that Blair, after eighteen years of Thatcherism, has not succeeded in stopping its dismantling even if it means to increase the taxes. As if, on the NHS, the Blair method of promising much without wanting to annoy the most conservative elements of the electorate had reached its limits.

4. **Cherie contre Tony.** Sur l'euro, ce Premier ministre qui ne prend que des risques contrôlés est confronté au même problème. Tony Blair s'est dit favorable à la monnaie unique mais comme il sait l'euro impopulaire, ni lui ni son gouvernement n'ont le courage de défendre ce grand dessein. Résultat : le *Guardian* faisait état hier d'un sondage montrant que jamais autant de Britanniques – 63% – étaient opposés à la monnaie européenne.

Cherie counters Tony. On the euro, this Prime Minister who does not only take controlled risks is confronted with the same problem. Tony Blair is known as favourable to the single currency but like he knows the unpopular euro, neither him nor his government have courage to defend this great intention. Result: Guardian made yesterday a survey showing that never as many British – 63% – was opposed to the European currency.

5. Autre souci pour Blair, la nomination du candidat à la mairie de Londres, qui risque, malgré tous ses efforts, de revenir à Ken Livingstone, surnommé « Red Ken », en raison de ses idées socialistes bon teint aux antipodes du New Labour. Mais Livingstone reste le plus populaire des candidats, et les Londoniens ne veulent pas de l'homme parachuté par le Premier ministre. Dernier problème – familial – pour Tony: sa femme Cherie, en sa qualité d'avocate de la confédération syndicale, le Trade Union Congress, et enceinte de cinq mois, a pris fait et cause contre une mesure prise par son époux limitant les congés maternité et a porté plainte...

Another concern for Blair, the nomination of the candidate for the town hall of London, which, despite all his efforts, is likely to go to Ken Livingstone, called "Red Ken", because of his socialist ideas good dye with the antipodes of New Labour. But Livingstone remains most popular of the candidates, and the Londoners do not want of the man parachuted by the Prime Minister. Last problem – family – for Tony: its Cherie wife, in her capacity as lawyer of the trade-union confederation, Trade Congress Union, and expecting five months, took fact and cause against a measure taken by her husband limiting the vacation maternity and lodged a complaint...

François Sergent, *Libération*
(503 mots)

1 *La méthode Blair grippée* (titre)
a – The Blair method seized *(text)*
b – The Blair method caught the flu
c – The Blair method hiccups
d – The Blair method on sick leave

2 *Il est des manchettes dont le PM se passerait* (§2)
a – It is cuffs whose the PM would do *(text)*
b – There are forearm smashes which the PM would refrain from
c – There are sleeves which the PM would take the place of
d – There are headlines the PM could well do without

3 *titrait hier le quotidien Guardian* (§2)
a – titled the daily Guardian yesterday *(text)*
b – the daily newspaper the Guardian titled yesterday
c – yesterday's Guardian newspaper proclaimed
d – headlined yesterday the everyday Guardian

4 *pourtant proche de ce parti* (§2)
a – however near to this party *(text)*
b – although generally sympathetic to this party
c – nevertheless a close relation to this party
d – even so similar to this party

5 *(sa popularité) jusqu'à présent inoxydable* (§2)
a – until now stainless *(text)*
b – rust-proof as far as the present-day
c – up to now non-oxidising
d – as yet untarnished

6 *un chiffre encore enviable après deux ans et demi de gouvernement* (§2)
a – a figure still enviable after two years and half of government *(text)*
b – a still desirable number after two years and a half of government.
c – a yet enviable amount halfway through their mandate
d – not a bad score after two and a half years in power.

7 *d'autant que la droite reste dans les choux* (§2)
a – the more so the right remains in the cabbages *(text)*
b – as much as the Tories stay in a mess
c – all the more so as the Tories are completely outdistanced
d – in proportion as the right-wing is finished

8 *à qui tout paraissait réussir* (§2)
a – with whom all appeared to succeed *(text)*
b – to whom nothing seemed impossible
c – who seemed unable to put a foot wrong
d – for whom everything came out successful

9 *l'état lamentable des services de santé* (§3)
a – the lamentable state health services *(text)*
b – the deplorable state of the health services
c – the mournful state services of health
d – the pathetic health state services

10 *condamnés à attendre des mois une opération salvatrice* (§3)
a – condemned to await months a saving operation *(text)*
b – sentenced to attend for months a blessed operation
c – obliged to wait for months for a life-saving operation
d – terminally ill to expect a hopeful operation

11 *se déclarant incapables de bien soigner* (§3)
a – declaring them unable to look after well *(text)*
b – declaring themselves unfit to take care.
c – who said they were incapable of looking after patients adequately.
d – admitting their incapacity to provide proper care.

12 *sentant l'orage* (§3)
a – feeling the storm *(text)*
b – scenting danger
c – smelling the clouds gathering
d – touching the thunder

13 *reconnaissant que le NHS était malade* (§3)
a – grateful that the NHS was sick *(text)*
b – admitting that the NHS was in poor shape
c – thankful that the NHS was not well
d – granting that the NHS had fallen ill

14 *« du berceau à la tombe »* (§3)
a – "from the cradle to the tomb" *(text)*
b – "from the cradle to the grave"
c – "from the crib to the tomb"
d – "from the birthplace to the place of burial"

15 *que Blair n'ait pas réussi à enrayer son démantèlement* (§3)
a – that Blair has not succeeded in stopping its dismantling *(text)*
b – that Blair did not succeed to stop its dismantling
c – that Blair would not have managed to halt it crumbling
d – that Blair might not have managed stopping its breakdown

16 *quitte à augmenter les impôts* (§3)
a – even if it means to increase the taxes *(text)*
b – even at the cost of increasing taxes
c – should it mean to increase the taxes
d – leaving aside taxes which are to increase

17 *Comme si sur le NHS, la méthode Blair de beaucoup promettre … avait trouvé ses limites* (§3)
a – As if, on the NHS, the Blair method of promising much … had reached its limits *(text)*
b – Like if on the NHS, the Blair method to promise much … had met his limitations.
c – Just as the Blair method full of promise … had bordered on the NHS
d – How if on the NHS the Blair method had found his limits.

18 *Cherie contre Tony* (§4)
a – Cherie counters Tony *(text)*
b – Cherie thwarts Tony
c – Cherie versus Tony
d – Cherie refutes Tony

19 *qui ne prend que des risques contrôlés* (§4)
a – who does not only take controlled risks *(text)*
b – who not only takes controlled risks
c – who only takes risks that have been checked
d – who never puts himself out on a limb

20 *est confronté au même problème* (§4)
a – is confronted with the same problem. *(text)*
b – is faced to the same problem.
c – is in front of the same problem.
d – faces up to the same problem.

21 *Tony Blair s'est dit favorable à la monnaie unique* (§4)
a – TB is known as favourable to the single currency *(text)*
b – TB is said to be in favour of the single currency
c – TB has declared himself to be in favour of the single currency
d – TB is thought to be for the single currency

22 *mais comme il sait l'euro impopulaire* (§4)
a – but like he knows the unpopular euro *(text)*
b – but as he knows the euro to be unpopular
c – but as he knows the euro unpopular
d – but since the euro became unpopular to his knowledge

23 *qui risque, malgré tous ses efforts, de revenir à Ken Livingstone* (§5)
a – which, despite all his efforts, is likely to go to Ken Livingstone *(text)*
b – which, despite of his efforts, will probably come back to Ken Livingstone
c – which, in spite of all his efforts, is to return to Ken Livingstone
d – which risks, even though his efforts, to revert to Ken Kivingstone

24 *ses idées socialistes bon teint* (§5)
a – its socialist ideas good dye *(text)*
b – his good dye socialist ideas
c – his dyed-in-the-wool socialism
d – his die-good socialism

25 *aux antipodes du New Labour.* (§5)
a – with the antipodes of New Labour *(text)*
b – which is everything that New Labour is not
c – on the opposite of New Labour
d – on the other side of the world from New Labour

26 *les Londoniens ne veulent pas de l'homme parachuté par le Premier ministre* (§5)
a – Londoners do not want of the man parachuted by the PM *(text)*
b – Londoners don't want anything from the PM's parachutist
c – Londoners won't hear of the PM's choice of candidate
d – Londoners bear a grudge to the PM's outsider

27 *et enceinte de cinq mois* (§5)
a – and expecting five months *(text)*
b – and with a five-month expectancy
c – and five months in labour
d – and five months pregnant

28 *a pris fait et cause contre une mesure* (§5)
a – took fact and cause against a measure *(text)*
b – took up somebody's cause against a measure
c – implored against a measure
d – stood out against a measure

29 *(limitant) les conges maternité* (§5)
a – the vacation maternity *(text)*
b – maternity leave
c – maternity holidays
d – motherhood vacations

30 *et a porté plainte* (§5)
a – and lodged a complaint *(text)*
b – and pressed charges
c – and took it to court
d – and undertook a protest

Such business practices hit the headlines in France with the €29m pension awarded to Daniel Bernard, ex-CEO of Carrefour.

Alongside the French text there is a draft translation containing several difficulties and errors in English. With the aid of the multiple-choice questions, decide whether the draft suggestion is correct (indicated by 'text') or choose the best suggestion available. Only the more blatant points are covered by the multiple-choice questions. A more polished translation with explanatory footnotes is provided later

Les actionnaires privent « Chat Gras » Garnier de parachute

Shareholders deprive fat cat Garnier of his golden parachute

1. « *Privons les 'chats gras' de crème* » : tel est le leitmotiv de la campagne des grands actionnaires britanniques qui, le 19 mai, ont refusé la rémunération royale versée au Français Jean-Pierre Garnier. Le directeur général du deuxième groupe pharmaceutique mondial, GlaxoSmithKline (GSK), il est vrai, s'est octroyé un « *parachute en or* » de 22 millions de livres (31 millions d'euros) à son départ, même en cas de renvoi pour mauvaise gestion. Sans parler d'une rémunération de 6 millions de livres ! Or la performance à la tête de la multinationale ne semble pas justifier ces émoluments : Garnier a fait perdre à ses actionnaires plus d'un tiers de leurs investissements.

2. Ce camouflet est une première dans le monde des affaires britannique depuis la promulgation, fin 2001, d'une législation obligeant les sociétés cotées en Bourse à consulter leurs actionnaires sur les salaires versés aux principaux dirigeants. « *L'impact de cette décision dépasse de loin GSK. Il faut désormais légiférer pour contrôler ces excès obscènes* » : le secrétaire général d'Amicus, le plus gros syndicat du groupe, juge parfaitement normal que le responsable d'un grand groupe reçoive un salaire très élevé pour soutenir une comparaison internationale, mais à condition que les

1. *"Let's steal the fat cats' cream":* this was the campaign war-cry from the large British shareholders who, on May 19, refused the royal remuneration paid to the French Jean-Pierre Garnier. The general manager of the second world pharmaceutical group, GlaxoSmithKline (GSK) admittedly had granted himself a golden parachute of 22 millions of pounds (31 million euros) on his departure, even in the event of severance as a result of mismanagement. Without speaking about a remuneration of 6 millions of pounds! However his performance at the head of the multinational does not seem to justify this payment: Garnier made his shareholders lose more than one third of their investments.

2. This comeuppance is a first in British business circles since the promulgation, at the end of 2001, of a legislation obliging companies quoted at the Stock Exchange to consult their shareholders on the wages paid to the principal leaders. "The impact of this decision outnumbers GSK by far. It is necessary from now on to legislate to control these obscene excesses": the general secretary of Amicus, the largest trade union in the group, judges perfectly normal that the responsible of a big group receives very high wages to support an international comparison, but provided

résultats soient eux aussi de classe internationale.

that the results are also of international class.

3. Le problème des *chats gras*, certes, n'est pas isolé. Mais qu'un pays traditionnellement plus aristocratique dans son approche des relations sociales et moins volontariste en matière économique que la France soit le théâtre de tels mouvements en dit long sur l'acuité de la question des différences de revenus en Grande-Bretagne. Ajoutez la bonne vieille habitude britannique consistant à démolir le succès, le déclin du respect de l'opinion pour toutes les institutions et une presse populaire en quête d'événements racoleurs, et vous avez tous les ingrédients du « Garniergate », qui défraie aujourd'hui la chronique des affaires.

3. The problem of the fat cats is certainly not isolated. But that a country traditionally more aristocratic in its approach of the social relations and less volontarist in economic matter that France is the theatre of such movements talks long about it on the acuity of the question of the revenue differences in Great Britain. Add the good old British custom of belittling success, the decline of the respect of the opinion for all the institutions and a popular press in quest of astounding events, and you have all the ingredients of the "Garniergate", which defrays today the chronicle of the businesses

4. « *Nous prenons ce vote très au sérieux* » : devant l'ampleur de la protestation de l'actionnariat, le président du groupe, Sir Christopher Hogg, s'est engagé à mettre en application le message de ses actionnaires.

Marc Roche, *Le Monde* (337 mots)

4. "We very take this vote very seriously": in front of the extent of the protest of the shareholding, the president of the group, Sir Christopher Hogg, committed himself to put in application the message of his shareholders.

1 *leitmotiv de la campagne* (§1)
- a – campaign war-cry *(text)*
- b – motto of the countryside activists
- c – motive of the campaign
- d – none of the above

2 *les grands actionnaires britanniques* (§1)
- a – the large British shareholders *(text)*
- b – important British shareholders
- c – majority British shareholders
- d – the great British shareholders

3 *ont refusé la rémunération royale versée au Français Jean-Pierre Garnier* (§1)
- a – refused the royal remuneration paid to the French Jean-Pierre Garnier *(text)*
- b – rejected the reward paid by the Queen to the Frenchman J-P Garnier
- c – refused to approve the princely sum to be paid to Frenchman J-P Garnier
- d – declined to accept the majestic bonus paid to French J-P Garnier.

4 *directeur général du deuxième groupe pharmaceutique mondial* (§1)
- a – general manager of the second world pharmaceutical group *(text)*
- b – director-general of the second world's pharmaceutical group
- c – top executive with the second global pharmaceutical company
- d – CEO of the world's second largest pharmaceutical group

5 *même en cas de renvoi pour mauvaise gestion* (§1)

a – even in the event of severance as a result of mismanagement *(text)*
b – even if he is made redundant for bad running of the company.
c – still if he is fired for improper accountability
d – yet if he is laid off for poorly managing.

6 *Sans parler d'une rémunération de 6 millions de livres* (§1)

a – Without speaking about a remuneration of 6 millions of pounds !*(text)*
b – And that's on top of a £6m annual salary !
c – Without negotiating a fee of £6 millions !
d – He even kept secret an allowance of 6 million pounds !

7 *Garnier a fait perdre à ses actionnaires plus d'un tiers de leurs investissements* (§1)

a – Garnier made his shareholders lose more than one third of their investments. *(text)*
b – Garnier was responsable of shareholders losing over one third of their investment.
c – shareholders saw their investments shrink by over one third under Garnier's stewardship
d – all of the above

8 *camouflet* (§2)

a – comeuppance *(text)*
b – slap in the face
c – backlash
d – all of the above

9 *une première dans le monde des affaires britannique* (§2)

a – a first in British business circles *(text)*
b – a prime in the British business associations
c – a première in British financial society
d – an initial step in the world of British business

10 *depuis la promulgation d'une législation* (§2)

a – since the promulgation of a legislation *(text)*
b – since the announcement of legislation
c – since the publication of an enactment
d – since the introduction of a law

11 *sociétés cotées en Bourse* (§2)

a – companies quoted at the Stock Exchange*(text)*
b – highly-thought-of firms
c – publicly-owned companies
d – societies valued by the Stock Exchange

12 *salaires versés aux principaux dirigeants* (§2)

a – wages paid to the principal leaders *(text)*
b – pay packages awarded to boardroom members
c – salaries given to the main executives
d – pay handed over to the most important staff members

13 « *L'impact de cette décision dépasse de loin GSK* » (§2)

a – "The impact of this decision far outnumbers GSK" *(text)*
b – "The effect of this decision overtakes GSK by a long way."
c – "This decision's impact can't be resolved by GSK alone"
d – "The shock waves of this vote will ripple far beyond GSK"

14 *que le responsable d'un grand groupe reçoive un salaire très élevé pour soutenir une comparaison internationale* (§2)

a – that the responsible of a big group receives very high wages to support an international comparison*(text)*
b – that the person charged with responsibility for a great group get a very high income to stand up to comparison internationally
c – that the chief executive of a major group should be paid a world-scale salary
d – that the general manager of an important group have a salary at an international level.

15 *Le problème des chats gras, certes, n'est pas isolé* (§4)

a – The problem of the fat cats is certainly not isolated *(text)*
b – The question of fat cats should surely not be separated out from others
c – Admittedly the topic of fat cats is not a flash in the pan
d – Fat cat pay is certainly not the only problem on the British horizon.

16 *son approche des relations sociales* (§3)

a – its approach of social relations *(text)*
b – its approach to social relationships
c – its approach to corporate affairs
d – its approach to industrial partnerships

17 *moins volontariste en matière économique que la France* (§3)

a – less volontarist in economic matter that France*(text)*
b – more *laissez-faire* than France when it comes to economic issues
c – less determined in its attitude to the economy in contrast to France
d – more liberally-minded as regards economical questions unlike France.

18 *en dit long sur l'acuité de la question des différences des revenus en Grande-Bretagne* (§3)

a – talks long about it on the acuity of the question of the revenue differences in Great Britain *(text)*
b – speaks lengthily about the acuteness of the question of British income differences
c – says a lot about how sharply the earnings gap is felt in Britain
d – is eloquent at length on the keenness of the topic of income differences in Britain

19 *démolir le succès* (§3)

a – belittling success *(text)*
b – tearing triumph to pieces
c – pulling down what has been built up
d – shattering achievement

20 *le déclin du respect de l'opinion pour toutes les institutions* (§3)
a – the decline of the respect of the opinion for all the institutions *(text)*
b – people's increasingly low regard for the Establishment
c – the down-turn in the respect for the opinion of all the institutions
d – the deterioration in respect of the opinion for any authority

21 *une presse populaire en quête d'évènements racoleurs* (§3)
a – a popular press in quest of astounding events*(text)*
b – a tabloid press hungry for sensationalism
c – a popular press in search of shocking happenings
d – a gutter press touting for headlines

22 *qui défraie aujourd'hui la chronique des affaires* (§3)
a – which defrays today the chronicle of the businesses *(text)*
b – which features currently in all the business sections of the newspapers
c – which reveals in full daylight the seamier side of the business world
d – which discredits the chronic state of business today

23 *devant l'ampleur de la protestation de l'actionnariat* (§4)
a – in front of the extent of the protest of the shareholding *(text)*
b – given the importance of the shareholders' revolt
c – face to the wide range of the protestation by the shareholders
d – in response to the scale of investor anger

24 *le président du groupe, Sir Christopher Hogg* (§4)
a – the president of the group, Sir Christopher Hogg*(text)*
b – Sir President Christopher Hogg
c – Group Chairman Sir Christopher Hogg
d – the chief officer of the group, Sir Christopher Hogg

25 *s'est engagé à mettre en application le message de ses actionnaires* (§4)
a – committed himself to put in application the message of his shareholders
b – promised to apply the message of his shareholders
c – undertook to pay heed to the message from the shareholders
d – engaged himself to enforce the shareholders' message

UNIT 6

Marketing strategy : a rather testing text from a general-public economic monthly introducing a new concept in store design. Thought and effort are required to interpret the French text.

Alongside the French text there is a draft translation containing several difficulties and errors in English. With the aid of the multiple-choice questions, decide whether the draft suggestion is correct (indicated by 'text') or choose the best suggestion available. Only the more blatant points are covered by the multiple-choice questions. A more polished translation with explanatory footnotes is provided later

APACHE

1. Ils ont moins de douze ans, ils savent ce qu'ils veulent et leurs parents sont prêts à tout pour leur arracher un sourire. Résultat : un nouveau marché !

1. They are less than twelve, they know what they want and their parents are ready for anything to tear a smile away from them. Result: a new market!

2. Au bout du tunnel secret interdit aux adultes, une usine à bonbons et une boutique « argent de poche ». Des ateliers pour apprendre à fabriquer du dentifrice ou des montgolfières miniatures, des rayons de jouets, des livres, des meubles pour chambres d'enfants... À mi-chemin entre le magasin, la boutique tous services et le parc d'attractions, la nouvelle enseigne Apache est un rêve de gamin conçu... par un gamin.

2. At the end of the secret tunnel forbidden to adults, a sweetie factory and a pocket money shop. Workshops to learn how to manufacture toothpaste or tiny hot-air balloons, toy departments, books, furnitures of rooms of children... A cross between the shop, the all-purpose store and the theme park, the new shop sign Apache is a dream of a kid conceived... by a kid.

3. Pendant ses huit premières années, rien qu'en jouets, chaque bambin touche près de 1.800 francs par an. Les 5,2 millions des 4-10 ans se partagent plus de 4 milliards de francs d'argent de poche, et leur pouvoir d'achat ne cesse d'augmenter. À la BNP, la moitié des clients mineurs ont moins de 12 ans et 2.000 francs en moyenne sur leur compte. Plus incroyable encore : d'après le président de l'Institut de l'Enfant (IDE) qui décortique depuis vingt-cinq ans les comportements des consommateurs en culottes courtes, 43% des dépenses annuelles des familles seraient directement ou indirectement sous l'influence des moins de 18 ans.

3. During his eight first years, nothing but in toys, each small child earns near of 1,800 francs a year. The 5.2 millions of 4-10 years old share more than 4 billions of francs of pocket money, and their buying power does not stop to augment. For the BNP, the half of the minor clients is less than twelve years and 2,000 francs on average on their account. Even more incredible : according to the president of the Institute of the Child (IDE, which peels for twenty-five years the behaviours of the consumers in shorts, 43% of the annual spendings of families would be directly or indirectly under the influence of least than 18 years.

4. Cela fait plus de quinze ans maintenant que les spécialistes du marketing labourent

4. It makes more than fifteen years now that the specialists in marketing are labouring

à coups de marques le marché des adolescents. Mais ils n'avaient pas encore défriché celui des tout-petits. D'après Christophe Parot, « la vente par correspondance a été le premier à proposer une offre à la fois globale et sélective qui accompagne l'enfant dès le premier âge ».

in the adolescents' market by fits of brands. But they had not cleared the ways for that of the toddlers yet. According to Christophe Parot, "mail order selling was the first to propose an offer at the same time global and effective which accompanies the child from the first age."

5. Aujourd'hui même les hypermarchés, jusque-là concentrés sur la ménagère de moins de 50 ans, découvrent les enfants. « L'usine à vendre des jouets, c'est fini. Il faut créer une atmosphère ludique, qui valorise l'enfant aux yeux de sa mère », souligne Joel-Yves Le Bigot.

5. Even today hypermarkets, up to there concentrated on the canteen of less than 50 years, discover the children. "The factory to sell toys, it is finished. It is necessary to create a playful atmosphere which values the child to the eyes of his mother," underlines Joel-Yves Le Bigot.

Capital (299 mots)

1 *Ils ont moins de douze ans* (§1)

a – They are less than twelve *(text)*
b – They are not yet twelve years old
c – They are under twelve
d – all of the above

2 *leurs parents sont prêts à tout* (§1)

a – their parents are ready for anything *(text)*
b – their parents are ready to make everything
c – their parents will stop at nothing
d – their parents will go to any lengths

3 *pour leur arracher un sourire* (§1)

a – to tear a smile away from them *(text)*
b – to make them smile
c – to get a smile out of them
d – to snatch a smile from them

4 *tunnel secret interdit aux adultes* (§2)

a – the secret tunnel forbidden to adults *(text)*
b – the secret tunnel prohibited to adults
c – a secret tunnel where adults may not enter
d – an adults' no entry secret tunnel

5 *une usine à bonbons* (§2)

a – a sweetie factory *(text)*
b – a candy store
c – a confectionery plant
d – all of the above

6 *ateliers* (§2)

a – workshops *(text)*
b – classes

c – play areas
d – studios

7 *fabriquer [du dentifrice]* (§2)
a – manufacture *(text)*
b – fabricate
c – elaborate
d – make

8 *[montgolfières] miniatures* (§2)
a – tiny *(text)*
b – model
c – miniature
d – all of the above

9 *rayons de jouets, livres* (§2)
a – toy departments, books *(text)*
b – some counters of toys and books
c – shelves filled with toys and books
d – toys and books radiating everywhere

10 *meubles pour chambres d'enfants* (§2)
a – furnitures of rooms of children *(text)*
b – kids' bedroom furniture
c – child-room furnishings
d – furniture for child's bedroom

11 *à mi-chemin entre le magasin* (§2)
a – A cross between a toy shop *(text)*
b – Across from the toy shop
c – Midway between the shop
d – Halfway across between the shop

12 *la nouvelle enseigne Apache est un rêve de gamin conçu … par un gamin* (§2)
a – the new shop sign Apache is a dream of a kid conceived … by a kid *(text)*
b – the new ensign 'Apache' is a dream by one child conjured up … by one child
c – the new Apache sign is a dream that has been imagined by a child.
d – the new Apache chain of stores is a kid's dream … dreamt up by a kid

13 *pendant ses huit premières années* (§3)
a – During his eight first years *(text)*
b – Since birth to the age of eight
c – In the first eight years of his life
d – While his eight prime years

14 *rien qu'en jouets* (§3)
a – nothing but in toys *(text)*
b – nothing only in toys
c – only in toys
d – in toys alone

15 *chaque bambin touche près de 1 800 francs par an* (§3)

a – each small child earns near of 1 800 francs a year *(text)*
b – every kiddie gets close on FF1,800 worth of toys a year
c – each toddler obtains toys for nearly 1,800 francs a year
d – every newborn picks up an annual 1 800 francs for toys.

16 *les 5,2 millions des 4-10 ans* (§3)

a – the 5.2 millions of 4-10 years old *(text)*
b – the five millions point two of four to ten years olds
c – the 5.2m four-to-ten-year-olds
d – the 5.2 million of the 4-10-year-olds

17 *leur pouvoir d'achat ne cesse d'augmenter* (§3)

a – their buying power does not stop to augment *(text)*
b – their disposable income does not cease increasing
c – their purchasing power continues to inflate
d – their spending power goes on growing

18 *À la BNP, la moitié des clients mineurs ont moins de 12 ans et 2000 francs en moyenne sur leur compte* (§3)

a – For the BNP, the half of the minor clients is less than twelve years and 2,000 francs on average on their account *(text)*
b – Half of the BNP's junior accountholders are under twelve and average FF2,000 on their accounts
c – One in two BNP youth clientele are below the age of 12 and in average 2,000 francs on their account.
d – At the BNP, one out of two minor customers have less than twelve years old and FF2,000 on average on their account.

19 *qui décortique depuis vingt-cinq ans les comportements des consommateurs en culottes courtes* (§3)

a – which peels for 25 years the behaviours of the consumers in shorts *(text)*
b – which hulls since 25 years the behaviour of short-panted consumers
c – which has analysed during 25 years the purchasing attitudes of youngsters
d – which has been monitoring over a period of 25 years young consumer trends

20 *43% des dépenses annuelles des familles* (§3)

a – 43% of the annual spendings of families *(text)*
b – 43% of the families' annual expense
c – 43% of annual household expenditure
d – 43% of the yearly outlay of the families

21 *seraient [directement ou indirectement] sous l'influence des moins de 18 ans* (§3)

a – would be under the influence of least than 18 years *(text)*
b – is influenced by the under-18s.
c – should be the responsibility of less than 18-year-olds.
d – has some bearing on children below the age of 18

22 *Cela fait plus de quinze ans maintenant* (§4)

a – It makes more than fifteen years now *(text)*
b – It is nowadays more than fifteen years that
c – For over fifteen years now
d – Since fifteen years today

23 *labourent à coups de marques le marché des adolescents* (§4)
a – are labouring in the adolescents' market by fits of brands *(text)*
b – have been flooding the teenagers' market with branded goods
c – have been making inroads into the teenager market by dint of designer labels
d – marketing well-known brand names in the adolescent market has proved difficult

24 *Mais ils n'avaient pas encore défriché celui des tout-petits* (§4)
a – but they had not cleared the way for that of the toddlers yet *(text)*
b – but they had not yet reclaimed that of the very young
c – but they had not until now worked out how to sell to toddlers
d – but the tiny tots' market was new territory for them

25 *la vente par correspondance* (§4)
a – mail order selling *(text)*
b – mail order firms
c – mail order sales
d – selling by mail

26 *une offre à la fois globale et sélective* (§4)
a – an offer at the same moment global and selective *(text)*
b – a selected bid and at the same time a worldwide one
c – a total and at the same time selective demand
d – a wide yet select range of goods

27 *qui accompagne l'enfant dès le premier âge* (§4)
a – which accompanies the child from the first age *(text)*
b – which goes along with the child as early as the first age
c – to suit every age from toddlers upwards
d – for all children since they are babies

28 *Aujourd'hui même les hypermarchés jusque-là concentrés sur la ménagère* (§5)
a – Even today hypermarkets, up to there concentrated on the canteen of less than 50 years *(text)*
b – Today even the hypermarkets, which up to then concentrated on the housewife of the under-fifties
c – Today even the superstores, which until recently targeted the middle-aged housewife
d – Nowadays still the superstores, up to now strengthened by under-fifties housewives.

29 *l'usine à vendre des jouets, c'est fini* (§5)
a – the factory to sell toys is finished *(text)*
b – the toy sales factory has closed down
c – the toy factory for sale is no longer there
d –the toyshop as a mass outlet is a thing of the past

30 *qui valorise l'enfant aux yeux de sa mère* (§5)
a – which values the child to the eyes of his mother *(text)*
b – enhances the status of the child in his mother's eyes
c – which projects a more grown-up image of the child to his mother
d – which makes the child the apple of his mother's eye

An incursion into the niceties of legal language, aimed at the middle-range employee, therefore a register which mixes everyday terms and legal technicalities.

Alongside the French text there is a draft translation containing several difficulties and errors in English. With the aid of the multiple-choice questions, decide whether the draft suggestion is correct (indicated by 'text') or choose the best suggestion available. Only the more blatant points are covered by the multiple-choice questions. A more polished translation with explanatory footnotes is provided later

Prime de Maternité

Un homme peut-il obtenir de son employeur une allocation de maternité ?

1. **Le cas :** Chez Renault, les femmes enceintes reçoivent une allocation de 7 500 francs lors de leur départ en congé de maternité[1]. Un salarié de sexe masculin, dont la femme attend un enfant, demande à bénéficier de cette disposition. Il invoque le principe communautaire d'égalité de traitement entre les hommes et les femmes pour les conditions d'emploi, de formation et de rémunération[2]. Refus de l'entreprise. L'employé porte plainte auprès du conseil de prud'hommes du Havre. L'affaire arrive devant la CJCE (Cour de Justice des Communautés européennes), qui donne tort au salarié.

2. **La réponse de l'avocat** : Dans cette affaire, l'argument du salarié de Renault était simple. Selon lui, si l'octroi d'un congé spécifique aux femmes enceintes se justifiait bien pour des raisons de santé, il n'en était pas de même pour l'allocation d'une somme d'argent: la naissance de l'enfant concerne aussi bien le père que la mère. En ne tenant compte de ce raisonnement, l'employeur se rendait coupable d'une discrimination abusive, contraire aux textes communautaires.

3. La Cour de justice des Communautés européennes n'a pas retenu cette analyse. Les magistrats ont considéré, au contraire, que le versement d'une allocation forfaitaire aux salariées ne violait pas le principe

Can a man obtain from his employer a maternity benefit?

Case history: At Renault, the pregnant women receive an allowance of FF 7 500 at the time of their departure on holidays for maternity. A male employee, whose the wife awaits a child, asks to profit from this provision. He calls upon the Community principle of equal treatment between the men and the women for the conditions of employment, formation and remuneration. The company refuses. The employee complains near the industrial tribunal in Le Havre. The business arrives in front of the CJCE (Court of Justice of the European Communities), which gives wrong to the employee.

The answer of the advocate: In this business, the argument of the Renault worker was simple. According to him, if the granting of a specific leave to the pregnant women was justified for reasons of health, it was not in the same way too for the allowance of an amount of money: the birth of a child concerns the father as well as the mother. While not taking account of this reasoning, the employer made himself guilty of an abusive discrimination contrary with the Community texts.

The Court of Justice of the European Communities did not retain this analysis. The magistrates considered, on the contrary, that the payment of a contractual allowance to the female employees did not violate

d'égalité de traitement entre hommes et femmes. En effet, selon les juges, le principe d'égalité de rémunérations présuppose que tous les travailleurs se trouvent dans des situations comparables.

the principle of equal treatment between men and women. Indeed, according to the judges, the principle of equal pay presupposes that all the workers are in comparable situations.

4. Ce n'est pas le cas durant un congé de maternité. Pendant cette période, les femmes sont, de façon évidente, désavantagées sur le plan professionnel : leur contrat de travail est suspendu et elles ne peuvent, par exemple, bénéficier d'une promotion ou d'une augmentation de salaire liée à leurs performances. Les hommes, eux, n'ont pas à subir une suspension de leur contrat de travail. Les magistrats ont donc estimé que les salariés masculins ne pouvaient prétendre aux compensations financières réservées aux femmes enceintes.

It is not the case during holidays for maternity. For this period, women are quite clearly at a disadvantage on the professional level: their employment contract is suspended and they cannot, for example, profit from a promotion or a wage increase connected to their performances. The men, them, do not have to undergo a suspension of their contract of employment. The magistrates thus estimated that the male employees could not pretend to the financial compensations reserved to the pregnant women.

5. A noter que, dans un précédent arrêt[3], la CJCE avait adopté une attitude inverse sur le problème du départ en retraite: selon la cour, fixer un âge différent de cessation d'activité pour les hommes et les femmes est contraire au principe absolu d'égalité de traitement entre les sexes.

To note that, in a preceding stoppage, the court had adopted an opposite attitude on the problem of retirement: according to the court, to fix a different age of suspension of activity for men and women is against the overriding principle of equal treatment between the sexes.

Capital (365 mots)

1. Article 18 de l'accord d'entreprise de Renault
2. Article 119 du traité de Rome et directive 75-11
3. CJCE, affaire C-262/88, Douglas Harvey Barber contre Guardian Royal Assurance Group, 17 mai 1990

1 *Chez Renault* (§1)

a – At Renault *(text)*
b – At Renault's
c – By Renault
d – In Renault's

2 *les femmes enceintes* (§1)

a – the pregnant women *(text)*
b – pregnant wives
c – women employees who become pregnant
d – female workers heavy with child

3 *lors de leur départ en conge de maternité* (§1)

a – at the time of their departure on holidays for maternity *(text)*
b – when they go off on maternity leave
c – on starting out for motherhood
d – during them leaving on pregnancy vacation

4 *un salarié de sexe masculin* (§1)
a – A male employee *(text)*
b – A manly staff member
c – A male sex salaried worker
d – A masculine executive

5 *dont la femme attend un enfant* (§1)
a – whose the wife awaits a child *(text)*
b – whose wife awaits a child
c – of whom the wife is waiting for a child
d – whose wife is expecting a child

6 *demande à bénéficier de cette disposition* (§1)
a – asks to profit from this provision *(text)*
b – requests to take advantage of this disposal
c – puts in a claim under this arrangement
d – demands to benefit from this disposition

7 *il invoque* (§1)
a – He calls upon *(text)*
b – He refers to
c – He pleads
d – He appeals to

8 *les conditions d'emploi, de formation et de rémunération*
a – the conditions of employment, formation and remuneration *(text)*
b – hiring, education and salaries requirements.
c – working conditions, training and pay
d – the circumstances of recruitment, practice and earnings

9 *porte plainte auprès [du]* (§1)
a – complains near *(text)*
b – lodges a complaint next to
c – takes his case to
d – registers his disapproval with

10 *le conseil de prud'hommes du Havre* (§1)
a – the industrial tribunal in Le Havre *(text)*
b – the Le Havre employment tribunal
c – the litigation council of Le Havre
d – both (a) & (b) but not (c)

11 *affaire* (§1)
a – business *(text)*
b – affair
c – concern
d – case

12 *Cour de Justice des Communautés Européennes* (§1)
a – Court of Justice of the European Communities *(text)*
b – European Court of Justice
c – Justice Court of the Communities of Europe
d – both (a) & (b) but not (c)

13 *donne tort au salarié* (§1)
a – gives wrong to the employee *(text)*
b – finds the employee guilty
c – finds against the employee
d – finds fault with the employee

14 *avocat* (§2)
a – advocate *(text)*
b – legal expert
c – attorney
d – barrister

15 *les femmes enceintes* (§2)
a – the pregnant women *(text)*
b – expectant mothers
c – matrons-to-be
d – both (b) & (c) but not (a)

16 *il n'en était pas de même pour* (§2)
a – it was not in the same way too for … *(text)*
b – it was not even so for …
c – there was no similarity with …
d – the same could not be said of …

17 *en ne tenant compte de ce raisonnement* (§2)
a – While not taking account of this reasoning *(text)*
b – By not following this reasoning
c – On not accounting for this reasoning
d – For ignoring this reasoning

18 *contraire aux textes communautaires* (§2)
a – contrary with the Community texts *(text)*
b – on the contrary to community texts
c – in breach of EU texts
d – opposed to the EU texts

19 *magistrats* (§3)
a – magistrates *(text)*
b – public prosecutors
c – judges
d – attorneys

20 *allocation forfaitaire* (§3)
a – a contractual allowance *(text)*
b – an ex gratia payment
c – a forfeited benefit
d – a set grant

21 *sur le plan professionnel* (§4)
a – on the professional level *(text)*
b – on the professional plane
c – occupationally speaking
d – career-wise

22 *promotion* (§4)
a – promotion *(text)*
b – special offer
c – succession
d – recommendation

23 *augmentation de salaire liée à leurs performances* (§4)
a – a wage increase connected to their performances *(text)*
b – a performance-related pay rise
c – an index-linked salary increase
d – an action-bound earnings bonus

24 *les hommes, eux* (§4)
a – The men, them *(text)*
b – Man himself
c – Male employees, on the other hand,
d – Those males

25 *ne pouvaient prétendre aux [compensations]* (§4)
a – could not pretend to *(text)*
b – could not aspire to
c – were not able to anticipate
d – were not entitled to

26 *réservées aux [femmes enceintes]* (§4)
a – reserved to *(text)*
b – booked for
c – intended for
d – aimed to

27 *A noter que* (§5)
a – To note that *(text)*
b – To be noted that
c – Noticeably
d – It is worth noting that

28 *arrêt* (§5)
a – stoppage *(text)*
b – arrest
c – decision
d – checking

29 *un âge différent de cessation d'activité* (§5)
a – a different age of suspension of activity *(text)*
b – different retirement ages
c – a different age to stop being active
d – different ages to close down

30 *principe absolu* (§5)
a – overriding principle *(text)*
b – unflinching principle
c – permanent principle
d – unmitigated principle

Right up your street! Though dated somewhat, a topic of central interest to all students, even if the wave of concern has receded for the time being. Ministers may come and go, the problems remain.

Alongside the French text there is a draft translation containing several difficulties and errors in English. With the aid of the multiple-choice questions, decide whether the draft suggestion is correct (indicated by 'text') or choose the best suggestion available. Only the more blatant points are covered by the multiple-choice questions. A more polished translation with explanatory footnotes is provided later.

Privatisation des Universités

Privatisation: la France encourage les étudiants européens à résister

1. PARIS (AFP) - La France a encouragé samedi les étudiants européens à résister aux menaces de privatisation qui pèsent sur les systèmes éducatifs de l'Union européenne (UE), en défendant notamment le principe de gratuité des études, pour parvenir à terme à un « Maastricht de l'éducation et de la culture ».

2. « Pour quelles raisons serait-on capable de déplacer des montagnes pour la création d'une monnaie unique et la libéralisation des marchés, et n'aurait-on pas la même énergie pour promouvoir le plurilinguisme et les échanges d'étudiants ? », s'est demandé samedi le ministre de l'Éducation, Jack Lang, en se déclarant favorable à un « Maastricht de l'Éducation » qu'il qualifie « d'utopie concrète ».

3. Le ministre, qui s'adressait à quelque 300 représentants de syndicats étudiants d'une trentaine de pays européens, réunis à Paris jusqu'à dimanche pour les premières « assises étudiantes européennes », a néanmoins reconnu qu'il s'agissait d'un « grand combat » qui « ne fait que commencer ».

4. « Si la gratuité de l'accès à l'enseignement est une valeur commune de vos

Privatisation : France incites the European students to resist

1. On Saturday France urged students throughout Europe to overcome the threat of privatisation which weighs over the educational systems of the European Union, while notably defending the principle of gratuitousness of the studies, to reach at term to a Maastricht of education and culture.

2. "For what reasons should we be capable of moving mountains in order to set up the single currency and to open up markets and yet not have the same energy to promote multilingualism and student exchanges" wondered Saturday the minister of Education, Jack Lang, declaring himself favourable to a Maastricht of Education which he qualified as a "concrete utopia."

3. The minister, who addressed himself to about 300 representatives of student syndicates of about thirty European countries, gathered at Paris as far as Sunday for the first "European Students Assizes" has nevertheless recognised that it was a question of a great combat which does nothing but begin.

4. If free access to higher education is a common value for your movements in

mouvements en Europe, il y a vraiment intérêt à ce que cela s'entende », a ajouté Jean-Luc Mélenchon, ministre de l'Enseignement professionnel, en appelant les étudiants à mieux s'organiser face aux instances européennes.

Europe, it is really interesting for it to be understood, added Jean-Luc Mélenchon, minister for professional education, calling the students to organise themselves better in front of the European authorities

5. « L'idée que l'éducation est une marchandise me scandalise et scandalise Jack Lang, mais c'est une idée qui incontestablement progresse à l'échelle du monde », a souligné M. Mélenchon, tandis que M. Lang soulignait qu'au sein de l'Union, « deux ou trois pays comme la Grande-Bretagne, les Pays-Bas et l'Allemagne ne sont favorables ni à des politiques publiques fortes de l'éducation, ni à une politique européenne forte de l'éducation ».

5. "The idea that education is a merchandise scandalises me and scandalises Jack Lang, but it is an idea that undoubtedly is progressing on the world scale" he underlined, while M. Lang underlined that within the EU "two or three countries like GB, the Netherlands and Germany are in favour of neither strong public policies for education nor of a strong European policy for education."

6. Le premier syndicat étudiant français, l'UNEF-ID, a souligné de son côté qu'il y a « aujourd'hui plus d'étudiants que d'agriculteurs en Europe, mais que l'Union consacre 41 milliards d'euros aux dépenses agricoles contre seulement quelques centaines de millions d'euros pour l'éducation".

6. The first French student trade union, UNEF-ID, underlined for its part that there are today more students than farmers in Europe, but the EU consecrates 41bn on agricultural spending as against only a few hundred million euros on education.

7. Néanmoins, avant de parvenir à une harmonisation générale des études et à l'avènement du diplôme unique, qui ne verra peut-être jamais le jour tant les résistances et les contradictions sont grandes à l'intérieur de chaque pays, la France souhaite faire avancer le chantier de la mobilité des étudiants pour « accentuer les brassages ».

7. Nevertheless, before reaching a general harmonisation of studies and the accession of the unique degree, which may never see the light of day so much are the resistances and the contradictions big inside each country, France wants to make advances on the work site of student mobility to "accentuate the brewings."

8. Actuellement, 120.000 étudiants européens bénéficient chaque année des bourses Erasmus pour participer à des échanges. « C'est trop peu », a estimé Jack Lang, qui veut faire adopter avant fin 2000 un plan d'action pour la mobilité sur 5 ans par le conseil des ministres européens, et compte sur le soutien des étudiants pour vaincre les résistances de certains États-membres.

8. Actually, 120,000 European students benefit each year from Erasmus bursaries to participate in exchanges. "It is too little" estimated Jack Lang, who wants to make adopt over five years an action plan by the Council of European Ministers , and counts on the support of the students to overcome the resistances of some member states.

9. Le plan français devrait ainsi permettre d'augmenter la proportion d'étudiants « mobiles » en Europe à 20 % (contre 5 %

9. The French plan should thus make it possible to increase the proportion of mobile students in Europe to 20 % (against

actuellement), grâce notamment à un doublement des bourses Erasmus, qui sont de 120 euros par mois pendant sept mois.

5% currently), thanks in particular to a doubling of Erasmus purses, which are of 120 euros by month during seven months.

10. Le ministre de l'Education s'est également déclaré favorable à une participation directe des étudiants au sein des instances européennes, et a « retenu » l'idée de la création « d'un parlement européen des étudiants » pour sensibiliser les opinions publiques sur les dangers des « forces de résistance et de conservatisme » qui menacent l'université en Europe.

10. The Minister of Education also declared himself favourable to a direct participation of the students within the European bodies, and he "retained" the idea of the creation of a "European parliament of the students" to sensitize the public opinions on the dangers of the "forces of resistance and conservatism which threaten the university in Europe.

AFP (502 mots)

1 *Privatisation : la France encourage les étudiants européens à résister* (titre)
a – Privatisation : France incites the European students to resist *(text)*
b – France cheers on the European students resisting privatisation
c – Privatisation : France encourages the European students to stand up.
d – France calls on students in Europe to stand out against privatisation

2 *qui pèsent sur les systèmes éducatifs de l'Union européenne (UE)* (§1)
a – which weighs over the education systems of the European Union (UE) *(text)*
b – which carries weight with the educational systems of the EU
c – which hangs over education in Europe
d – which is weighing down the educational systems of the European Union

3 *en défendant notamment* (§1)
a – while notably defending *(text)*
b – on above all supporting
c – at the same time noticeably endorsing
d – by first and foremost standing out in favour of

4 *le principe de gratuité des études* (§1)
a – the principle of gratuitousness of the studies *(text)*
b – the principle of state funding of education
c – the principle of the freedom of studies
d – the principle of free access to education

5 *pour parvenir à terme à un Maastricht de l'éducation et de la culture* (§1)
a – to reach at term to a Maastricht of education and culture*(text)*
b – with the long-term goal of an educational and cultural Maastricht
c – to manage forward to a Maastricht for education and culture
d – to bring to an end an educational and cultural Maastricht

6 *pour quelles raisons serait-on capable de déplacer des montagnes* (§2)
a – For what reasons should we be capable of moving mountains *(text)*
b – Why would they be capable to move mountains
c – To what purpose ought we to be able to move mountains
d – How come we can move mountains

7 *pour la création d'une monnaie unique et la libéralisation des marchés* (§2)
a – to set up the single currency and to open up markets *(text)*
b – to create the single money and the liberal trade
c – to establish only one currency and one market
d – to coin the single coin and the single market

8 *s'est demandé samedi le ministre de l'Education* (§2)
a – wondered Saturday the minister of Education Jack Lang *(text)*
b – enquired about himself the Education minister Jack Lang on Saturday
c – the minister for Education, Jack Lang, asked of his audience on Saturday
d –the minister for education, Jack Lang, asked himself on Saturday

9 *utopie concrète* (§2)
a – concrete utopia*(text)*
b – achievable utopia
c – realisable aim
d – practical paradise

10 *qui s'adressait à quelque 300 représentants de syndicats étudiants* (§3)
a – who addressed himself to about 300 representatives of student syndicates *(text)*
b – who aimed his speech at an audience of about 300 student trade union stewards
c – who appealed to almost 300 representative union students
d – who was speaking in front of some 300 student union delegates

11 *réunis à Paris* (§4)
a – gathered at Paris as far as Sunday *(text)*
b – meeting in Paris until Sunday
c – brought together to Paris till Sunday
d – assembled in Paris right up to Sunday

12 *il s'agissait d'un grand combat qui ne fait que commencer* (§3)
a – it was a question of a great combat which does nothing but begin *(text)*
b – it was about a big fight that is does only begin.
c – the issue was a major struggle that was only just beginning
d – at stake was a huge bout which kept on at the beginning

13 *une valeur commune de vos mouvements en Europe* (§4)
a – a common value for your movements in Europe *(text)*
b – a value common to all your European movements
c – a value shared by all your organisations throughout Europe
d – an everyday value in your organisations in Europe

14 *il y a vraiment intérêt à ce que cela s'entende* (§4)
a – it is really interesting for it to be understood *(text)*
b – there is a real interest in its understanding
c – it is in your interest to make this heard loud and clear
d – it is truly of interest that you come to an agreement

15 *ministre de l'Enseignement professionnel* (§4)
a – minister for professional education *(text)*
b – minister for vocational training
c – minister for job-oriented teaching
d – minister for business learning

16 *en appelant les étudiants à mieux s'organiser face aux instances européennes* (§4)
- a – calling the students to organise themselves better in front of the European instances *(text)*
- b – advising students they had better organise themselves to face up to European authorities
- c – appealing to students to set themselves up better facing the European bodies
- d – encouraging the students to adopt a common stance to present to the European authorities

17 *l'éducation est une marchandise (§5)*
- a – education is a merchandise *(text)*
- b – education is a good
- c – education is something that can be bought and sold
- d – all of the above

18 *une idée qui incontestablement progresse à l'échelle du monde (§5)*
- a – an idea that undoubtedly is progressing on the world scale *(text)*
- b – an idea that is without doubt gaining ground throughout the world
- c – an idea that is not being progressively contested on a world scale
- d – an idea that is going forward up the world ladder

19 *politiques publiques fortes de l'éducation (§5)*
- a – strong public policies *(text)*
- b – a proactive role for the state in education
- c – powerful government ministers of education
- d – public politicians whose strong point is education

20 *le premier syndicat étudiant français (§6)*
- a – the first French student union *(text)*
- b – the prime French student union
- c – the foremost French student union
- d – the leader French student union

21 *a souligné de son côté (§6)*
- a – underlined for its part *(text)*
- b – stressed on its side
- c – emphasized in its own way
- d – accentuated in an aside

22 *seulement quelques centaines de millions d'euros (§6)*
- a – only a few hundred million euros *(text)*
- b – only some hundreds of millions of euros
- c – almost only hundred millions euros
- d – only nigh on a hundred million euros

23 *l'avènement du diplôme unique (§7)*
- a – the accession of the unique diploma *(text)*
- b – the coming of an only degree
- c – the introduction of a Europe-wide degree
- d – the advent of the single certificate

24 *tant les résistances et les contradictions sont grandes à l'intérieur de chaque pays (§7)*

a – so much are the resistances and the contradictions big inside each country *(text)*
b – so strong is the hostility and the internal wrangling within each member state
c – as bitter are the resistances and the disagreements inside each country
d – as long as the Resistance and the controversy are considerable within each country

25 *la France souhaite faire avancer le chantier de la mobilité des étudiants (§7)*

a – wants to make advances on the work site of student mobility *(text)*
b – is willing to help further the shambles of student mobility
c – would like to make a start to student mobility
d – aims to move forward on the question of student mobility

26 *accentuer les brassages (§7)*

a – to accentuate the brewing *(text)*
b – to encourage the intermingling of European youth.
c – to stress the mixture of university populations.
d – to bring about an amalgamation of European countries.

27 *qui veut faire adopter un plan d'action pour la mobilité sur 5 ans par le conseil des ministres européens (§8)*

a – who wants to make adopt over five years an action plan by the Council of European Ministers *(text)*
b – who aims to have the European Council of Ministers adopt a five-year mobility plan
c – who wishes to make the European Ministers' Council adopt a plan of action for five years' mobility.
d – (a) & (b) but not (c)

28 *grâce notamment à un doublement des bourses Erasmus, qui sont de 120 euros par mois pendant sept mois (§9)*

a – thanks in particular to a doubling of Erasmus purses which are of 120 euros by month during seven months *(text)*
b – thanks to a doubling of the value of Erasmus scholarships, which are 120 euros monthly for seven months
c – by doubling the number of Erasmus grants, which are currently worth 120 euros per month over a seven-month period
d – thanks to a folding in half of Erasmus bursaries which start at 120 euros a month for seven months

29 *a retenu l'idée (§10)*

a – he retained the idea *(text)*
b – he accepted wholeheartedly the idea
c – he withheld the idea
d – he took note of the idea

30 *pour sensibiliser les opinions publiques sur les dangers (§10)*

a – to sensitize the public opinions on the dangers (*text*)
b – to make public opinion sensitive of the dangers
c – to sharpen the public's attitudes over the dangers
d – to heighten public awareness of the dangers

R.I.P. : an obituary for this soon-to-become defunct item, so much an essential part of our everyday life. Often seen hanging outside the windows of the Cité Universitaire dormitories (in northern climes), for students the plastic bag has a second life as substitute for a fridge. Legitimate ecological concerns have ensured its demise, but that will not prevent us from missing it and wondering how to replace it.

A full translation with explanatory footnotes is to be found later.

Polluant mais indispensable

1. *Dans les années 60 avec la grande distribution, le "sac sortie de caisse" est vite devenu l'emblème de la nouvelle société de consommation et du gaspillage. On en fabrique aujourd'hui en France 14 milliards par an pour un public qui le décrie mais ne peut pas s'en passer. A quand le sac biodégradable?*

2. Il est transparent, sauf le nom du magasin imprimé avec une encre à l'eau, biodégradable, photodégradable et miscible dans l'eau. Lui, c'est le « sac sortie de caisse » parfaitement écologique. Incinéré, il brûle sans laisser de résidus. Oublié dans la nature par un promeneur négligent ou déposé sur l'eau par un coup de vent, il s'évapore en quelques mois sans laisser d'autres traces que des molécules de carbone et d'hydrogène. Ce sac magique, les industriels savent le fabriquer, mais son coût de revient est jugé trop élevé par les distributeurs. Il reste donc dans les cartons.

3. Depuis son apparition, il y a une quarantaine d'années, le sac plastique souffre de sa mauvaise renommée. En 1963, Carrefour inaugure le premier hypermarché français à Sainte-Geneviève-des-Bois (Essonne). Très vite, les sacs en papier kraft sans poignées se révèlent inadaptés. Il faut des sacs dotés de poignées et moins chers à fabriquer. «Avec les sacs plastiques, on divisait le coût de fabrication par trois», précise Daniel Valeri, directeur d'Alplast, la deuxième entreprise française du secteur. Aujourd'hui, le prix de revient d'un tel produit est de 6 centimes environ. Aux Etats-Unis, les premiers sacs plastiques apparaissent au milieu des années 70. En France, l'explosion du «sac sortie de caisse» accompagne l'expansion de la grande distribution. Remplaçant les cabas, les paniers et autres filets, le sac plastique devient l'emblème de cette nouvelle société de la consommation et du gaspillage. Gratuit, il est distribué sans compter et jeté sans complexes. Chaque année, les commerçants en donnent 14 milliards environ.

4. En quarante ans, le sac de caisse a aussi maigri. Les plus légers font 8 microns contre 40 à 50 dans les années 70; dès lors, leur fabrication nécessite moins de pétrole.

(343 mots)
François Dagognet, *Libération*

1 *avec la grande distribution* (§1)

a – with the big distribution
b – together with the major distributors
c – with the advent of superstores
d – along with mass marketing

2 *sac « sortie de caisse »* (§1)

a – the way-out from the cashdesk bag
b – the bag you get when you leave the shop
c – the cashpoint bag
d – the supermarket checkout bag

3 *la nouvelle société de consommation et du gaspillage* (§1)

a – the new throwaway, consumer society
b – the brand-new consumption society and of waste
c – the new-fangled wasting consumption society
d – the innovative consumer and disposable age

4 *on en fabrique aujourd'hui en France 14 milliards par an* (§1)

a – people in France today fabricate 14 billion of bags every year
b – we turn out today in France 14 billions of it yearly
c – 14 billion of them are manufactured nowadays in France every year
d – 14 billions a year are produced nowadays in France

5 *[un public qui] le décrie* (§1)

a – hasn't got a good word to say for them
b – criticizes them
c – disparages them
d – looks down on them

6 *A quand le sac biodégradable ?* (§1)

a – For when the biodegradable bag ?
b – How long before we get the environmentally-friendly bag ?
c – Until when will we see the ecological bag ?
d – When is the ecological bag for ?

7 *imprimé* (§2)

a – stamped
b – embossed
c – imprinted
d – printed

8 *miscible dans l'eau* (§2)

a – miscible in the water
b – water-soluble
c – solvant
d – mixable

9 *Oublié dans la nature par un promeneur négligent* (§2)

a – Forgotten in nature by a negligent walker
b – Unwittingly left behind in natural surroundings by a casual stroller
c – Overlooked in the countryside by a careless hiker
d – Thoughtlessly discarded by an inconsiderate rambler

10 *déposé sur l'eau* (§2)

a – deposited on the water
b – left on the water
c – put on the water
d – blown onto the water

11 *un coup de vent* (§2)

a – a blow of wind
b – a gale
c – a gust of wind
d – a blast of wind

12 *Ce sac magique, les industriels savent le fabriquer* (§2)

a – This magic bag, industrials know to make it.
b – Manufacturers have the know-how to produce this wonder bag
c – Industrialists know how to make this bag magic
d – none of the above

13 *Il reste donc dans les cartons.* (§2)

a – so it stays in the boxes
b – so it remains on the drawing-board
c – it is still therefore in its carton packaging
d – therefore it is put away on the shelves

14 *Depuis son apparition, il y a une quarantaine d'années* (§3)

a – Since its apparition since about forty years
b – There are forty years since it's appeared
c – Since it first came on the scene some forty years ago
d – Since it made its first appearance for fourty years

15 *souffre de sa mauvaise renommée* (§3)

a – suffers of its bad reputation
b – has suffered from its notoriety
c – bears its ill repute
d – has had to live down its poor image

16 *Très vite, les sacs en papier kraft sans poignées se révèlent inad*aptés (§3)

a – Very fast, the kraft paper bags without handles show themselves not adapted
b – Very quickly the ordinary brown paper grocery bags proved to be unsuitable
c – Very quickly it seemed that the brown wrapping paper bags were maladjusted
d – Within a short space of time, the handless brown paper bags appeared unfitting

17 *Alplast, la deuxième entreprise française du secteur* (§3)

a – Alplast, the second French company in the sector
b – Alplast, the number two French firm of the segment
c – Alplast, the second largest French manufacturer in this field
d – Alplast, the second French manufacturer in the activity.

18 *Remplaçant les cabas, les paniers et autres filets* (§3)

a – Replacing the shopping bag, the pannier and other net bags
b – Supplanting the fabric shopper, the wicker basket and string bag, to name but a few
c – Standing in for either shopping bags, hampers or otherwise punnets
d – Substituting for bags, baskets and nets

19 *Gratuit, il est distribué sans compter et jeté sans complexes* (§3)

a – It is allotted in mass not counting and thrown into the dustbin with no complex
b – It is handed out freely and free of charge, and thrown away without a second thought
c – Free, it is distributed disinterestedly and discarded without hang-ups
d – It is shared out freely and dropped shamelessly

20 *dès lors* (§4)

a – from then on
b – seeing that
c – as from that point
d – consequently

News in Brief : the sort of item you could be asked to translate – or at least give an account of – at a moment's notice. A full translation with explanatory footnotes is to be found later.

Abeilles chercheuses d'explosifs

1. Des scientifiques américains sont en train de travailler, à la demande du Pentagone, sur un moyen de dresser des abeilles à repérer des traces d'explosifs, ce qui pourrait permettre un jour de détecter ainsi des bombes, a affirmé lundi le New York Times.

2. Le projet, démarré il y a trois ans, en est encore à son stade initial mais a franchi une étape. Les abeilles ont d'abord été entraînées pour aider à repérer des mines, elle sont maintenant dressées à détecter un camion portant des traces d'explosifs.

3. Le sens olfactif des abeilles, selon un laboratoire de recherche de l'armée de l'air au Texas, est sûr à plus de 99%, selon des essais récents.

4. Ainsi, des essaims pourraient être placés près des points de contrôles de sécurité et beaucoup plus tard, les abeilles pourraient également servir à repérer des attaques biologiques ou chimiques, selon les chercheurs.

5. Les chercheurs envisagent par la suite d'équiper les abeilles de transmetteurs gros comme un grain de riz. Elles pourront ainsi être suivies à la trace, ajoute le journal. Pour les récompenser, les chercheurs de l'université du Montana, également sur le projet, leur donnent du sucre.

6. Les responsables du Pentagone reconnaissent que ces expériences peuvent susciter le scepticisme ou la moquerie mais sont sûrs qu'elles peuvent amener des résultats.

7. Depuis cinq ans, le Pentagone a dépensé 25 million de dollars sur ce projet et d'autres projets équivalents impliquant des animaux.

(237 mots)
AFP

1 *Abeilles chercheuses d'explosifs* (titre)

a – Explosive researcher bees
b – Sniffer bees
c – Bees searching explosives
d – Homing bees

2 *à la demande du Pentagon* (§1)

a – at the request of the Pentagon
b – on the demand of the Pentagon
c – under contract to the Pentagon
d – by application from the Pentagon

3 *dresser des abeilles* (§1)

a – to train bees
b – to tame bees
c – to break in bees
d – to make bees perform

4 *à repérer des traces d'explosifs* (§1)

a – to spot tracks of explosives
b – to locate explosive traces
c – to detect traces of explosives
d – to pinpoint the tracks of bombs

5 *ce qui pourrait permettre un jour [de détecter]* (§1)

a – what could permit one day to ..
b – with the long-term aim of ..
c – which could allow one day for ..
d – which could enable a day to ...

6 *a affirmé lundi le New York Times* (§1)

a – affirmed on Monday the New York Times
b – the New York Times confirmed Monday
c – the New York Times pretended in Monday's newspaper
d – the New York Times claimed in its Monday edition

7 *en est encore à son stade initial* (§2)

a – is still at its initial stage
b – is in its early days yet
c – is still at its starting-point
d – has only just passed through its prime juncture

8 *Le projet, démarré il y a trois ans* (§2)

a – The project that got under way since three years
b – It is three years now that the project took off
c – That makes three years that the project was booted
d – which started up three years ago

9 *a franchi une étape* (§2)

a – has reached a milestone
b – has gone beyond a stopping-point
c – has completed a first stage
d – has cleared a hurdle

10 *d'abord* (§2)

a – at first
b – first of all
c – primarily
d – (b) & (c) but not (a)

11 *Le sens olfactif des abeilles* (§3)

a – The olfactory sense of bees
b – The bees sense of scent
c – Bees' sense of smell
d – The bee's odorous sense

12 *est sûr à plus de 99%* (§3)

a – is sure to more than 99%
b – is accurate at more than 99%
c – is precise by 99%
d – is 99% reliable

13 *selon … selon* (§3)

a – according to … according to
b – so says … pointing to
c – on the authority of … as maintained by
d – consistent with … in conformity with

14 *par la suite* (§5)

a – in the more distant future
b – as a follow-up
c – in the ensuing time
d – furthermore

15 *[transmetteurs] gros comme un grain de riz.* (§5)

a – no bigger than a grain of rice
b – large like a grain of rice
c – as big as a grain of rice
d – fat as rice grains

16 *Elles pourront ainsi être suivies à la trace* (§5)

a – They will be able to be followed as a result by their tracks
b – Thus it will be possible to follow in their footsteps
c – In this way their movements could be tracked
d – By this fashion they will be kept up with their displacements

17 *pour les récompenser, les chercheurs de l'université du Montana leur donnent du sucre* (§5)

a – To compensate them, the searchers of the University of Montana give them some sugar
b – The researchers from the University of Montana reward them with sugar
c – Sugar is the recompense of the Montana University researchers .
d – As a retribution, the researchers give sugar to them.

18 *Les responsables du Pentagone* (§6)

a – Officials at the Pentagon
b – The responsables of the Pentagon
c – The persons responsible for the Pentagon.
d – People in charge of the Pentagon

19 *ces expériences peuvent susciter le scepticisme ou la moquerie* (§6)

a – these experiments may provoke disbelief and even some leg-pulling
b – these experiments may spark off expressions of incredulity or ridicule
c – these experiments could raise a few eyebrows or even a titter
d – all of the above

20 *Depuis cinq ans, le Pentagone a dépensé 25 millions de dollars* (§7)

a – For five years, the Pentagon has been spending 25 millions of dollars
b – Since five years the Pentagon has spent 25 million dollars
c – During five years, the Pentagon is spending \$25m
d – Over the past five years, the Pentagon has spent \$25m

A delightfully amusing little text... which is guaranteed to cause you problems. It goes to show that it's not always the shortest texts that are the easiest to deal with. Keep in mind that behind sociologist Jean-Claude Kaufmann's vocabulary lies a social observation with which you are familiar. He is describing what is going on around you, perhaps you yourself are in this situation.

Express these ideas with everyday words in English and do not fall into the trap of translating word-for-word ! It is an excellent illustration of how English and French differ in their conceptions – English remains down-to-earth, uses concrete terms and is rooted in empiricism where French prefers to conceptualise and philosophise. English speakers "call a spade a spade" and militate in favour of "Plain English" (www.plainenglish.co.uk). Consequently, the language of English-speaking researchers also remains much closer to general English than is the case for French academics.

A full translation with explanatory footnotes is to be found later.

Le Lave-linge : un oui pour la vie

1. Les couples d'aujourd'hui ? Ils se mettent en ménage à petits pas : c'est d'abord le « chacun chez soi », puis la cohabitation.

2. L'engagement vient avec l'achat d'appareils ménagers. Le four ou le réfrigérateur ne les impliquent guère, ils sont liés aux repas et le plaisir gomme la contrainte.

3. Le lave-linge, en revanche, joue un rôle essentiel ! Parce que laver son linge se réfère à l'intime et nécessite un système de propreté collective.

4. Résister à l'achat du lave-linge, en dehors des raisons financières, c'est un peu hésiter à se lancer dans la vie à deux.

5. S'en doter, au contraire, met en marche la machine conjugale. Et affirme l'existence du nid, sans Lavomatic ou détour chez les parents.

6. En fait, cet appareil ménager est un intermédiaire : de couple débutant, on devient couple installé. Prêt à se projeter dans l'avenir.

(144 mots)
Jean-Claude Kaufmann

1 *un oui pour la vie* (titre)

a – Washing-machine : say 'yes' to life
b – Saying 'yes' to a washing-machine for ever after
c – When a washing machine means 'I do'
d – When a washing-machine is a vote for life

2 *les couples d'aujourd'hui* (§1)

a – the young couples of today
b – young couples nowadays
c – today's young couples
d – all of the above

3 *ils se mettent en ménage à petits pas* (§1)

a – they live together in short steps
b – they set up house in stages
c – little by little they make a household
d – they toddle into a home together

4 *c'est d'abord le « chacun chez soi »* (§1)

a – it's first the 'each at its own'
b – at the beginning, each goes on living at their own place
c – for a start, they live apart
d – first and foremost, it's each for himself

5 *puis la cohabitation* (§1)

a – then comes cohabitation
b – then they share lodgings
c – then they move in together
d – then they become flatmates

6 *l'engagement* (§2)

a – the engagement
b – the undertaking
c – the beginning
d – the commitment

7 *ne les impliquent guère* (§2)

a – do not hardly implicate them
b – hardly imply them
c – do not really tie them down
d – do not concern them much

8 *ils sont liés aux repas* (§2)

a – they are bound to meals
b – they are associated with eating
c – they are connected to menus
d – they are limited to lunch hours

9 *le plaisir gomme la contrainte* (§2)

a – the pleasure erases the constraint
b – the enjoyment of the meal outweighs the chore of cooking
c – the delight of taste smoothes out that of obligation
d – the idea of a pleasing purchase masks the sense of compulsion

10 *en revanche* (§3)

a – on the other hand
b – to the contrary
c – as a revenge
d – in return

11 *laver son linge se réfère à l'intime* (§6)

a – to wash one's linen refers to the intimate
b – washing their clothes is personal
c – doing the washing is an individual task
d – washing your smalls implies intimacy

12 *nécessite un système de propreté collective* (§3)

a – entails a system of collective cleanliness
b – works better when shared
c – requires a team cleaning scheme
d – needs everyone to be responsible for hygiene

13 *résister à l'achat du lave-linge* (§4)

a – to resist to the purchase of the washing-machine
b – withstanding buying a washing-machine
c – to stand up to the purchase of a washing-machine
d – holding back from buying a washing-machine

14 *en dehors des raisons financières* (§4)

a – financial considerations apart
b – besides the question of cost
c – money problems aside
d – all of the above

15 *se lancer dans la vie à deux* (§4)

a – to take the plunge
b – to both embark upon life
c – to throw oneself into life as a twosome
d – to launch themselves wholeheartedly in twos

16 *s'en doter* (§5)

a – to endow oneself with one
b – equipping oneself of it
c – acquiring one
d – to grant oneself one

17 *met en marche la machine conjugale* (§5)

a – starts up married life
b – gets the marriage working
c – is the first step towards togetherness
d – turns on the love machine

18 *sans Lavomatic ou détour chez les parents* (§5)

a – without laundromat or diversion at the parents'
b – with neither laundrette nor detour via the parents'
c – neither automatic machines nor parents do the washing
d – no more trips to the laundrette or taking the dirty washing back home

19 *intermédiaire* (§6)

a – stepping-stone
b – go-between
c – negotiator
d – halfway house

20 *de couple débutant, on devient couple installé* (§6)

a – from a couple of novices, one becomes a well-fitted couple
b – from being a young couple starting out in life, they put down their roots
c – after two newlyweds, they become a well-established couple
d – after being debutantes, they turn into a stay-at-home couple

UNIT 12

Sport too is of capital importance in our leisure society of today, and its economic impact transcends borders, as is shown here. Manchester United FC, for example, often proclaimed as being the world's richest club, has an annual turnover of some £170 million, with financial interests and activities far beyond the actual playing pitch. Merchandising and media are the most obvious, but MU also offers car & home insurance deals, credit cards, and stock exchange financial services, etc., etc.

A full translation with explanatory footnotes is to be found later.

Le foot en danger

1. A force de surenchère, le football professionnel aurait-il empoisonné sa poule aux œufs d'or, sa très chère télévision ? L'inflation des droits télévisuels du football est directement mise en cause derrière la faillite de KirchMedia, la filiale du groupe Kirch qui a déposé son bilan lundi 8 avril, faillite qui survient moins de deux semaines après celle d'ITV Digital, une chaîne numérique payante britannique. Le groupe allemand s'était engagé à verser 1,5 milliard d'euros sur quatre ans à la fédération et aux clubs de la Bundesliga. ITV Digital avait acheté pour plusieurs centaines de millions d'euros les droits de retransmission des matches des deuxième, troisième et quatrième divisions anglaises pour une durée de trois ans. Aujourd'hui, les deux sociétés sont exsangues. Les recettes escomptées ne sont jamais arrivées.

2. Trop de football tue le football télévisé. A force de diffuser des rencontres sans réel intérêt et de verser des sommes démesurées pour s'assurer simplement que telle ou telle compétition ne tomberait pas dans l'escarcelle du bouquet concurrent, ces télévisions se sont brûlé les ailes et ont provoqué leur propre chute. Devenu un produit vendu en masse par les hypermarchés médiatiques, le football s'est banalisé. L'excitation des soirées européennes s'est diluée dans les rencontres de seconde zone dont le téléspectateur se trouve abreuvé à longueur d'année. La France semble – pour l'instant – l'une des moins touchées par la morosité qui gagne l'Europe télévisuelle : en Italie et en Espagne, les plates-formes numériques sont également au bord de l'étouffement.

3. Le football sait qu'il risque d'être la première victime du remodelage du paysage audiovisuel qui s'est amorcé. En Angleterre, le nombre de clubs de D2, D3 et D4 menacés de faillite par le dépôt de bilan d'ITV Digital est estimé entre trente et cinquante. Les administrateurs de la chaîne payante négocient actuellement avec la Football League pour ramener de 300 à 83 millions d'euros la somme due pour conserver les droits. En Allemagne comme en France, les budgets des plus petits clubs des divisions supérieures dépendent pour plus de moitié de la manne télévisuelle. Celui de Sankt-Pauli, actuellement dernier du championnat allemand, est alimenté à 69 % par les droits télé.

4. Seuls les grands clubs ont su anticiper les événements en cours en faisant de la diversification de leurs recettes une priorité. L'envolée des salaires des joueurs les place néanmoins dans des situations difficiles, au point que leurs dirigeants sont de plus en plus nombreux à se prononcer pour un plafonnement de la masse salariale. Ils ont été aussi

les premiers à réclamer la propriété individuelle pour chaque club des droits télévisuels. Mais la sélection est cruelle : en Italie, la moitié des clubs de l'élite n'ont pas réussi à vendre leurs droits. La loi du marché préfère les gros clubs aux petits. Le football professionnel, qui a tant réclamé le droit de s'y soumettre, est en train d'apprendre qu'elle élimine les faibles.

(484 mots)
Le Monde

1 *A force de surenchère* (§1)
a – Through outbidding each other
b – By dint of escalation
c – As a result of excessiveness
d – By raising the stakes too high

2 *le foot professionnel aurait-il empoisonné sa poule aux œufs d'or* (§1)
a – the professional football would have poisoned its hen and its eggs of gold
b – would professional football have slaughtered the chicken with the golden eggs
c – has professional football perhaps killed the goose that laid the golden eggs
d – professional football may have poured out the baby with the bath-water

3 *très chère* (§1)
a – very expensive
b – high-priced
c – highly-prized
d – beloved

4 *mise en cause* (§1)
a – questioned behind
b – responsable for
c – implicated in
d – charged with

5 *survient* (§1)
a – arises
b – occurs
c – turns up
d – arrives

6 *celle de ITV Digital* (§1)
a – that of ITV Digital
b – the one of Digital ITV
c – this of Digital ITV
d – the latter of ITV Digital

7 *une chaîne numérique payante britannique* (§1)
a – a British paying digital chain
b – a paying British digital channel
c – a British paying numerical chain
d – a British digital pay channel

8 *plusieurs centaines de millions d'euros* (§1)
a – several hundreds of millions euros
b – several hundred million euros
c – several hundreds of millions of euros
d – several hundred million of euros

9 *Aujourd'hui, les deux firmes sont exsangues* (§1)
a – Today both societies are wan
b – Today the two companies are bloodless
c – Today the both firms are anaemic
d – Today both companies have been bled white

10 *Les recettes escomptées ne sont jamais arrivées* (§1)
a – the discounted receipts never arrived
b – the cut-price income never happened
c – the hoped-for revenue never materialised
d – the expected recipes never reached them

11 *A force de diffuser des rencontres sans réel intérêt* (§2)
a – Due to spreading meetings without real interest
b – With force to diffusing matches without real interest
c – By broadcasting contests with no real interest
d – As a result of televising boring encounters

12 *ne tomberait pas dans l'escarcelle du bouquet concurrent* (§2)
a – would not fall in the moneybag of the concurrent bouquet
b – would not fall into the purse of the rival bunch
c – would not fall in the offer of the competitor
d – would not fall into the hands of the rival operator

13 *ces télévisions se sont brûlé les ailes et ont provoqué leur propre chute.* (§2)
a – these televisions burned wings and provoked their own fall
b – these televisions flapped their wings and caused their proper failure.
c – these television companies got their fingers burnt and brought about their own downfall.
d – these television channels burned their wings and roused their own failing

14 *Devenu un produit vendu en masse par les hypermarchés médiatiques* (§2)
a – Become a product sold en masse by the media hypermarkets
b – Having become a consumer good on sale in the medias
c – Turned into an everyday item by the media moguls
d – Growing to be a mediatised mass market merchandise

15 *dont le téléspectateur se trouve abreuvé à longueur d'année* (§2)
a – whose televiewer is watered with length of year
b – with which the viewer is soaked all year round
c – in which the television spectator immerses himself for twelve months
d – with which the viewer is bombarded throughout the year

16 *La France semble l'une des moins touchées par la morosité qui gagne l'Europe télé visuelle* (§2)

a – France seems one of the least touched by the gloom which wins television Europe
b – France seems to be one of those least hit by the low spirits spreading through Europe's televisions
c – France seems one of the least hit by the moroseness which gains televisual Europe
d – France seems to be one of the least affected by the melancholy that is on the television screens of Europe

17 *au bord de l'étouffement* (§2)

a – at the edge of the breathlessness
b – on the verge of smothering
c – about to be hushed up
d – on the brink of financial ruin

18 *Le football sait qu'il risque d'être la première victime du remodelage du paysage audiovisuel qui s'est amorcé.* (§3)

a – Football knows he risks to be the first victim of the replanning of the audiovisual landscape which began
b – Football knows it is likely to be the first victim of the reshaping of broadcasting which has begun
c – Football is aware that it risks being the chief victim from the remodelling of the television scenery which has started.
d – Football recognizes there is a chance it will be the principal victim of the transformation of the television world scene that is under way

19 *pour ramener de 300 à 83 millions d'euros la somme due pour conserver les droits* (§3)

a – to return 300 to 83 millions of euros the sum owed to keep the rights.
b – to reduce by 300 to 83 million euros the amount outstanding to conserve the rights.
c – to bring back from 300 to 83 million of euros the amount due to preserve the rights.
d – to cut from 300 to 83 million euros the sum due to retain the rights.

20 *les budgets des plus petits clubs des divisions supérieures dépendent pour plus de la moitié de la manne télévisuelle.* (§3)

a – the budgets of the smallest clubs of the superior divisions depend for more half of the television basket
b – the budgets of the smallest clubs in the higher divisions are more than 50% dependent on the income from television
c – the budgets of the smaller clubs in the higher divisions owe more than half to the televised manna
d – the budgets of the smallest clubs in the upper divisions are answerable for more than the half of the television godsend.

21 *Celui de Sankt-Pauli, actuellement dernier du championnat allemand, est alimenté à 69 % par les droits télé.* (§3)

a – That of Sankt-Pauli, at present last of the German championship, is fed in 69 % by right TV

b – The one of Sankt Pauli, actually bottom of the German championship, is powered to 69 % by television rights.

c – The latter of Sankt-Pauli, currently last from the German championship, is fed at 69 % by the tele-rights.

d – That of Sankt Pauli, at present in bottom place in the German championship, is funded for 69% by the television rights.

22 *L'envolée des salaires des joueurs.* (§4)

a – The inspiration of the salaries of the players

b – The flight of player's salaries.

c – The spiralling players' wage bill.

d – The take-off of players' salaries.

23 *au point que leurs dirigeants sont de plus en plus nombreux à se prononcer pour un plafonnement de la masse salariale.* (§4)

a – to the point that their leaders are more and more numerous to pronounce for an upper limit of the salary mass

b – so much so that their leaders are increasingly numerous to decide for a levelling off of the wage bill

c – so much so that more and more chairmen are coming out in favour of capping the wage bill

d – to the point where a number of managers want a ceiling of the salary amounts.

24 *Ils ont été aussi les premiers à réclamer la propriété individuelle pour chaque club des droits télévisuels.* (§4)

a – They were also the first to claim individual ownership for each club of the television rights

b – They were also the first ones to demand the individual property for every club of the televisual rights.

c – They were also the first ones to complain of the individual transparency for all clubs of the television laws.

d – They were also the leading ones to reclaim the individual assets for every club of the televised rights.

25 *La loi du marché* (§4)

a – The law of the market

b – Market forces

c – The dictates of supply and demand.

d – The principles of trade

Setting the cat among the pigeons! The foundations of London's international status and reputation are here seriously rocked by a fact-finding investigation. Some might say that this is a case of "the pot calling the kettle black" or that "people in glasshouses shouldn't throw stones," but that would be being petty.

La City, « lieu de placement » pour les terroristes

1. Un rapport de députés français, publié mercredi, accuse la City de Londres comme étant un « lieu de placement par les organisations terroristes » et présente les îles anglo-normandes sont de « véritables usines à blanchir l'argent du crime ». La plus grande place financière du monde est « très attrayante pour les blanchisseurs d'argent » en raison notamment « de la permissivité de la législation sur les trusts qui garantit l'anonymat des bénéficiaires réels des fonds et de l'absence de réglementation de certaines professions financières », souligne la mission d'information de l'Assemblée nationale sur le blanchiment d'argent.

2. Cet « État dans l'Etat », où sont accumulés près de 3.800 milliards d'euros d'avoirs bancaires, affiche une « superbe indifférence à l'égard du risque de blanchiment », ajoute ce rapport rédigé par le député socialiste Arnaud Montebourg et intitulé « La Cité de Londres, Gibraltar et les dépendances de la Couronne : des centres offshore, sanctuaires de l'argent sale ». Au moment où la « cruelle démonstration » vient d'être faite que des organisations liées à Oussama ben Laden ont « su utiliser à leur profit la déréglementation financière », poursuit-il, il n'y a « nulle surprise à constater l'importance, pour les organisations criminelles à visée terroriste, de la place de Londres et des territoires offshore ». Le rapport pointe également du doigt les îles anglo-normandes (Jersey, Guernesey...). « Les choix stratégiques en matière fiscale et bancaire » des autorités, « avec l'appui tacite, si ce n'est le soutien explicite, du Royaume-Uni », font de ces territoires « de véritables trous noirs de la finance mondiale ».

3. Les députés français stigmatisent aussi « le manque de coopération judiciaire » de la Grande-Bretagne, pas seulement pour les affaires financières mais pour « l'ensemble des crimes et délits » (extraditions...). Le Home Office (ministère de l'Intérieur), déplore le document, « continue dans sa tradition obstinée à nuire aux enquêtes des pays européens et ralentit, lorsqu'il ne paralyse pas, la lutte contre le blanchiment ». Et de noter que si le gouvernement travailliste de Tony Blair a décidé, en 1997, de « réagir » pour renforcer sa législation financière, avec la création notamment d'un organisme de régulation (FSA), « le bilan de la lutte anti-blanchiment au Royaume-Uni reste, quatre ans plus tard, bien maigre ».

(352 mots)
Le Monde

1 *La City, lieu de placement pour les terroristes* (titre)
a – The City : a savings place for the terrorists
b – The City : a safe place for terrorists
c – The City : an investment haven for terrorists
d – The City : a placing centre for terrorists

2 *Un rapport de députés français* (§1)
a – a study of French deputies
b – a French Parliamentary report
c – a study from French representatives
d – a report realised by French MPs

3 *accuse la City de Londres comme étant [un lieu de placement]* (§1)
a – charges London City with being ...
b – accuses the City of London to be ...
c – castigates London's City as being ...
d – all of the above

4 *véritables usines à blanchir l'argent du crime* (§1)
a – true factories for whitening the money of crime
b – veritable money-laundering plants for the proceeds of crime
c – real workshops to recycle criminal money
d – actual manufactories to whitewash money from crime

5 *La plus grande place financière du monde est très attrayante pour les blanchisseurs d'argent* (§1)
a – The stronghold of world finance is highly attractive to money launderers
b – The biggest financial place of the world is very attractive for cleaners of money.
c – The world's largest stock exchange is appealing greatly to money laundry workers.
d – The largest financial centre in the world appeals much to whitewashers of money.

6 *en raison de la permissivité de la législation* (§1)
a – because of the permissiveness of the legislation
b – owing to what the laws tolerate
c – according to the magnanimity of the laws
d – by virtue of its lax legislation

7 *souligne la mission d'information de l'Assemblée nationale sur le blanchiment d'argent* (§1)
a – underlines the mission of information of the French National Assembly over the whitening of money
b – the French National Assembly news commission about money recycling underscores
c – the French parliamentary financial crime committee underlines
d – stresses the legislative whitewashing task force

8 *Cet « État dans l'État »* (§2)
a – This "state within the state"
b – This "state in the state"
c – This "law unto itself"
d – This "state inside the state"

9 *où sont accumulés près de 3.800 milliards d'euros d'avoirs bancaires* (§2)

a – where are accumulated close to 3.800 billions of euros of bank holdings
b – where some €3,800bn worth of assets are invested
c – where almost €3 800 billion are piled up in credit notes
d – where nigh on €3,800bn of bank dues are hoarded

10 *affiche une superbe indifférence* (§2)

a – cocks a snoot at
b – flaunts a disdainful disregard
c – pays scant regard to
d – all of the above

11 *rédigé* (§2)

a – written
b – drawn up
c – drafted
d – all of the above

12 *il n'y a nulle surprise à constater* (§2)

a – there is not a surprise to notice
b – it does not have any surprise to see
c – it comes as no surprise to note
d – it is hardly surprising to remark

13 *les organisations criminelles à visée terroriste* (§2)

a – criminal organizations for terrorist purposes
b – underworld groups bent on terrorism
c – guilty bands with terrorist aims
d – crime syndicates with designs on terrorism

14 *Les choix stratégiques en matière fiscale et bancaire des autorités* (§2)

a – the strategic choices in fiscal and banking matters of their authorities
b – the fiscal and banking strategies of their authorities
c – the strategic choices of their authorities as regards fiscals and banks
d – (a) & (b) but not (c)

15 *de véritables trous noirs de la finance mondiale* (§2)

a – veritable black holes of world finance
b – real black deficits in worldwide finances
c – true depths of despair for the world of finance
d – global banking's credit gap.

16 *continue dans sa tradition obstinée à nuire aux enquêtes des pays européens* (§3)

a – persists in its habit of putting spokes in the wheels of judicial investigations abroad
b – remains steadfast in its traditional stubbornness to damage inquests into European countries
c – goes on, as is its wont, to prejudice enquiries from European countries
d – carries on with its customary insistence on harming surveys of European countries

17 *[Le Home Office] ralentit, lorsqu'il ne paralyse pas, la lutte contre le blanchiment* (§3)
a – slows down, when it does not paralyse the fight against financial crime
b – hampers, and even totally frustrates, the battle against money-laundering
c – obstructs, and brings to naught the war against the recycling of illegal funds.
d – all of the above

18 *Et de noter que si le gouvernement travailliste de Tony Blair a décidé en 1997…* (§3)
a – And to notice that if the Labour government of Tony Blair has decided in 1997…
b – And the report goes on to note that if the Labour government under Tony Blair decided in 1997…
c – Furthermore the document notices that if the Labour Blair government came to the decision in 1997…
d – And of note is that if the Tony Blair's 1997 Labour government decided in 1997…

19 *avec la création notamment d'un organisme de régulation (FSA)* (§3)
a – by setting up first and foremost a watchdog
b – with the creation of a noted control organism
c – above all by settling an organization of regulation
d – with notably creating a regulation body

20 *le bilan […] au Royaume–Uni reste, quatre ans plus tard, bien maigre* (§3)
a – the balance-sheet in the United Kingdom [for this subject] remains after four years, lean
b – the statement by the United Kingdom [on this topic] stays skinny for four years
c – four years on, the UK's track record [in this field] is lacklustre
d – four years later, Britain's state of affairs continues to be slight

Even a text about the older generation can throw up a few pitfalls of expression – and may even cause youngsters a few wrinkles. Pay particular attention to how you refer to your 'elders and betters' (some of them may read your text) and also to your choice of terms for the various activities mentioned.

A full translation with explanatory footnotes is to be found later.

Des « seniors » créateurs

1. En Grande Bretagne le nombre de sociétés créées par des personnes du troisième âge a augmenté l'an dernier de 23 %. Selon une étude de l'unité de recherche de la Barclays Bank, 23 600 entreprises ont été fondées par des Britanniques âgés de 55 à 64 ans, alors même que la moyenne des créations d'entreprises en GB est en baisse !

2. Au total, 50% des nouvelles entreprises ont été lancées par des personnes de plus de 50 ans : secrétariat, cours de piano, travaux d'intérieur, études de marché, commerces... « L'évolution du système social, ajoutée à l'allongement de la vie, incite la frange la plus âgée de la population à trouver de nouvelles occupations, surtout pour ceux qui n'ont pas pu accumuler suffisamment d'épargne via un système de retraite », explique Mike Davis, directeur de la division PME de Barclays.

3. Qui sont donc ces créateurs d'entreprises d'un genre nouveau ? Certains ont été licenciés du fait de restructurations, et ont dû trouver un moyen de subsister en attendant d'atteindre l'âge de la retraite. Mais nombreux sont ceux qui sont passés volontairement du salariat au travail en indépendant. Ils peuvent ainsi travailler moins (36 heures en moyenne) et prendre davantage de vacances (quatre à six semaines) que leurs jeunes concurrents. Le chiffre reste modeste : 110 000 euros par an (contre une moyenne globale de 220 000 euros).

4. L'entreprise est généralement de petite taille, et est gérée à partir du domicile. Ce qui est d'autant plus confortable que les entrepreneurs du troisième âge ne sont pas « technophobes ». L'utilisation d'un ordinateur est fréquente de même que le fax et l'accès à l'Internet.

(270 mots)
Le Point

1 *le nombre de sociétés [créées] a augmenté l'an dernier de 23 %* (§1)

a – the proportion of business start-ups grew by 23 % last year
b – the share of firms has increased last year of 23 %
c – the amount of companies was put up from 23 % last year
d – last year the number of societies went up to 23 %

2 *créées par des personnes du troisième âge* (§1)

a – created by some third age individuals
b – funded by old folk
c – set up by people in their late middle-age
d – launched by senior citizens

3 *fondées* (§1)

a – founded
b – established
c – floated
d – registered

4 *des Britanniques âgés de 55 à 64 ans* (§1)

a – by British aged from 55 to 64 years
b – by British 55-to-64 year olds
c – by over 55 British people
d – by British people 55 to 64 years

5 *la moyenne des créations d'entreprises est en baisse* (§1)

a – the average of firm creations is falling
b – the acceptable standard for launching new undertakings is on the wane
c – the mean of created companies is dropping
d – generally speaking the number of company start-ups year-on-year is in decline

6 *Au total,* (§2)

a – Overall,
b – Completely
c – Summed up,
d – To cut a long story short

7 *secrétariat* (§2)

a – secretary's office
b – secretaryships
c – secretarial services
d – posts of secretary

8 *travaux d'intérieur* (§2)

a – inside works
b – interior decorating
c – household tasks
d – homework

9 *études de marché* (§2)

a – market researches
b – merchandising studies
c – marketing consultancies
d – product designs

10 *commerces* (§2)

a – retailing
b – businesses
c – trades
d – stores

11 *l'évolution du système social* (§2)
a – the evolution of the social system
b – the improvements in working conditions
c – changes in the welfare system
d – the development of social security

12 *ajoutée à l'allongement de la vie* (§2)
a – plus greater life expectancy
b – on top of the lengthening of living
c – added to an extension of livelihood
d – all of the above

13 *incite [la frange ...population] à trouver de nouvelles occupations* (§2)
a – incites [them] to find new hobbies
b – is encouraging [them] to take up different leisure activities
c – is spurring [them] to start a second career
d – is exhorting [them] to discover new-fangled occupations

14 *la frange la plus âgé de la population* (§2)
a – the eldest section of the population
b – the mature fringe of the workforce
c – the uppermost swathe of people
d – the oldest among the citizens

15 *accumuler suffisamment d'épargne via un système de retraite* (§2)
a – spare enough by means of a pension scheme
b – build up a nest-egg through a pension fund scheme
c – hoard enough money using a retirement arrangement
d – amass enough savings via a retirement system

16 *directeur de la division PME de la Barclays* (§2)
a – director of the PME division of Barclays
b – manager of the SME section at Barclays
c – Barclay's small business manager
d – head of businesses from Barclays

17 *Qui sont donc ces créateurs d'entreprise d'un genre nouveau ?* (§3)
a – Who then are this new breed of entrepreneurs?
b – Who are so those new-style firms' founders?
c – Who are therefore these company creators of a new type?
d – Thus who are those new-fangled businessmen?

18 *Certains ont été licenciés du fait de restructurations* (§3)
a – Some have been dismissed for restructuring
b – Certain of them were fired as a result of streamlining
c – Some have been made redundant in the wake of a corporate downsizing
d – Some have been laid off by means of a reorganisation

19 *ont dû trouver un moyen de subsister* (§3)

a – were bound to find a method to stay alive
b – must have found a means to subsist
c – have been obliged to find a mean of survival
d – have had to find a way to earn a living

20 *Nombreux sont ceux qui sont passés volontairement du salariat au travail en indépendant* (§3)

a – But quite a lot of them have switched, of their own free will, from working for someone else to being their own boss
b – But many are those who have moved from wage-earner to independent.
c – But a great number have willingly gone from being in employment to freelance work
d – But many of them have volunteered to pass from a nine-to-five job to self-made man.

21 *leurs jeunes concurrents* (§4)

a – their younger counterparts
b – their young rivals
c – their junior competitors
d – their youthful adversaries

22 *Le chiffre reste modeste* (§3)

a – the figure remains modest
b – the salary is unpretentious
c – the turnover is moderate
d – the total keeps on unassumingly

23 *L'entreprise est généralement de petite taille et gérée à partir du domicile* (§4)

a – The business is on the whole under-sized and managed as from their home
b – Such ventures are as a rule small and run from home
c – This kind of company is generally little and controlled to start from their house
d – These smallholdings are usually administered at home

24 *Ce qui est d'autant plus confortable que* (§4)

a – which is so much more comfortable than
b – which is all the easier as
c – what is especially relaxing that
d – that which is all the more so likeable since

25 *de même que* (§4)

a – as are
b – likewise
c – and the same is true of
d – all of the above

Throughout Western Europe, governments are having to face up to the problems brought about by an ageing population – the topic is being widely discussed, but beware that solutions which bear similar names may hide different realities from one country to another. Sooner or later, all of us are directly involved in the issue.

A full translation with explanatory footnotes is to be found later.

Chirac donne le coup d'envoi de la réforme des retraites

1. Jacques Chirac a donné lundi le coup d'envoi de la réforme des retraites, l'un des dossiers les plus sensibles du Premier ministre Jean-Pierre Raffarin, en demandant au gouvernement de fixer ses choix d'ici l'été.

2. « Le gouvernement suivra la voie du dialogue avec les partenaires sociaux pour arrêter, avant l'été, les décisions nécessaires », a dit M. Chirac au cours de la cérémonie des vœux des « forces vives », quelque 1 500 responsables syndicaux, économiques et associatifs.

3. Le chef de l'État a réaffirmé sa volonté de sauvegarder le principe de la retraite par répartition qui constitue « un pacte entre générations ». Mais il a jugé nécessaire de la compléter par l'épargne retraite qui ne peut être qu'un « mécanisme d'appoint ». « Il s'agira de rendre accessible à tous les Français ce qui est encore l'apanage d'un petit nombre », a-t-il dit, évoquant les systèmes dont bénéficient actuellement les fonctionnaires.

4. Alors que l'une des grandes difficultés de la réforme réside dans l'alignement de la durée de cotisation du secteur public sur celle du privé, Jacques Chirac a insisté sur « l'exigence absolue de l'équité ».

5. Tout en maintenant le principe du départ à la retraite à 60 ans, il a souligné qu'il fallait aussi « donner la liberté et la possibilité à ceux qui le souhaitent de travailler plus longtemps ».

6. Pour le chef de l'État, les pré-retraites sont un « gâchis humain » et « économique ». « Finissons-en avec ce gâchis », a-t-il dit, en demandant aux partenaires sociaux de prendre « à bras le corps ce problème » pour élaborer « un véritable pacte social pour l'emploi des plus de 50 ans ».

7. Jacques Chirac s'est dit confiant dans les chances de convaincre. « La tâche est exigeante, mais le mur n'est pas infranchissable », a-t-il dit.

8. Il a défini la méthode qui doit être celle du gouvernement et qui passe par le dialogue et, au-delà des négociations entre partenaires sociaux, par le « débat ». Toutes les solutions « doivent être examinées sans a priori. Rien n'est décidé à l'avance. Chacun devra être écouté ».

9. « Réformer les retraites, c'est renouer les fils de la solidarité. Ce n'est pas dresser les Français les uns contre les autres, actifs contre retraités, secteur public contre secteur privé, salariés contre professions indépendantes », a déclaré Jacques Chirac, gardant à l'esprit l'échec de la tentative de 1995 par le gouvernement d'Alain Juppé.

10. « Si nous voulons bien d'un effort partagé et juste, vous verrez que les évolutions nécessaires seront en réalité à notre portée », a-t-il ajouté.

11. Les premières réactions ont été plutôt positives. « C'est une feuille de route qui va bien à la CFDT », a déclaré le secrétaire général François Chérèque. « On nous promet la négociation, allons-y maintenant ».

12. D'accord pour négocier « des modalités différentes et nouvelles », mais seulement « pour assurer un progrès social », a dit le secrétaire général de la CGT Bernard Thibault.

13. M. Chirac « a bien posé les principes: équité, liberté, garantie des retraites », a commenté le patron du Medef Ernest-Antoine Seillière.

14. Jacques Chirac a également insisté sur la nécessité de rendre à la France sa compétitivité pour conforter son « attractivité durable ». Poursuivre la baisse de l'impôt sur le revenu et des charges sociales, contenir les dépenses de l'État, réorganiser les services publics, simplifier les réglementations: tels sont les moyens qu'il a suggérés pour restaurer « la confiance ».

Yahoo Actualités, Agences

1 *Chirac donne le coup d'envoi* (Titre)
- a – Chirac gives the start
- b – Chirac kicks off
- c – Chirac activates
- d – Chirac sends off

2 *réforme des retraites* (Titre)
- a – reform of the retirements
- b – reformation of withdrawals
- c – pensions reform
- d – reforming of the retreats

3 *en demandant* (§1)
- a – while asking
- b – in requesting
- c – requiring
- d – on asking

4 *d'ici l'été* (§1)
- a – from here the summer
- b – by the summer
- c – until the summer
- d – between now on till the summer

5 *les partenaires sociaux* (§2)
- a – both sides of industry
- b – the social partners
- c – the industrial partnership
- d – work colleagues

6 *quelque 1500 responsables syndicaux, économiques et associatifs* (§2)

a – some 1,500 persons in charge of trade, economic and associative unions
b – almost 1,500 union, economic and associated responsibles
c – some 1,500 representatives from trade unions, industry and the voluntary sector
d – nearly 1,500 syndicalists, managers and associates

7 *a réaffirmé sa volonté* (§3)

a – reaffirmed his will
b – expressed once again his willingness
c – reasserted his wish
d – restated his firm intention

8 *la retraite par répartition* (§3)

a – the pension by distribution
b – the sharing-out of pension funds
c – the contributory pension scheme
d – pension by apportionment

9 *qui ne peut être qu'un mécanisme d'appoint* (§3)

a – which can be only one "auxiliary mechanism"
b – which can be simply one of several instruments
c – which may be only an optional extra.
d – which can't be anything other than a top-up scheme

10 *ce qui est encore l'apanage d'un petit nombre* (§3)

a – what was as yet the prerogative of the few
b – what was still the birthright of a small number
c – which was more the privilege of few people
d – that which was moreover the monopoly of small people

11 *fonctionnaires* (§3)

a – civil servants
b – functionaries
c – public sector employees
d – bureaucrats

12 *réside* (§4)

a – resides in
b – lies in
c – inhabits
d – dwells on

13 *l'alignement de la durée de cotisation du secteur public sur celle du privé* (§4)

a – bringing the number of qualifying years for public sector employees in line with that of the private one
b – lining up the duration of the public sector contributions over the private ones.
c – balancing the length of subscription in the public sector on the private one's one.
d – all of the above

14 *l'exigence absolue de l'équité* (§4)

a – the absolute need for a fair deal for all
b – the indisputable requirement of equity
c – the unmitigated demand for even-handedness
d – the absolved strictness for impartiality

15 *les pré-retraites sont un gâchis humain et économique* (§6)
a – The premature retirements are a human and economic waste
b – Untimely pensions are a humane and economic mess
c – Early retirement is a waste of economic and human potential
d – Prepaid pensions are an economic and human nonsense.

16 *prendre à bras le corps ce problème* (§6)
a – take with arm the body this problem
b – take in their arms the body of the problem.
c – tackle the problem head on
d – clasp the problem to its chest

17 *un véritable pacte social pour l'emploi des plus de 50 ans* (§6)
a – a true social pact for the use of more than 50 year-old workers
b – a commitment to keeping the over-fifties in work.
c – a genuine work contract for those aged 50 or more
d – a joint undertaking to get fifty-year-olds back to work

18 *Chirac s'est dit confiant dans les chances de convaincre* (§7)
a – Chirac is known as trustful in the chances to convince.
b – Chirac confided to himself his chance of convincing
c – Chirac was self-confident that he would prove convincing
d – Chirac expressed his confidence in the prospects of winning everyone over to a solution

19 *Il a défini la méthode qui doit être celle du gouvernement* (§8)
a – He defined the method which must be the one of the government
b – He exposed the method that must be that of the government
c – He laid out the approach the government should take
d – He specified the methodology the government is due to adopt.

20 *qui passe par le dialogue* (§8)
a –which passes by the dialogue
b – which passes dialogue by
c – which involves conversations
d – which demands consultations

21 *sans a priori* (§8)
a – without a priori
b – without priorities
c – with an open mind
d – with hindsight

22 *Chacun devra être écouté* (§8)
a – Each one will have to be listened
b – Every one will have an audience
c – All should be heard
d – Everyone must be able to have their say

23 *Réformer les retraites, c'est renouer le fil de la solidarité* (§9)
a – To reform the retirement, it is to join again wires of solidarity
b – Reforming retirement is to re-tie comradeship.
c – To reform pensions we must take up again the thread of common purpose
d – Pensions reform is a renewed expression of social inclusion

24 *actifs contre retraités, salariés contre professions indépendantes* (§9)

a – those in work opposed to pensioners, employees opposed to the self-employed
b – workers versus the retired, wage-earners versus independent professions
c – assets up against those pensioned off, salaried workers up against sole traders.
d – active against non-active, working men against liberals

25 *Si nous voulons bien d'un effort partagé et juste* (§10)

a – If we want well an effort shared and right
b –If we are all willing to do our fair share
c – If we wish a fair and mutual solution well.
d – If we really want just a shared effort.

26 *Les premières réactions étaient plutôt positives* (§11)

a – The initial reactions were rather positive
b – First reactions were on the whole favourable
c – Early comments were somewhat encouraging
d – all of the above

27 *C'est une feuille de route qui va bien à la CFDT* (§11)

a – It is a waybill which goes well with the CFDT
b – It is a warrant which is good to the CFDT
c – It is a roadmap which suits the CFDT
d – It is a framework which fits the CFDT

28 *la nécessité de rendre à la France sa compétitivité pour conforter son « attractivité durable »* (§14)

a – the necessity of returning France to competitiveness in order to comfort its sustainable attractiveness.
b – the obligation to give France back its fighting spirit so as to strengthen its long-lasting charm.
c – the need to restore France's competitiveness in order to bolster its continuing appeal for investors
d – all of the above

29 *Poursuivre la baisse de l'impôt sur le revenu et des charges sociales* (§14)

a – To pursue the fall of income tax and the social charges
b – To further the lowering of tax on revenues and on entrepreneurial expenses
c – To prosecute lower income tax and company overheads
d – To go on bringing down income tax and employers' contributions

30 *simplifier les réglementations* (§14)

a – doing away with red tape
b – simplifying rules
c – making regulations easier to understand
d – easing laws

Sit back and relax with this tongue-in-the cheek look at most iconic of all British symbols.

A full translation with explanatory footnotes is to be found later.

La « cup of tea » n'est plus la tasse de thé des Britanniques

1. La célèbre *cup of tea* ne serait plus la tasse de thé des Britanniques ! D'après une étude publiée le 16 juin par le consultant londonien Datamonitor, les sujets de Sa Majesté préfèrent désormais les tisanes au thé. "*Autrefois, la tisane était associée aux hippies. De nos jours, cette infusion est préférée au thé par ceux qui se préoccupent avant tout de leur santé*", affirme le chercheur John Band.

2. A écouter l'auteur de ce rapport réalisé à partir d'analyses des ventes de boissons dans les grandes surfaces, l'effet de mode et une campagne astucieuse de marketing expliquent l'engouement suscité auprès de la population par la menthe, la camomille, le cassis. Fini le rituel de l'eau versée avant son point d'ébullition dans une théière amenée à la bouilloire et non l'inverse ? Sans parler de la dégustation dans un mutisme calculé, le petit doigt en l'air, summum des bonnes manières ?

3. "*Ce document est ridicule*, réplique William Gorman, directeur du Tea Council, le conseil du thé du Royaume-Uni, *le consultant ne tient pas compte de la forte consommation de thé dans les cafés, les restaurants, les avions.*" Pour ce défenseur de la boisson nationale, l'infusion n'est qu'un vulgaire mélange de fruits, de plantes et d'épices. Rien à voir avec l'ainsi dénommé "Camillia Sinensis", cette noble feuille qui protège des maladies cardio-vasculaires et qui peut aider à prévenir le cancer.

4. Mise sur pied de clubs de connaisseurs, octroi d'étoiles style Michelin, aide aux jeunes designers pour mettre au point la théière du futur : le Tea Council a contre-attaqué. Dans les entreprises, la fameuse pause-thé est menacée, mais la City découvre le *power tea*, qui rivalise avec les déjeuners du même nom. A l'instar de la reine, des pop stars comme Boy George, Robbie Williams ou le mannequin Kate Moss emportent en tournée leurs propres sachets de Twining.

5. Un nouveau site Internet baptisé nicecupofteaandasitdown.com ("une bonne tasse de thé et une pause"), consacré au plaisir de la *cuppa* accompagnée d'un léger biscuit sec, fait un tabac auprès des super-branchés.

(349 mots)
Marc Roche, *Le Monde*

ne serait plus la tasse de thé (§1)

would no more be the cup of tea (of …)

cup of tea be still a favourite

should no longer find favour (with …)

[…] cup of tea is no longer to the taste (of …)

b – After

c – Following

d – In line with

5 *les sujets de Sa Majesté* (§1)

a – Her Majesty's subjects

b – Her Britannic Majesty's subjects

c – the subjects of the British monarch

d – all of the above

6 *Autrefois, la tisane était associée aux hippies* (§1)

a – In the past, herbal and fruit teas conjured up images of hippies

b – Fruit teas were once looked down upon as a drink for hippies

c – Drinking herbal teas used to be seen as part of the hippy scene

d – all of the above

7 *l'effet de mode et une campagne astucieuse de marketing* (§2)

a – the result of style and of crafty marketing

b – the effect of mode and a cunning nature for marketing.

c – trends in fashion and a shrewd marketing campaign

d – a craze and a marketing drive

8 *l'engouement* (§2)

a – the popularity

b – the passing fancy

c – the fad

d – all of the above

9 *avant son point d'ébullition* (§2)

a – before its boiling point
b – when it is hardly boiling
c – just coming to the boil
d – just as it simmers

10 *et non l'inverse* (§2)

a – and not the other way round
b – and not outside in
c – and not counter-wise
d – and not contrarily

11 *Sans parler de la dégustation dans un mutisme calculé* (§2)

a – Without speaking about the sampling in a calculated dumbness
b – Testing it without talking in a well-timed silence
c – Not to mention savouring it in appreciative silence
d – Without talking of tasting it speechlessly.

12 *summum des bonnes manières* (§2)

a – the pinnacle of good ways
b – the height of good manners
c – the last word in refinement
d – (b) & (c) but not (a)

13 *la forte consommation de thé dans les cafés* (§3)

a – the strong consumption of tea in cafés
b – all the tea drunk in tea-shops
c – the strong demand for tea in restaurants
d – the high levels of tea in cafés

14 *Rien à voir avec l'ainsi dénommé 'Camellia Sinensis'*(§3)

a – Nothing in common with the plant known as 'Camellia Sinensis'
b – Nothing to see with the so-called 'Camellia Sinensis' plant
c – Nothing to do with the thus-named 'Camellia Sinensis' leaf
d – No connection with the 'Camellia Sinensis' thus cited.

15 *qui peut aider à prévenir le cancer* (§3)

a – which may help to warn cancer
b – which can help foresee cancer
c – which can help ward off cancer
d – which possibly anticipates cancer

16 *clubs de connaisseurs* (§4)

a – specialist clubs
b – gourmet clubs
c – expert groups
d – connaisseur's circles

17 *octroi* (§4)

a – toll booth
b – award

c – tax
d – licensing

18 *mettre au point* (§4)
a – adjust
b – bring into focus
c – finalize
d – develop

19 *dans les entreprises* (§4)
a – in the workplace
b – in the companies
c – in the enterprise
d – in any business

20 *fameuse pause-thé* (§4)
a – famous tea-stop
b – first-class pause for tea
c – traditional tea-break
d – well-known tea time out

21 *A l'instar de la reine* (§4)
a – Following the example of the Queen
b – Like the Queen
c – Taking their cue from the Queen
d – all of the above

22 *consacrée* (§5)
a – consecrated
b – given over to
c – established for
d – dealing with

23 *un léger biscuit sec* (§4)
a – a light dry biscuit
b – a low-fat biscuit
c – a plain biscuit
d – a wafer

24 *fait un tabac* (§5)
a – is a big hit
b – makes a tobacco
c – makes a splash
d – gets a kick

25 *auprès des super-branchés* (§5)
a – next to the jet set
b – in the opinion of the trendies
c – with the in-crowd
d – near those really turned on

There never was in Britain a nationwide project along the lines of 'Informatique pour Tous' in France. Nor is it clear today whether this announcement was ever put into effect – an example of political cant perhaps.

A full translation with explanatory footnotes is to be found later.

Le gouvernement britannique veut louer des ordinateurs aux pauvres

1. LONDRES, 28 oct. (AFP) - Les familles britanniques qui n'ont pas les moyens de s'acheter un ordinateur pourront en louer un à bas prix et ainsi éviter de passer à côté de la « révolution du savoir » et de l'Internet, a annoncé jeudi le gouvernement.

2. « Nous allons lancer un système qui permettra aux plus pauvres de louer des ordinateurs et des logiciels au siècle prochain, de la même façon que les bibliothèques municipales ont prêté des livres au cours du siècle écoulé », a déclaré le ministre des Finances Gordon Brown lors d'une conférence sur l'internet à Londres.

3. Le plan doit permettre à au moins 100 000 familles défavorisées d'accéder à l'informatique et à l'Internet à domicile d'ici la fin de l'année 2004.

4. Le prix de la location n'est pas encore fixé mais le gouvernement espère qu'il pourra descendre jusqu'à 5 livres par mois (7,5 euros, 8 dollars).

5. L'opposition a reproché à cette initiative de laisser de côté le problème du coût de la connexion à l'Internet. Une étude récente a estimé qu'un internaute se connectant chaque jour pendant une heure ajoute 30 livres (47 euros) à sa facture mensuelle.

6. « Il ne sert à rien d'offrir aux gens un peu de matériel bon marché s'ils se retrouvent avec une énorme facture de téléphone à la fin du mois », a affirmé Alan Duncan, porte-parole du parti conservateur pour les questions de technologie.

7. M. Brown a assuré que le renforcement de la concurrence sur ce marché, encouragée par le gouvernement, va continuer à faire baisser les prix.

8. Le ministre compte sur les entreprises, les collectivités locales et les associations pour fournir des ordinateurs de seconde main qui seront remis à niveau avec l'aide du gouvernement.

9. « Alors que nous entrons dans un nouveau siècle, nous devons faire en sorte que personne ne reste à l'écart de la révolution informatique », a déclaré Gordon Brown. Le gouvernement de Tony Blair veut éviter que « l'inégalité de l'accès aux ordinateurs mène à l'inégalité dans la vie ».

(344 mots)
Yahoo Actualités, Agences

1 *Le gouvernement britannique veut louer des ordinateurs aux pauvres* (titre)

a – praise computers for the poor
b – hire computers from the poor
c – rent out computers to the poor
d – let computers to the poor

2 *Les familles britanniques* (§1)

a – The British families
b – Families in Britain
c – Britain's families
d – (b) and (c) but not (a)

3 *qui n'ont pas les moyens de s'acheter un ordinateur* (§1)

a – don't have the means to buy a computer
b – who can't afford a computer
c – who aren't well enough off to purchase their own computer
d – all of the above

4 *à bas prix* (§1)

a – at a low price
b – for a modest sum
c – cut-price
d – for a bargain

5 *éviter de passer à côté de la révolution du savoir* (§1)

a – avoid to pass next to the "learning revolution"
b – avoid passing by the "learning curve"
c – avoid the "knowledge revolution" passing them by
d – avoid passing close by the "science revolution"

6 *lancer un système* (§2)

a – start up a system
b – launch a proposal
c – kick-start a method
d – pioneer a scheme

7 *permettra aux plus pauvres de louer des ordinateurs* (§2)

a – will allow to the poorest to hire out computers
b – will allow the impoverished hiring computers
c – will allow the less well-off to rent computers
d – will permit the most down-and-out that they let out computers

8 *logiciels* (§2)

a – logicians
b – softwares
c – software
d – logistics

9 *les bibliothèques municipales* (§2)
a – public libraries
b – municipal libraries
c – township bookstores
d – local bookshops

10 *au cours du siècle écoulé* (§2)
a – during the century passed
b – in the century just ending
c – in the course of the elapsed century
d – (a) & (b) but not (c)

11 *lors d'une conférence sur l'internet* (§2)
a – at the time of a conference on the Internet
b – on the occasion of an Internet conference
c – while conferring on the Internet
d – during a conference over the Internet

12 *Le plan doit permettre à au moins 100.000 familles défavorisées* (§3)
a – The plan must allow to at least 100,000 disadvantaged families
b – The programme should at the least permit that 100,000 underprivileged families
c – The scheme will enable at least 100,00 less well-off families
d – The project has to permit to 100,000 penalized families at the least

13 *accéder à l'informatique et à l'Internet* (§3)
a – accede to data processing and the Internet
b – to get into IT and the Internet
c – to access computer science and the Internet
d – to attain informatics and the Internet

14 *à domicile d'ici la fin de l'année 2004* (§3)
a – from home by the end of 2004
b – at their house from now till the end of 2004
c – to their home between now and end 2004
d – at place of abode from here to the end of 2004

15 *le prix de la location* (§4)
a – the prize of the hiring
b – the cost of the rent
c – the price of the lease
d – the rental charge

16 *le gouvernement espère qu'il pourra descendre jusqu'à 5 livres par mois* (§4)
a – the government hopes it will go down as far as 5 pounds a month
b – the government hopes to bring it down to £5 a month
c – the government hopes to make it as little as £5 a month
d – the government hopes he will be able to come down until £5 a month

17 *L'opposition a reproché à cette initiative de laisser de côté* (§5)
a – The opposition reproached the initiative to let on the side
b – The opposition criticized the scheme because it leaves aside
c – The opposing party blamed the initiative for letting [the question] sideways
d – The other side charged the initiative for leaving out

18 *a estimé* (§3)
a – esteemed
b – evaluated
c – guesstimated
d – concluded

19 *se connectant chaque jour pendant une heure* (§5)
a – connecting up each day during one hour
b – who has an hourly daily connection to the Internet
c – spending an hour a day on the Internet
d – linking up for one hour a day on the Internet

20 *facture mensuelle* (§5)
a – monthly invoice
b – month's expense account
c – monthly bill
d – month's financial statement

21 *Il ne sert à rien d'offrir aux gens* (§6)
a – It serves nothing to offer people
b – There's little point in giving folk
c – It doesn't help anyone to make available
d – all of the above

22 *porte-parole du parti conservateur pour les questions de technologie* (§6)
a – press secretary of the Conservative party for questions about technology
b – Tory spokesman for technological questions
c – Conservative technology mouthpiece.
d – Shadow Minister for Technology

23 *Mr. Brown a assuré que le renforcement de la concurrence sur ce marché* (§7)
a – Mr. Brown assured that the reinforcement of the concurrence on this market …
b – Mr. Brown concurred that the stronger market …
c – Mr. Brown insured that the strengthening of competition in this market …
d – Mr. Brown was confident that tougher competition in this sector …

24 *faire baisser les prix* (§7)
a – make lower prices
b – make prices drop
c – have prices fall
d – bring prices down

25 *les collectivités locales et les associations* (§8)
a – local authorities and voluntary associations
b – the localities and the associations collectively
c – the local communities and the partnerships
d – local citizens as a body and clubs

26 *pour fournir des ordinateurs de seconde main* (§8)
a – to furnish second-hand computers
b – to donate obsolete computers
c – to come up with occasional computers
d – to produce used computers

27 *qui seront remis à niveau avec l'aide du gouvernement* (§8)
a – which will be put to level once again with the help of the government
b –which will be brought up to standard with the help of the government
c – which will be upgraded with government aid
d – which will be refreshed with government assistance

28 *Alors que nous entrons dans un nouveau siècle* (§9)
a – Whereas we enter into a new century
b – While we come into the new age
c – As we move into the new millennium
d – When we enter this brave new world

29 *faire en sorte que personne ne reste à l'écart* (§9)
a – do it so that nobody doesn't stand out of the way
b – see to it that somebody isn't kept to the side
c – make sure that no-one stays in the gap
d – ensure that no-one is left out

30 *éviter que « l'inégalité de l'accès aux ordinateurs mène à l'inégalité dans la vie »* (§9)
a – avoid that unequal access to computers leads to unequal access to life
b – avoid a society divided between the information haves and the have-nots
c – avoid inequality spreading from the Internet to the whole of society
d – avoid unjust access to computers leading to injustice in life

This text addresses a classic socio-economic issue, thus providing the opportunity for you to hone your skills in this field.

A full translation with explanatory footnotes is to be found later.

L'Allemagne paye les chômeurs pour travailler

Objectif de la prime : inciter à accepter les emplois peu payés.

1. Face à la remontée du chômage allemand, qui devrait repasser la barre des 4 millions de demandeurs d'emploi ce mois-ci, Gerhard Schröder a ressorti une arme qu'il voudrait remède miracle : le *Kombilohn,* le « salaire combiné ». Il consiste à subventionner les chômeurs qui acceptent un emploi mal payé à moins de 900 euros mensuels. Pendant une durée limitée à trois ans, l'État prend en charge une partie des cotisations sociales que devraient normalement verser ces nouveaux salariés. Un célibataire peut ainsi se voir rembourser jusqu'à 67 euros par mois, plus 77 euros par enfant à charge. « *Les salariés conservent ainsi une plus grande partie de leur revenu brut,* expliquait hier le chancelier Schröder. *Pour eux, cela vaut ainsi davantage la peine d'accepter un travail.* »

2. Le Kombilohn tente de s'attaquer ainsi, en douceur, à l'un des problèmes de fond du marché de l'emploi allemand: convaincre les chômeurs de reprendre le travail quand le niveau et la durée des indemnités chômage leur garantissent un niveau de vie pratiquement aussi élevé. Dans l'ouest de l'Allemagne, d'après les agences pour l'emploi, les deux tiers des chômeurs sont des travailleurs peu qualifiés et/ou en chômage de longue durée qui ne peuvent espérer retrouver que des emplois peu rémunérés et ne se donnent pas toujours beaucoup de mal pour travailler.

3. Expérimenté sous différentes formes depuis déjà des années en Allemagne, le Kombilohn n'est pourtant ni vraiment nouveau ni vraiment efficace, observent la plupart des experts. « *Mieux vaudrait un modèle où une partie de la subvention va aux employeurs, pour les inciter aussi à créer des emplois* », plaide Klaus Zimmermann, président du DIW, l'institut de recherches économiques de Berlin. « *Mieux vaudrait aussi réduire les charges sociales pesant sur les bas salaires, comme le gouvernement Jospin l'a fait en France en 1997,* observe de son côté Thomas Hueck. *Mais cela coûterait beaucoup plus cher, entre 1 et 2 milliards d'euros. Et les syndicats allemands, clientèle du gouvernement Schröder, y sont opposés, car ils craignent l'établissement durable d'un large secteur de bas salaires.* »

(349 mots)

Lorraine Millot, *Libération*

1 *l'objectif de la prime* (§1)

a – the prime purpose
b – target of the bonus
c – the premium's aim
d – reason for the incentive

2 *inciter à accepter les emplois peu payés* (§1)

a – to incite to accept badly-paid placements.
b – to persuade those out of work to take up low-paid jobs
c – to encourage the unemployed to accept poorly-paid employments
d – to convince to agree to little-paid works.

3 *Face à la remontée du chômage* (§1)

a – In front of the rise in unemployment
b – Facing an increase of unemployment once more
c – In response to a new upswing in unemployment
d – Opposite increasing joblessness

4 *qui devrait repasser la barre des 4 millions de demandeurs d'emploi* (§1)

a – which really ought to go over the four millions of jobseekers this month
b – which should pass over the bar of four millions unemployed
c – which will probably rise once more above the 4 million mark this month
d – which might have to come back over the four million people out of work

5 *a ressorti une arme qu'il voudrait remède miracle* (§1)

a – has brought out once again an arm that he would wish to be a miracle drug
b – has come up with a scheme he hopes will do miracles
c – has another time wielded a secret weapon which he is proposing as a panacea
d – has revealed a plan he would like as a wonder cure

6 *Pendant une durée limitée à trois ans* (§1)

a – For up to three years
b – During a period limited to three years
c – During three years of limited duration
d – all of the above

7 *l'Etat prend en charge une partie des cotisations sociales* (§1)

a – the State takes charge of one part of the welfare subscriptions
b – the State will pay part of the employee's contributions
c – the State partially takes care of social security
d – the State will pick up to some extent the burden of social payments

8 *Un célibataire peut ainsi se voir rembourser jusqu'à 67 euros par mois* (§1)

a – a bachelor can thus see himself refunding as far as € 67 every month
b – a spinster can so be paid off monthly till € 67
c – an unmarried man can as a result redeem as much as € 67 a month
d – a single person can in this way claw back up to € 67 per month

9 *par enfant à charge* (§1)

a – for each dependant
b – per child in charge
c – by each child taken care of
d – none of the above

10 *cela vaut ainsi davantage la peine d'accepter un travail* (§1)

a – that is worth the trouble thus more of accepting a work
b – it is worth so more to accept an employment
c – it is more worthwhile their accepting a job offer
d – it's more expensive for them to go back to work

11 *Le Kombilohn tente de s'attaquer en douceur [à]* (§2)

a – The Kombilohn tries to creep up on
b – The Kombilohn attempts to attack gently
c – The Kombilohn is a softly-softly approach to tackling
d – The Kombilohn endeavours to be attacked carefully

12 *l'un des problèmes de fond du marché de l'emploi allemand* (§2)

a – one of the base problem of the German job market
b – one of the difficulties from the bottom of the German work market
c – one fundamental dilemma from the German employment exchange.
d – one of the issues that lie at the heart of the German labour market

13 *niveau de vie* (§2)

a – level of life
b – standard of living
c – livelihood
d – lifestyle

14 *les deux tiers des chômeurs sont des travailleurs peu qualifiés et/ou en chômage de longue durée* (§1)

a – the two thirds of the jobless are little qualified workers and/or unemployed for a long duration.
b – two out of three unemployed are hardly qualified to work and/or out of work since a long time
c – two-thirds of those out of work are poorly-skilled and/or the long-term unemployed
d – two in three unemployed workers are not very well educated and/or have no immediate job prospects

15 *ne se donnent pas toujours beaucoup de mal pour travailler* (§2)

a – don't always go out of their way to find a job
b – don't always harm themselves working
c – often don't find a job without difficulty
d – don't always bother working

16 *Expérimenté sous différentes formes depuis déjà des années* (§3)

a – Experimented under different shapes years beforehand
b – Tested in various forms since already many years
c – Conducted research on diverse forms years and years long
d – Tried out in many guises for a number of years now

17 *de son côté* (§3)

a – from his viewpoint
b – for his part
c – on his side
d – sideways on

18 *les charges sociales pesant sur les bas salaires* (§3)

a – the social burdens weighing on low salaries
b – the welfare charges pressing down on the low wage-earners
c – the industrial costs hanging over low pay
d – employers' contributions that weigh heavily on low-paid jobs

19 *clientèle du gouvernement Schröder* (§3)

a – customers of the Schröder government
b – the Schröder's government's patrons
c – the stock-in-trade of Schröder's government
d – the Schröder government's electoral base

20 *ils craignent l'établissement durable d'un large secteur de bas salaires* (§1)

a – they fear the durable establishment of a broad sector of low wages
b – they fear the long-term creation of an extensive low-paid workforce
c – they are afraid to set up a large, indestructible, low-wage sector
d – they can't bear the thought of the sustainable development of widespread low wages

A topic close to the hearts of most students as this becomes an accepted means of communication. However, with only 75 % of the population having a mobile phone, France lags well behind other western European countries where market penetration rate is closer to 97 % (based on number of active SIM cards).

A full translation with explanatory footnotes is to be found later.

SMS : la guerre des mots

1. Dimanche 9 mai, *l'UFC-Que choisir* a appelé au boycott des SMS, tant les mini-messages sont devenus une manne pour Orange, SFR et Bouygues Télécom.

2. Ce qui au début n'était que simple phénomène de mode chez les ados, s'étend progressivement depuis à peu près trois ans à toutes les couches de la société.

3. Votes d'émissions de téléréalité, prévisions météo... : le nombre de SMS progresse chaque année de 35%.

4. D'après l'association de consommateurs, les 11 milliards de SMS émis cette année généreraient un chiffre d'affaires de 1,4 milliard d'euros, pour un bénéfice qui dépasse le milliard, soit une marge de près de 80 %...

5. Les SMS, dont le coût de revient s'élève à 2,21 centimes d'euro, sont facturés en moyenne 15 centimes d'euro aux abonnés français, contre 5 centimes seulement aux Danois.

6. Cet écart de prix montre à quel point les bénéfices réalisés par les opérateurs sont importants, et pas seulement en France.

7. Une étude de CDC-Ixis indique, en effet, que la rentabilité des capitaux employés par les sociétés de téléphonie mobile – dont beaucoup ont payé cher les licences UMTS-3G – atteint souvent 150 %.

8. Leur marge opérationnelle varie de 14 % pour Bouygues, quatrième opérateur européen, jusqu'à 34 % pour le premier opérateur mondial Vodaphone, qui les vend 18 centimes d'euro à ses clients britanniques.

9. Depuis quelque temps, cet écart soulève des suspicions croissantes chez les régulateurs nationaux, de sorte qu'il y a deux mois Vodaphone a unilatéralement annoncé une baisse de 15 % du prix hors TVA à partir de septembre.

10. Parmi les autres sujets chauds, outre les SMS, figure le *roaming* – le prix que l'utilisateur paie pour émettre un appel de l'étranger – qui serait aussi largement supérieur aux coûts réels.

11. L'arrivée prochaine d'«opérateurs mobiles virtuels» qui achèteront aux opérateurs classiques des minutes par millions pour les revendre jouera en faveur des consommateurs.

(301 mots)

1 *a appelé au boycottt* (§1)
a – called for a boycott
b – has called to a boycott
c – has been calling on a boycott
d – calls at a boycott

2 *tant les mini-messages sont devenus une manne pour Orange* (§1)
a – as much as the text messages have become a godsend to Orange
b – to the extent that text messaging becomes heaven-sent manna for Orange
c – so much has text messaging become a moneyspinner for Orange
d – so much so that texting became a lucky strike for Orange

3 *Ce qui au début n'était que simple phénomène de mode chez les ados* (§2)
a – Which at the start was only a simple adolescent fashion phenomenon
b – That which firstly was a simple tendency of adolescent fashion
c – Which at the beginning was just a passing fashion for teenagers
d – What started out as nothing more than a teenage fashion fad

4 *s'étend progressivement depuis à peu près trois ans* (§2)
a – stretches out progressively since nearly three years
b – has gradually spread over the past three years or so
c – for three years now has been widening bit by bit
d – is expanding itself step by step since approximately three years

5 *toutes les couches de la société* (§2)
a – throughout all the social classes
b – all social strata
c – every section of society
d – all of the above

6 *Votes d'émissions de téléréalité, prévisions météo …* (§3)
a – Votes of real TV broadcasts, wether expectations …
b – Given voting for TV reality output, meteorological predictions …
c – What with reality show polls, weather forecasts and all the rest
d – Votes of real TV shows, weather forecasts, etc

7 *le nombre de SMS progresse chaque année de 35%* (§3)
a – the number of text messages increases each year of 35%
b – the number of text messages goes up every year by 35%
c – the number of text messages rises year after year to 35%
d – there is a year-on-year text message improvement of 35%

8 *d'après l'association des consommateurs, les 11 milliards de SMS généreraient un chiffre d'affaires de 1,4 milliards d'euros* (§4)
a – According to the consumers association, these 11 billions of text messages could engender a turnover of 1,4 billions of euros
b – Going by the association of consumers, the 11 billion text messages would generate a sales figure of € bn1.4
c – In accordance with the consumer association, the 11 billion text messages are going to provide sales reaching 1,4bn euro
d – In the opinion of the consumers' association, the 11 billion text messages will produce a turnover of €1.4bn

9 *Les SMS, dont le coût de revient s'élève à 2,21 centimes d'euro* (§5)

a – text messages, whose the cost price rises as high as 2,21 eurocent
b – text messages, whose cost to the operator is 2.21 eurocent
c – text messages of which the manufacturing price stands at 2.21 cents euro
d – text messages which raise € 0.221 for the operator

10 *abonnés* (§5)

a – phone users
b – regular customers
c – subscribers
d – all of the above

11 *Cet écart de prix montre à quel point les bénéfices réalisés sont importants* (§6)

a – This difference of price shows to what extent the benefits realised are important
b – This split in pricing illustrates the important profit margins made
c – This disparity demonstrates just how high profits are
d – This price gap makes one realise the significant advantages

12 *une étude de CDC-Ixis* (§7)

a – a study of CDC-Ixis
b – a CDC-Ixis's analysis
c – a report from CDC-IXIS
d – a research by CDC-Ixis

13 *la rentabilité des capitaux employés* (§7)

a – the profitability of the employed capital
b – the return on investment
c – the cost-effectiveness from the funds used
d – the yield of the principal

14 *dont beaucoup ont payé cher les licences UMTS-3G* (§7)

a – of which a lot have paid dear their UMTS-3G licences
b – whom several paid the UMTS-3G licences expensively
c – many of whom have paid a fortune for the UMTS-3G licences
d – whose UMTS-3G licences many cost the earth

15 *leur marge opérationnelle varie de 14 % pour Bouygues [...] jusqu'à 34 % pour Vodaphone* (§8)

a – Their operating margin varies by 14 % for Bouygues as far as 34 % for Vodaphone
b – Their profit margins range between 14 % for Bouygues up to 34 % for Vodaphone
c – Their operating margin goes from 14 % for Bouygues until 34 % for Vodaphone
d – Their operational margin fluctuates from 14 % for Bouygues to the amount of 34 % for Vodaphone

16 *Bouygues, quatrième opérateur européen* (§8)

a – Bouygues, fourth operator on the european market
b – Bouygues, the European forth operator
c – Bouygues, operator number four at the European level
d – Bouygues, the fourth largest operator in Europe

17 *Vodaphone, premier opérateur mondial* (§8)

a – Vodaphone, the first operator in the world
b – Vodaphone, the world's leading operator

c – Vodaphone, the world's prime operator
d – Vodaphone, the first global operator

18 *depuis quelque temps* (§9)
a – for some time now
b – since a little time
c – for sometimes
d – for a little while

19 *à partir de septembre* (§9)
a – as from September
b – from September onwards
c – starting in September
d – all of the above

20 *parmi les autres sujets chauds, outre les SMS* (§10)
a – another hot potato, apart from text messages
b – among the other heated subjects, text messages not included
c – amid other hot topics regardless of text messages
d – among polemic issues beyond text messages

21 *émettre un appel de l'étranger* (§10)
a – to call a foreign country
b – to phone from abroad
c – make an international call
d – all of the above

22 *qui serait largement supérieur aux coûts réels* (§10)
a – which would be largely superior to the real costs
b – that would be hardly higher than the real costs
c – which is apparently also well above the real cost
d – what might be greater than the true cost

23 *L'arrivée prochaine* (§11)
a – The next arrival
b – The arrival in the near future
c – The soon coming
d – The nearest appearance

24 *achèteront aux opérateurs classiques des minutes par millions* (§11)
a – will buy to the standard operators minutes in their millions
b – will buy minutes in their millions from the regular operators
c – will buy for classic operators minutes by millions
d – will buy traditional operators millions of minutes

25 *jouera en faveur des consommateurs* (§11)
a – will be to the benefit of consumers
b – will work to the favour of consumers
c – will play in favour of the consumers
d – will act on behalf of consumers

The other face of Britain today, what is often referred to in France as "la fracture sociale". With some 4 million children (30 % +) living in poor families, Britain has one of the highest child poverty rates in Europe. It would not be fair to lay all the blame at Tony Blair's door, since there has been little change since the beginning of the '90s, but ironically the economic boom is a contributory factor to this state of affairs.

A full translation with explanatory footnotes is to be found later.

À Londres, un enfant sur deux sous le seuil de pauvreté

1. Charles Dickens, s'il vivait aujourd'hui, aurait encore de quoi nourrir sa veine littéraire. Il trouverait matière à s'indigner dans le plus inattendu des résultats d'une enquête remise au maire de Londres, mardi 19 novembre, à la veille de la Journée internationale des droits de l'enfant : 53 % des enfants de la capitale britannique vivent sous le seuil de pauvreté. Ainsi, la plus riche, la plus opulente, la plus dispendieuse des capitales européennes abrite en son sein, à côté de ses nombreux millionnaires – en livres sterling –, plus de 300 000 enfants officiellement « pauvres ».

2. Ils ne vivent pas dans les lointaines banlieues mais au centre de la ville, au cœur du « Londres intérieur » qui compte près de trois millions d'habitants et possède le plus haut revenu d'Europe *per capita*.

3. Ils habitent les secteurs les plus démunis des subdivisions administratives *(boroughs)* de Hackney, Lambeth, Southwark ou Tower Hamlets, à quelques stations de métro des quartiers les plus prospères – Chelsea ou Kensington –, là où les prix de l'immobilier atteignent des sommets.

4. Autre surprise : la pauvreté affecte proportionnellement plus d'enfants dans le centre de Londres que dans toute autre région du pays. En Grande-Bretagne est « pauvre » toute personne vivant dans une famille disposant d'un revenu inférieur à 60 % du revenu moyen. Et l'enquête remise au maire repose sur les chiffres officiels du ministère du travail et des retraites. Par souci d'équité, elle prend en compte le revenu familial diminué des impôts, des prélèvements sociaux et des frais de logement, très inégaux selon les régions. La pauvreté infantile à Londres est la plus forte (73 %) parmi les minorités d'origine pakistanaise et bangladeshie. Le très faible taux de chômage national – à peine plus de 3 % – masque d'énormes disparités. Chaque année, Londres accueille quelque 150 000 nouveaux arrivants.

5. La grande majorité d'entre eux occupent un emploi très peu qualifié, ou n'en trouvent aucun. En termes réels, les revenus des travailleurs manuels n'ont progressé à Londres que de 9 % en dix ans, ceux des travailleuses de 12 %. Le « Inner London » souffre aujourd'hui du plus fort taux de chômage, parmi toutes les « sous-régions » du pays. Les enfants pauvres appartiennent aux familles où le chômage frappe l'un des parents ou les deux. Enfin, la tuberculose est entre trois et huit fois plus répandue à Londres que dans le reste du royaume. Ce qui, décidément, ne surprendrait pas Dickens.

(402 mots)

J-P. Langellier, *Le Monde*

1 *Charles Dickens, s'il vivait aujourd'hui* (§1)

a – Were he living today, Charles Dickens
b – Charles Dickens, if he lived today,
c – If Charles Dickens was still alive today, he
d – (a) & (c) but not (b)

2 *aurait encore de quoi nourrir sa veine littéraire* (§1)

a – would have to feed his literary vein.
b – would find plenty to write about.
c – would have the wherewithal to feed his literary imagination.
d – (b) & (c) but not (a)

3 *trouverait matière à s'indigner* (§1)

a – would find material so as to become indignant
b – would find plenty to get worked up about
c – should find matter to get on his high horse
d – ought to discover subjects so as to vent his ire

4 *une enquête remise au maire de Londres* (§1)

a – an investigation submitted to the London mayor
b – an inquest transferred to the Lord Mayor of London
c – a report handed over to the Mayor of London
d – an enquiry delivered to the London's mayor

5 *ainsi* (§1)

a – thus
b – in other words
c – so
d – in this way

6 *abrite en son sein* (§1)

a – harbours in its breast
b – accommodates close to its heart
c – provides warm-hearted lodgings for
d – shelters in its bosom

7 *à côté de ses nombreux millionnaires en livres sterling* (§1)

a – next to its numerous millionaires in pounds sterling
b – besides the large number of pound sterling millionaires
c – alongside its many £ sterling millionaires
d – rubbing shoulders with its many sterling millionaires

8 *les lointaines banlieues* (§2)

a – the far-flung outskirts
b – the outlying dormitory towns
c – the distant suburbs
d – the faraway suburbia

9 *qui compte près de trois millions d'habitants* (§2)
a – which counts up to close on three millions of inhabitants
b – with its 3,000,000 townspeople
c – with a population nigh on 3 million
d – which accounts for almost 3m citizens

10 *et possède le plus haut revenu d'Europe per capita* (§2)
a – which has the highest per capita income in Europe
b – with the most important European revenue per head
c – where everyone earns more than elsewhere in Europe
d – and gets the topmost European salary per head of population

11 *à quelques stations de métro des quartiers les plus prospères* (§3)
a – at some subway stations of the most prosperous quarters
b – at a few underground stops far from the richest parts of town
c – only a short tube ride away from the most upmarket residential areas
d – to some metro stations' distance from the best-off districts

12 *là où les prix de l'immobilier atteignent des sommets* (§3)
a – there where the real estate business costs reach the peak
b – where property prices go through the roof
c – where the cost of housing hits an all-time high
d – where estate costs attain the top spot

13 *dans une famille disposant d'un revenu inférieur à 60% du revenu moyen* (§4)
a – in a family disposing of a 60% average income
b – in a household whose income is below 60% of the national average
c – in a home where the income is 60% less than that of the medium one
d – in a family with an income inferior to 60% of the mean

14 *repose* (§4)
a – is based on
b – rests on
c – is supported by
d – lies on

15 *par souci d'équité* (§4)
a – out of a sense of even-handedness
b – in order to compare like with like
c – so as to be fair
d – with a concern for equity

16 *diminué des impôts* (§4)
a – diminished by taxes
b – lightened of taxes
c – net of tax
d – after tax reductions

17 *prélèvements sociaux* (§4)

a – social security payments
b – national insurance contributions
c – direct debit deductions
d – industrial levies

18 *Le très faible taux de chômage national – à peine plus de 3 %* (§4)

a – The very weak rate of national unemployment – with difficulty more than 3 %
b – The very slight rate of domestic jobless ones - a little over 3%
c – The very low nationwide unemployment rate – hardly more than 3%
d – (b) & (c) but not (a)

19 *Enfin, la tuberculose* (§5)

a – At last, tuberculosis
b – Tuberculosis is finally
c – In the end, tuberculosis
d – And, too cap it all, tuberculosis

20 *la tuberculose est trois à huit fois plus répandue à Londres que dans le reste du royaume* (§5)

a – tuberculosis is three to eight times as prevalent in London as in the rest of the country
b – tuberculosis is three to eight times more common in London than in the rest of the kingdom
c – tuberculosis is between three and eight times as widespread in London as elsewhere in the country
d – all of the above

An idea that London borrowed from capital cities elsewhere in the world, but which was rejected by the citizens of Edinburgh in a referendum in 2005. Particular attention should be paid to the figures in this text.

A full translation with explanatory footnotes is to be found later.

Taxe d'embouteillage : 30% de voitures en moins dans le centre de Londres

1. Le nombre de voitures circulant au centre de Londres a baissé de 30 % depuis l'introduction de la taxe d'embouteillage en février 2003, a annoncé mardi le maire de la capitale britannique, Ken Livingstone, en dressant le premier bilan annuel de ce péage électronique controversé.

2. L'objectif initial de cette taxe quotidienne de 5 livres (environ 7,5 euros), réduire les traditionnels embouteillages londoniens, a ainsi été atteint selon lui, avec une réduction du nombre d'embouteillages évaluée à 30 %.

3. Parallèlement, le nombre de voitures particulières à circuler dans le centre de Londres a baissé aussi de 30 %. Compte tenu d'une augmentation du nombre des taxis et des bus, le trafic global est en baisse de 18 %, de nombreux voyageurs optant désormais pour les transports en commun.

4. Selon les chiffres dévoilés mardi par le maire de Londres, le trafic des taxis et des bus a ainsi augmenté de 20 % dans la zone de 20 km^2 visée par la « *congestion charge* », les bus comptant 29 000 passagers supplémentaires aux heures de pointe, le matin, entre 07 h 00 et 10 h 00.

5. Niant que cette taxe d'embouteillage ait un impact négatif sur l'économie londonienne, Ken Livingstone a au contraire estimé qu'elle avait permis de fluidifier le trafic dans le centre de la capitale. Un effet positif qu'il a évalué à 50 millions de livres pour les entreprises travaillant à Londres.

6. Le bénéfice escompté de la nouvelle taxe est moindre que prévu, avec 68 millions de livres dégagés, contre 130 millions de livres escomptés au départ. M. Livingstone a mis cela sur le compte d'un effet dissuasif plus fort que prévu.

7. En moyenne, 110 000 automobilistes acquittent cette taxe chaque jour pour entrer dans le centre de Londres, et 165 000 amendes sont infligées chaque mois aux fraudeurs.

(295 mots)
Agences

1 *Taxe d'embouteillage* (titre)

a – Bottle-neck tax
b – Hold-up duty
c – Traffic-jam tax
d – none of the above

2 *30 % de voitures en moins* (titre)

a – Cars down 30 %
b – 30 % less cars
c – 30 % fewer cars
d – (a) and (c) but not (b)

3 *Le nombre de voitures circulant au centre de Londres a baissé de 30 %* (§1)

a – The amount of cars travelling into the centre of London has dropped of 30 %
b – The number of cars circulating in central London fell to 30 %
c – The volume of car traffic in central London has decreased by 30 %
d – The number of cars in circulation in the centre of London has fallen from 30 %

4 *en dressant le premier bilan annuel* (§1)

a – when presenting the first year's report
b – while drawing up the first balance sheet of the year
c – on raising firstly the annual statement of accounts
d – by putting down the first annual toll

5 *ce péage électronique controversé* (§1)

a – the debatable electronic turnpike
b – this controversed electronic toll
c – this much-discussed electronics tollgate
d – this highly-controversial electronic toll

6 *quotidienne* (§2)

a – daily
b – everyday
c – by day
d – day-to-day

7 *les traditionnels embouteillages* (§2)

a – habitual hold-ups
b – traditional traffic jams
c – time-honoured snarl-ups
d – conventional bottle-necks

8 *voitures particulières* (§3)

a – individual cars
b – private cars
c – personal cars
d – particular cars

9 *Compte tenu d'une augmentation du nombre des taxis* (§3)

a – Thanks to a boosting of the number of the taxis
b – Taken into account of the proliferation of taxis
c – Despite an increase in the number of taxis
d – Even taking account of the rise of the frequency in taxis

10 *voyageurs* (§3)

a – voyagers
b – commuters
c – holidaymakers
d – commercial travellers

11 *transports en commun* (§3)

a – common transports
b – public transport
c – communal transport
d – municipal transports

12 *la zone de 20km² visée par…* (§4)

a – the 20 square kilometer zone aimed at by…
b – the designated 20 km² sector…
c – the 20 sq. km. area covered by…
d – (b) and (c) but not (a)

13 *les bus comptant 29 000 passagers supplémentaires* (§4)

a – the buses counting on 29 000 supplementary passengers
b – with the busses numbering 29,000 additional travellers
c – with bus patronage up by 20,000
d – the buses tallying an extra 29,000 voyagers

14 *Niant que* (§5)

a – Dismissing the notion that
b – Denying the fact that
c – Refuting the idea that
d – (a) & (c) but not (b)

15 *ait [un impact négatif]* (§5)

a – is having
b – may have
c – should have
d – (a) & (b) but not (c)

16 *Le bénéfice escompté* (§6)

a – the profit counted on
b – the revenue generated
c – the hoped-for benefit
d – the profit discounted

17 *En moyenne 110.000* (§7)

a – In average, 110.000
b – By average, 110,000
c – On the average, 110 000
d – An average of 110,000

18 *acquittent* (§7)

a – acquit
b – get off
c – pay
d – are discharged

19 *165.000 amendes sont infligées* (§7)

a – 165,000 fines are handed out
b – 165.000 taxes are inflicted
c – 165 000 amends are made
d – 165,000 amendments are delivered

20 *fraudeurs* (§7)

a – dodgers
b – tax evaders
c – smugglers
d – swindlers

A company profile : a classic presentation of the sort of corporate image that every major international company produces.

A full translation with explanatory footnotes is to be found later.

Carrefour : je positive

1. Par ce slogan, apparu en 1988, Carrefour tend à décrire à ses clients sa façon d'exercer son métier de commerçant. Il symbolise le comportement, l'état d'esprit de l'ensemble des salariés, mobilisés pour trouver des solutions, anticiper les besoins. « Positiver », parfois encore taxé de néologisme, est entré dans le dictionnaire.

2. Il est Savoyard. Il est né en 1914. Il s'appelle Marcel Fournier. Aîné d'une famille de dix enfants, il va succéder à ses parents et à cinq générations de Fournier dans l'exploitation du magasin familial, une mercerie-bonneterie du centre d'Annecy, maison fondée en 1822. Commerce traditionnel s'il en est, et qu'on croirait immuable ! Mais l'homme est de ceux qui ne s'endorment pas sur les situations acquises. Il a des charges et de l'ambition, de quoi penser qu'on risque de tout perdre en ne voulant pas gagner assez. En vingt ans, il transforme l'affaire en une sorte de grand magasin de mille mètres carrés, avec succursale à Annemasse.

3. C'est le début des années cinquante, avec le boom des techniques, les nouveaux textiles, la machine à laver et, dans d'autres branches, les plastiques, le réfrigérateur, la télévision, en attendant mieux. Tout devrait favoriser le commerce, à condition de donner à une clientèle aux appétits de confort tout nouveaux les moyens d'acheter, en cherchant à vendre meilleur marché grâce à la vente en masse d'articles de grande consommation, en somme à pratiquer le « discount ». C'est aussi le début de la concentration urbaine. L'automobile est encore rare; en une décennie elle va tout envahir, et Marcel Fournier situe très vite les limites à l'expansion rêvée de son commerce : l'impossibilité de stationner devant son magasin.

4. Un jour, au cours d'une rencontre professionnelle, il s'ouvre de ces problèmes auprès de Louis Defforey et de son fils Denis, succursalistes alimentaires à Lagnieu, dans l'Ain.

5. Le 3 juin 1960, Marcel Fournier et les Defforey ouvrent, avenue de Parmelan, dans un immeuble en construction que son promoteur a baptisé "Carrefour", un supermarché "discount" de six cent cinquante mètres carrés affecté – c'est en France une nouveauté sensationnelle – d'un parking de soixante-dix places. Le succès, immédiat, transforme en vérités expérimentales les vues qui ont présidé à sa naissance : primo, le meilleur service que le magasin de l'avenir rendra à sa clientèle, c'est le bas prix; secundo, cette clientèle est disposée à prendre sa voiture pour aller chercher ce bas prix.

6. Forte de ce succès, la jeune société Carrefour ouvre, le 15 juin 1963, en pleine nature, à Sainte-Geneviève-des-Bois, au sud de la région parisienne, le premier hypermarché français dont Jacques Defforey, frère de Denis, prend la direction : deux mille cinq cents mètres carrés et quatre cents places de parking. On crie au fou ! Mais dès la première année, le magasin réalise le double des ventes prévues. le troisième, ouvert un peu plus tard à Bassens près de Chambéry, révèle encore autre chose : Carrefour a ses fanas, une

clientèle fidèle qui entretiendra des rapports affectifs avec son magasin. Dès lors, rien n'arrêtera le développement de ce nouveau type de commerce ni la marche en avant de la société.

7. A la mort de Marcel Fournier, au début de l'année 1985, Carrefour gérait cinquante-sept magasins en France, dix-huit en Espagne, neuf au Brésil, deux en Argentine. Vingt ans plus tard, en 2005, ils sont 179 en France et 810 dans 23 pays dans le monde à porter l'enseigne Carrefour, avec toute la signification que cela comporte.

(569 mots)
Journal de Carrefour

1 *Par ce slogan, apparu en 1988, Carrefour tend a décrire à ses clients sa façon d'exercer son métier de commerçant* (§1)

a – By means of this slogan, appeared in 1988 Carrefour tends to describe to its clients its way to exercise its trade of shopkeeper.
b – Through this motto which made its apparition in 1988, Carrefour stretches towards explaining to its customers its way of carrying on its business of salesman.
c – This corporate byword, adopted in 1988, sums up for shoppers the Carrefour approach to the art of retailing
d – The catchphrase that was coined in 1988 tries to portray Carrefour as a professional merchant for its customers

2 *l'état d'esprit de l'ensemble des salariés, mobilisés pour [...] anticiper les besoins* (§1)

a – the state of mind of the whole employees, working in order to anticipate needs
b – the attitude of the all workforce called up to think ahead of the needs
c – the commitment of the whole workforce to anticipating new consumer trends
d – the predisposition of all members of staff, constantly on the alert for new requirements

3 *parfois encore taxé de néologisme* (§1)

a – sometimes even today decried by purists as a new coinage
b – looked down on disparagingly in some circles as being a neologism
c – sometimes still disapproved of as a nonce word
d – all of the above

4 *Il est Savoyard. Il est né en 1914. Il s'appelle Marcel Fournier* (§2)

a – He is a Savoyard, born in 1914 and called Marcel Fournier
b – Marcel Fournier was born in Savoy in 1914
c – He comes from Savoy. He is born in 1914. His name is Marcel Fournier
d – He was a Savoyman, born in 1914 and baptised Marcel Fournier

5 *Il va succéder à ses parents et à cinq générations de Fournier* (§2)

a – He will succeed his parents and five Fournier generations
b – He would succeed to his parents and to 5 generations of Fournier
c – He is going to step into the shoes of his parents and five Fournier generations
d – In due time he was to take over from his parents and five generations of Fourniers

6 *dans l' exploitation du magasin familial* (§2)
a – in the exploitation of the family shop
b – in the running of the family business
c – in turning to best advantage the family's store
d – all of the above

7 *Commerce traditionnel s'il en est, et qu'on croirait immuable !* (§2)
a – If it is a traditional trade, we would believe it to be eternal.
b – The sort of long-established small business that seems set to stay as it is for ever and ever
c – A customary shop if there are any, and that one would have thought unchanged
d – A venerable company if ever there was one that one would believe permanent.

8 *l'homme est de ceux qui ne s'endorment pas sur les situations acquises* (§2)
a – he was not one to sit back and let the business run itself.
b – he was of the stuff of men who do not rest on their laurels
c – this man was not one of those who go to sleep on their assets
d – all of the above

9 *il a des charges* (§4)
a – he had overheads to pay
b – he had responsabilities to look after
c – he had a family to support
d – he had burdens to carry

10 *on risque de tout perdre en ne voulant pas gagner assez* (§2)
a – All may be lost unless strong-minded enough to earn
b – Who dares wins
c – Nothing ventured, nothing gained
d – Faint heart never won fair lady

11 *en vingt ans il transforme l'affaire* (§2)
a – in a mere twenty years he had transformed the business
b – in twenty years time he was to transform the company
c – over a period of twenty years he was changing the concern
d – by twenty years he will refurbish the enterprise

12 *C'est le début des années cinquante, avec le boom des techniques* (§3)
a – It's the beginning of the 50's, with the boom of technics
b – It's now the start of the fifty years and of the technical boom
c – The early Fifties was a time of technological expansion
d – We are at the beginning of the 50s and the explosion of techniques.

13 *en attendant mieux* (§3)
a – while waiting for better
b – with plenty more innovations still to come
c – that's enough to be going on with
d – at the same time expecting an improvement

14 *Tout devrait favoriser le commerce* (§3)

a – Everything was in place for retailing to flourish
b – All should support trade
c – Every one should have encouraged the business
d – Nothing ought to stop business

15 *à condition de donner à une clientèle […] les moyens d'acheter* (§3)

a – provided customers […] could afford to buy
b – on condition of giving customers […] the wherewithal to purchase
c – so long as customers […] were given the means of buying
d – provided customers […] were allowed to make purchases

16 *une clientèle aux appétits de confort tout nouveaux* (§3)

a – a clientele with the very new appetites for comfort
b – consumers with a newly-acquired taste for material comforts
c – customers showing a craving for innovative forms of comfort
d – a customer base that has just recently demanded comfort

17 *en cherchant à vendre meilleur marché grâce à la vente en masse d'articles de grande consommation* (§3)

a – while seeking to sell cheaper thanks to selling mass market products
b – through trying to sell more cheaply by selling a lot of articles
c – by trying to inundate the market with staple goods
d – by offering lower prices through volume sales of everyday items

18 *C'est aussi le début de la concentration urbaine* (§3)

a – It is also the beginning of the urban concentration
b – This is too the start of town growth
c – Conurbations date from this time
d – This period also marks the beginning of town centre congestion

19 *au cours d'une rencontre professionnelle* (§4)

a – in the course of a professional get-together
b – during an occupational date
c – in the run of a skilled conference
d – on the occasion of a business meeting

20 *il s'ouvre de ces problèmes auprès de Louis Defforey* (§4)

a – he opened his heart about these problems to Louis Defforey
b – he aired his concerns to Louis Defforey
c – he entrusted Louis Defforey with the difficulties he was having
d – he got these problems off his chest by talking to Louis Defforey

21 *dans un immeuble en construction que son promoteur a baptisé « Carrefour »* (§5)

a – in a newly-constructed complex that the property developer had named "Carrefour"
b – in a building under construction that its promoter has baptised "Crossroads"
c – in a block of flats being built that its builder nicknamed "Carrefour"
d – in a real estate that the building engineer called "Crossroads"

22 *affecté d'un parking de soixante-dix places* (§5)

a – affected by a parking of seventy places
b – with parking for seventy cars
c – allocated to a seventy place car park
d – alongside a parking lot of seventy places

23 *Le succès, immédiat, transforme en vérités expérimentales les vues qui ont présidé à sa naissance* (§5)

a – It was an overnight success and confirmed the wildest dreams
b – Immediate success converts into experimental truths the views which chaired its birth
c – It was an instantaneous success and changed into untried facts the sights which governed its conception
d – Immediately the achievement remodelled the original plans as hypothetical realities.

24 *Forte de ce succès* (§6)

a – Confident of success
b – Bolstered by this success
c – Knowledgeable about this achievement
d – Strengthened by this success

25 *en pleine nature* (§6)

a –in a natural beauty spot
b – in the middle of nowhere
c – on a greenfield site
d – right in the countryside

26 *On crie au fou !* (§6)

a – Everyone thought it was madness
b – People cried out to stop the madman
c – All protested that he was a fool
d – We shouted out to the idiot

27 *dès la première année le magasin réalise le double des ventes prévues* (§6)

a – as soon as the first year the shop realised the double of the forecast sales
b – from the first year onwards, the supermarket achieved the expected sales two times over
c – in its first year, the store doubled its target takings
d – from the outset, the turnover was twice as important as foreseen

28 *rien n'arrêtera le développement de ce nouveau type de commerce ni la marche en avant de la société.* (§6)

a – nothing will stop the development of this new style of commerce nor social progress
b – nothing could halt the spread of this new form of retailing or prevent Carrefour from going from strength to strength
c – nothing will stand in the way of the growth of this new kind of business neither the onward march of society.
d – nothing was to hamper this innovative style of business nor walk in front of the company

29 *ils sont 179 en France [...] à porter l' enseigne Carrefour* (§7)

a – they are 175 superstores in France [...] to carry the Carrefour shop sign
b – Carrefour counts 175 superstores in France [...] which display the Carrefour ensign
c – 175 superstores in France [...] trade under the Carrefour banner
d – all of the above

30 *Carrefour a ses fanas, une clientèle fidèle qui entretiendra des rapports affectifs avec son magasin* (§5)

a – Carrefour discovers customer loyalty : regular shoppers ready to return time and time again to the same store.
b – Carrefour has its fans, a faithful clientele which keeps up affective relations with its shop.
c – Carrefour has its supporters, loyal clients which will maintain the emotional link with their store.
d – Carrefour has its addicts, reliable consumers who will support a sentimental relationship with their store.

A personal indulgence taking me back to my own schoolboy days in the home town of Barbour & Sons. Though it may go back many years now, this product profile is not in the least 'dated'. If anything, the product has gone on to even greater success, and as an exercise the text remains pertinent.

A full translation with explanatory footnotes is to be found later.

Le Barbour, classique tous temps

1. Les rues des villes sont envahies depuis peu de silhouettes vert bouteille. Lycéens des beaux quartiers, hommes d'affaires et élégants des boulevards arborent le même imperméable d'aspect luisant quel que soit le temps : le Barbour. Étonnant succès pour un vêtement qui symbolise au contraire la tradition.

2. Il ne pouvait naître qu'outre-Manche. Au nord-est de l'Angleterre, il y a un siècle exactement John Barbour, un petit tailleur de Newcastle eut l'idée de couper des vêtements pour ses clients agriculteurs dans une toile enduite, destinée aux voiles de bateau.

3. Ce n'est qu'en 1930 que sa boutique, qui avait prospéré grâce à ce produit, l'a remplacée par un coton d'Egypte, teinté ensuite en vert anglais. Quelques modèles ont alors été conçus pour les pêcheurs, les chasseurs et même pour les premiers motards, qui réclamaient tous un vêtement parfaitement étanche. De cette époque date la première veste d'extérieur à fermeture éclair, la Solway Zipper, qui figure toujours dans le catalogue de la marque.

4. Jusqu'à la fin des années 60, le nom de Barbour, dont le siège et l'unité de fabrication sont installées à South Shields n'a été connu que des seuls Britanniques. En particulier des grandes familles aristocratiques qui ne concevaient pas d'aller à la pêche ou à la chasse sans leur Spey Wading jacket ou leur Gamefair. La marque, qui fournissait la Cour, obtint alors le label de « *fournisseur de Sa Majesté la Reine, du duc d'Edimbourg et du prince de Galles* » et en quelques années, le vêtement envahit les rues londoniennes.

5. À la fin des années 80, avec le retour à l'« authentique », au durable et au fonctionnel, la demande de vêtements solides, les premiers Barbour importés sur le continent ont connu le succès en Italie, en Allemagne, puis en France, malgré leur réputation de « haut de gamme ».

6. Créée en 1989, la filiale française a vu ses ventes multipliées par sept en l'espace de seulement quatre ans: soixante mille imperméables ont été distribués en 1993. L'an dernier, Barbour France, qui emploie aujourd'hui dix-huit personnes, a réalisé un chiffre d'affaires de 9 millions d'euros pour son exercice, dont le cinquième avec d'autres produits comme les chapeaux, les chemises et les bottes. Curieusement le modèle d'imperméable le plus vendu actuellement à travers le monde, le Beaufort, a été créé il y a une quinzaine d'années à la demande des chasseurs français. Son carnier est jugé très pratique par les lycéens.

7. Aujourd'hui, J. Barbour & Sons expédie les deux tiers de sa production vers l'étranger, et a été sacré deux fois meilleur exportateur britannique de l'année. Mais tout reste

fabriqué dans les cinq usines. Chaque modèle, qui comporte entre trente et quarante pièces de tissu, nécessite quinze mille points de couture. Cette technique de fabrication et la graisse qu'il faut régulièrement appliquer, et dont la composition est gardée secrète, assurent à ces vêtements une imperméabilité totale sous les pires averses.

8. Cet entretien régulier, comme pour une belle paire de chaussures, est le seul moyen de conserver sa solidité à une toile qui, sinon, devient cassante en se desséchant : un manuel et une boîte de graisse sont remis au client. Cependant, Barbour assure dans ses ateliers la réimperméabilisation, les réparations éventuelles, comme toutes les modifications souhaitées par les clients. Un dixième des sept cents salariés de la firme travaillent à ce service après-vente : « *C'est devenu un de nos arguments de vente, mais nous devons l'expliquer à nos revendeurs. Ils craignaient de ne revoir leurs clients que pour des réparations, alors que ceux-ci font au contraire, la publicité de la solidité de produits qui coûtent en général moins de 300* », explique le directeur de Barbour France.

9. Rançon du succès, Barbour est devenu un nom générique et les copies se multiplient. Mais Margaret Barbour, qui dirige l'entreprise familiale, est intransigeante. Personne d'autre que Barbour n'a le droit d'afficher le logo aux trois couronnes de la firme. Rien que pendant le dernier trimestre, la filiale française a engagé quarante-sept procédures contre des détaillants qui vendaient du vulgaire coton huilé sous la marque centenaire.

(675 mots)
Christophe de Chenay, *Le Monde*

1 *Le Barbour, classique tous temps* (titre)

a – Barbour, the all-weather classic
b – The Barbour, one of the all-time greats
c – Barbour, the all-purpose standard.
d – The all-day model Barbour

2 *Les rues des villes sont envahies depuis peu de silhouettes vert bouteille* (§1)

a – The streets of the towns are invaded since a little time by green bottle silhouettes
b – Town streets have been flooded for a short time with bottle green shadows.
c – Our city streets have recently been invaded by figures in bottle green
d – The streets of our towns were overrun a moment ago by bottle green shapes

3 *lycéens des beaux quartiers* (§1)

a – high-school kids in the beautiful quarters
b – schoolboys from well-to-do families
c – pupils from good secondary schools
d – posh estate pupils

4 *élégants des boulevards* (§1)

a – boulevard dandies
b – elegant men-in-the-street
c – fashionable men-about-town
d – chic avenues

5 *arborent* (§1)
a – display
b – sport
c – carry
d – hoist

6 *le même imperméable d'aspect luisant* (§1)
a – the same shiny-looking raincoat
b – the same dull outlook waterproof
c – the same glistening mackintosh
d – the same rainproof outdoor wear with its dull sheen

7 *quel que soit le temps* (§1)
a – in all weathers
b – whatever the weather
c – come rain come shine
d – all of the above

8 *Étonnant succès pour un vêtement qui symbolise au contraire la tradition.* (§1)
a – A singular success for an item of clothing that is the byword for tradition.
b – Astonishing success for a clothing which on the opposite stands up for tradition.
c – An incredible bestseller that contrarily symbolises custom.
d – A hit which surprisingly for clothes represents habits.

9 *Il ne pouvait naître qu'outre-Manche* (§2)
a – It could be born only cross-Channel
b – It couldn't be anything but English
c – It could only be born on the other side of the Channel
d – It could only spring up in England

10 *un petit tailleur* (§2)
a – a small tailor
b – a humble tailor
c – a modest tailor
d – a little tailor

11 *couper des vêtements [...] dans une toile enduite, destinée aux voiles de bateau* (§2)
a – cut clothes in a smeared canvas, intended for ship's sails
b – cut clothing from coated sail made for boats' sails
c – cut clothes out of oiled sailcloth
d – cut clothes from waxed cloth, destined to become sails for a boat

12 *teinté ensuite en vert anglais* (§3)
a – then dyed moorland green
b – shaded later English green
c – tinted furthermore with Saxon green
d – subsequently given a light green hue

13 *pêcheurs* (§3)
a – anglers
b – sinners
c – fishers
d – fishermen

14 *étanche* (§3)
a – watertight
b – weatherproof
c – impermeable
d – leak-proof

15 *qui figure toujours dans le catalogue de la marque* (§3)
a – which yet figures in the brand catalogue
b – which always stays in the firm's catalogue
c – which is still available to this day in the Barbour catalogue
d – all of the above

16 *le nom de Barbour [...] n'a été connu que des seuls Britanniques* (§4)
a – the name of Barbour was not known to the only British
b – Barbour's name was not known of the British people alone
c – Barbour was known solely to the British consumer
d – the name of Barbour was known by the British public on their own.

17 *En particulier des grandes familles aristocratiques* (§4)
a – in particular great aristocratic families
b – and then only to members of the upper classes
c – moreover by some grandees
d – privately large families of high birth

18 *dont le siège et l'unité de fabrication sont installées à South Shields* (§4)
a – of which the seat and the factory are settled in South Shields
b – whose the head office and manufacturing unit are set up in South Shields
c – of which the headquarters and production plant are established in South Shields
d – whose main office and workshop are located in South Shields

19 *la marque, qui fournissait la Cour* (§4)
a – The brand, which furnished the Court
b – The company, which supplied the Royal Household
c – The make which equipped the Royal Court
d – The trademark, which provided for the Court of St. James

20 *le vêtement envahit les rues londoniennes* (§4)
a – The clothes invaded the Londonian streets
b – The garment invaded London's streets
c – The jacket was to be seen everywhere on the streets of London
d – The item of clothing overran the London streets

21 *avec le retour à l'authentique, au durable et au fonctionnel* (§5)

a – with the move back to items true to life, rugged and workaday
b – with the "back to basics" fashion for hard- wearing, practical clothing
c – with the return to the authentic, the durable and the functional clothes
d – with the turnabout to everything genuine, tough and purpose-made

22 *malgré leur réputation de "haut de gamme"* (§5)

a – despite their upmarket image
b – although their reputation is expensive
c – in spite their reputation of top of range
d – despite that they are reputed to be top-class

23 *Créée en 1989* (§6)

a – Set up in 1989
b – Established in 1989
c – Spun off in 1989,
d – all of the above

24 *la filiale française a vu ses ventes multipliées par sept en l'espace de seulement quatre ans* (§6)

a – the French subsidiary saw its sales multiply by seven over a four-year period.
b – sales through the outlets in France soared sevenfold within a mere four years.
c – the French side of the business increased its sales seven times over in four years.
d – all of the above

25 *soixante mille [imperméables] ont été distribués en 1993* (§6)

a – sixty thousand were distributed in 1993
b – 60,000 were sold in 1993
c – 60,000 were handed out in 1993
d – 60,000 were allocated in 1993.

26 *L'an dernier, Barbour France qui emploie aujourd'hui 18 personnes, a réalisé un chiffre d'affaires de 9 millions d'euros pour son exercice* (§9)

a – Barbour France, which employs eighteen people today, realised sales of 9 millions of euros for the latest exercise.
b – Barbour France and its eighteen current employees produced a turnover of € 9 millions for the last exercise.
c – Barbour France, which today has taken on eighteen employees, turned in 9 million € in revenues during its last trading year.
d – Barbour France, now with a workforce of 18, had a turnover of €9m for the last financial year.

27 *dont le cinquième avec d'autres produits comme les chapeaux, les chemises et les bottes* (§6)

a – whose the fifth with other products like hats, shirts and boots
b – of which the fifth with other items as the hats, the vests and the marching shoes
c – a fifth of which with accessories such as hats, casual shirts and wellington boots
d – whose one fifth with other casuals like caps, country checks and field boots

28 *le modèle le plus vendu actuellement à travers le monde, le Beaufort, a été créé à la demande de chasseurs français* (§6)

a – the Beaufort, at present the best-selling model worldwide, was designed with French hunters in mind.
b – the model the most sold today across the world, the Beaufort, was introduced at the demand of French huntsmen.
c – the Beaufort model of the most sold coat presently in the world was crafted at the request of French gamekeepers.
d – the model more currently sold throughout the world, the Beaufort, was created on order from the French huntsmen.

29 *il y a une quinzaine d'années* (§6)

a – that makes it almost fifteen years
b – about fifteen years since
c – some fifteen years ago
d – approximately for fifteen years

30 *Aujourd'hui Barbour expédie les deux tiers de sa production vers l'étranger* (§7)

a – Today Barbour expedites the two thirds of its products towards foreign countries
b – Nowadays Barbour exports two thirds of its output
c – At present Barbour dispatches for the two thirds its production overseas
d – Barbour now sends abroad two thirds of its manufacture

31 *a été sacré deux fois meilleur exportateur britannique de l'année* (§7)

a – was twice sacred year's Better British Exporter.
b – was consecrated two times the year's Best British Exporter.
c – has twice been crowned a Better British Exporter of the Year.
d – has on two occasions won the annual Best British Exporter Award.

32 *Mais tout reste fabriqué dans les cinq usines* (§7)

a – But all remains made in the five factories
b – But everything stays made in the five plants
c – But everything is still produced in the five workshops
d – But all items are yet carried out in the five works

33 *qui comporte entre trente et quarante pièces de tissu* (§7)

a – which is composed between 30 and 40 bits of material.
b – which includes thirty to fourty pieces of fabric.
c – which is made up from anything between thirty and forty pieces of cloth
d – which comprises thirty or forty scraps of cloth

34 *nécessite* (§7)

a – necessitates
b – calls on
c – needs
d – requires

35 *qui, sinon, devient cassante en se desséchant* (§8)
a – which otherwise cracks as it dries out
b – which, if not, becomes breakable by becoming parched.
c – which, unless, becomes fragile while it gets dry.
d – which except for becoming brittle while being desiccated

36 *un manuel et une boîte de graisse sont remis au client* (§8)
a – a manual and a box of fat are handed over to the client
b – a textbook and a box of grease are given to the buyer
c – an instruction booklet and a tin of wax are supplied to the customer.
d – a handbook and a tin of fat are presented to the customer

37 *Un dixième des sept cents salariés de la firme travaillent à ce service après-vente* (§8)
a – a tenth of the seven hundred salaried workers of the firm work on this after-sales service.
b – one in ten of the firm's seven-hundred strong workforce is employed in this after-sales department
c – every tenth worker in the firm is affected to this after-sales service.
d – all of the above.

38 *alors que ceux-ci font au contraire la publicité de la solidité de produits qui coûtent en général moins de 300 euros* (§8)
a – while these latter make on the contrary the publicity of the solidity of products which cost in general less that 300 euro
b – even though quite the reverse these promote the fastness of goods which are priced below 300 €
c – when on the contrary these do the advertising of the sturdiness of items that cost us less than 300 euro
d – whereas in fact they provide living proof of the durability of garments which sell on average for under € 300

39 *Rançon du succès, Barbour est devenu un nom générique et les copies se multiplient* (§8)
a – Ransom of success, Barbour became a generic name and the copies multiply
b – The price to pay is that Barbour has become a household name and imitations abound
c – The pay-off is that Barbour is now a non-proprietary name and forgeries proliferate.
d –The price of success : Barbour is becoming a general name and the copies increase

40 *qui dirige l'entreprise familiale* (§8)
a – who manages this family firm
b – who steers this family company
c – who runs the familial undertaking
d – (a) & (b) but not (c)

41 *Margaret Barbour est intransigeante* (§9)
a – Margaret Barbour is uncompromising.
b – Margaret Barbour is stubborn.
c – Margaret Barbour takes a firm line
d – (a) & (c) but not (b)

42 *Personne d'autre que Barbour n'a le droit d'afficher le logo aux trois couronnes de la firme* (§9)

a – Nobody other that Barbour does not have the right to stick up the logo with the three crowns of the firm
b – Nobody else than Barbour has the right to show the three crowns' symbol of the firm
c – No-one other than Barbour is legally entitled to use the firm's triple crown trademark
d – No company other than Barbour is eligible for the three crown brand.

43 *Rien que pendant le dernier trimestre* (§9)

a – Nothing but during the latest term
b – Only during the last quarter
c – In the last three months alone
d – Simply in the latest trimester

44 *la filiale française a engagé quarante-sept procédures contre des détaillants* (§9)

a – the French subsidiary took out forty-seven court actions against retailers
b – the French subsidiary committed forty-seven lawsuits against dealers
c – the French branch engaged forty-seven procedures against shopkeepers
d – the branch in France introduced forty-seven proceedings against merchants

45 *qui vendaient du vulgaire coton huilé sous la marque centenaire.* (§9)

a – who sold vulgar cotton oiled under the centenarian brand.
b – who were passing off common-or-garden oilskin as the genuine, century-old article.
c – who traded in ordinary oiled cotton for the centenary-long make.
d – who were fraudulently retailing waxed base cotton by the hundred-years-old trade-name.

Another topic that is constantly in the news that is of immediate concern to students. Statistics may be on a rollercoaster, government policies come and go, but the phenomenon remains with us. A full translation with explanatory footnotes is to be found later.

Les jeunes et le tabac

1. Les adolescents se sont remis à fumer. Une étude réalisée en avril auprès d'un millier de jeunes de 12 à 18 ans pour le compte de la Caisse nationale d'assurance – maladie (CNAM) révèle que 35 % des 12-18 ans grillent une cigarette, au moins de temps en temps. Cette proportion est en hausse de 4,5 points par rapport à la dernière enquête et à peine inférieure à celle des adultes, qui sont 36 % à fumer.

2. Malgré cette rechute, la tendance globale est orientée à la baisse depuis 1987, date à laquelle près de la moitié (46 %) des adolescents fumaient. En outre, d'autres chiffres démontrent qu'à l'évidence le tabac a moins la cote auprès des jeunes que par le passé. Le nombre de fumeurs réguliers, c'est-à-dire consommant au moins une cigarette par jour, est lui aussi en diminution : 74 % de l'ensemble des jeunes fumeurs sont des fumeurs réguliers, contre 77,5 % l'an passé.

3. L'âge moyen d'initiation au tabac est retardé, qui est passé de 12,5 ans il y a quatorze ans à 14,5 ans aujourd'hui. Enfin, les jeunes fumeurs souhaitent de plus en plus souvent arrêter de fumer, et près des deux tiers affirment avoir déjà fait une tentative d'arrêt avec, pour motivations, la santé (81 %), la dépendance (62 %) et le coût (48 %).

4. Pourtant, dans le même temps, l'image du fumeur se dégrade. Les deux tiers des adolescents interrogés se disent persuadés que le fumeur est une personne « *triste* », alors que le non-fumeur, lui, passe pour « *énergique* » (75 %), « *à forte personnalité* » (44 %), « *sympathique* » (39 %). Dans ce contexte, comment les adolescents viennent-ils au tabac ? Sous l'influence de leurs copains, mais aussi de leurs parents. 45 % des jeunes dont les deux parents fument sont eux-mêmes fumeurs, contre 31 % de ceux dont aucun des deux parents n'est adepte de la cigarette. L'attitude plus ou moins répressive des adultes à l'égard de la cigarette joue grandement : on trouve 18 % de fumeurs parmi les adolescents auxquels leurs parents interdisent de fumer, 90 % parmi ceux qui disposent d'une autorisation parentale...

5. Quelle que soit l'influence de l'environnement, le tabagisme des adolescents s'accentue avec l'âge, de même que les quantités de cigarettes grillées. La consommation moyenne des fumeurs réguliers passe de 2,2 cigarettes par jour chez les 12-13 ans à 8,9 chez les 16-17, et 10,7 pour les jeunes de 18 ans.

6. Selon deux autres enquêtes auprès des médecins généralistes et du personnel hospitalier, 34 % des médecins généralistes sont fumeurs. Ils sont néanmoins 88 % à se sentir investis d'une mission de prévention, et 84 % à affirmer mettre systématiquement en garde les parents fumeurs des dangers du tabac pour leurs enfants. Quant aux personnels hospitaliers, s'ils estiment qu'ils doivent avoir une attitude exemplaire vis-à-vis des malades, ils ne sont que 37 % à penser que la prévention fait partie de leurs fonction.

(461 mots)
Pascale Kremer, *Le Monde*

1 *une étude réalisée en avril auprès d'un millier de jeunes de 12 à 18 ans* (§1)
a – a study realised in April near a thousand of young 12 to 18 years old
b – a paper conducted in April with a thousand youngs of 12-18
c – a research led by approximately one thousand young people aged 12 to 18
d – a survey carried out in April involving some one thousand 12-18-year-olds

2 *pour le compte de la CNAM* (§1)
a – commissioned by the French Health Insurance Department (CNAM)
b – for the French Health Insurance Department's account (CNAM)
c – on account of the French Social Security (CNAM)
d – put down on the bill of the French Social Security (CNAM)

3 *grillent une cigarette* (§1)
a – burn a coffin nail
b – toast a butt
c – light up a fag
d – singe a cancer stick

4 *par rapport à la dernière enquête* (§1)
a – with respect to the latest report
b – compared to the previous study
c – with regard to the final investigation
d – in relation to the last enquiry

5 *à peine inférieure à celle des adultes* (§1)
a – scarcely inferior to the one of adults
b – hardly under that adult's one
c – only slightly lower than that of adults
d – with difficulty below the adults' one

6 *qui sont 36 % à fumer* (§1)
a – who are 36 % to smoke
b – who smoke at 36 %
c – 36 % of which smoke
d – of whom 36 % smoke

7 *la tendance globale est orientée à la baisse depuis 1987* (§2)
a – the global movement shows a bearish tendency since 1987
b – the overall trend since 1987 has been downwards
c – the worldwide swing is directed in the decline since 1987
d – the total inclination has been in decline since 1987

8 *date à laquelle près de la moitié des adolescents fumaient* (§2)
a – date at which nearly the half of the adolescents smoked
b – date on which close on half of the teenagers were smoking
c – when almost half of all youngsters smoked
d – at a time when near to half of the teenagers used to smoke

9 *En outre, d'autres chiffres démontrent qu'à l'évidence le tabac a moins la cote auprès des jeunes que par le passé* (§2)

a – Besides, other figures demonstrate that obviously tobacco has less the quotation near young people than in the past.
b – Moreover other figures in the evidence show that teenagers fancy less tobacco than before.
c – Furthermore other figures confirm that smoking really is less popular amongst youngsters than it used to be.
d – What's more, other statistics clearly prove that cigarettes are less considered by teenagers than formerly.

10 *c'est à dire consommant au moins une cigarette par jour* (§2)

a – that's to say, consummating for the least a cigarette per day
b – i.e. smoking at least one cigarette a day
c – in other words, consuming at least one cigarette every day
d – that is going through a minimum of a cigarette a day

11 *L'âge moyen d'initiation au tabac est retardé* (§3)

a – The average age of initiation to tobacco is delayed
b – The mean age of introduction to cigarettes is backward.
c – Young people take up smoking later
d – Youngsters on average hold back to begin to smoke.

12 *Enfin les jeunes fumeurs souhaitent de plus en plus souvent arrêter de fumer* (§3)

a – At last, young smokers hope more and more often to stop to smoke
b – Finally, more and more young smokers want to stop smoking
c – At long last, teenagers who smoke wish over and over again they could stop smoking.
d – Eventually, under-age smokers aspire more frequently to give up smoking.

13 *Pourtant, dans le même temps, l'image du fumeur se dégrade* (§4)

a – And yet, at the same time, the smoker is less and less socially accepted
b – Nonetheless, concurrently, the representation of the smoker is showing signs of wear and tear.
c – However, at the same time , the image of the smoker is degrading.
d – Even so, concomitantly, the smoker's self-respect is debased.

14 *Les deux tiers des adolescents interrogés* (§4)

a – Two thirds of the adolescents interrogated
b – The two thirds of the teenagers questioned
c – Two out of three adolescents polled
d – Two in three teenagers examined

15 *le non-fumeur passe pour « énergique »* (§4)

a – the non-smoker passes for energetic
b – the non-smoker is seen as being "full of life"
c – the non-smoker is made out to be boisterous
d – the non-smoker is put over as invigorating

16 *sympathique* (§4)

a – sympathetic
b – considerate
c – well-disposed
d – nice to know

17 *Dans ce contexte, comment les adolescents viennent-ils au tabac* (§4)

a – In this context, how the teenagers do they come to the tobacco first ?
b – On that point, how come they start to smoke ?
c – If this is so, how do teenagers come to take up smoking in the first place ?
d –In this respect, how do adolescents come to smoking to begin with ?

18 *sous l'influence de leurs copains* (§4)

a – By emulating their friends
b – Through taking the lead from their pals
c – As a result of peer group pressure
d – all of the above

19 *45 % des jeunes dont les deux parents fument sont eux-mêmes fumeurs* (§4)

a – 45 % of youngsters both of whose parents smoke are themselves smokers
b – 45 % of youngsters whose both parents smoke are smokers themselves
c – 45 % of youngsters with two smoking parents smoke too
d – 45 % of youngsters of which the two parents smoke smoke also

20 *contre 31% de ceux dont aucun des deux parents n'est adepte de la cigarette* (§4)

a – as against 31% of those, neither of whose parents smokes
b – against 31% of the ones whom none of both parents is a cigarette addict
c – compared to 31% for those whose neither of the two parents is a supporter of the cigarette.
d – opposed to 31% of those of whom neither parent is adept at smoking.

21 *L'attitude plus ou moins répressive des adultes à l'égard de la cigarette joue grandement* (§4)

a – Just how strict parents are about smoking plays a determining role
b – The more or less repressive attitude of the parents with regard to the cigarette plays greatly
c – The widespread restrictions imposed by parents are more or less prohibitive.
d – (a) & (c) but not (b)

22 *ceux qui disposent d'une autorisation parentale* (§4)

a – those who obtain parental consent
b – those whose parents' approval is obtained
c – those whose parents tolerate their smoking
d – all of the above

23 *Quelle que soit l'influence de l'environnement, le tabagisme des adolescents s'accentue avec l'âge* (§4)

a – Irrespective of the environmental influences, the nicotine habit is growing with the youngsters' age.
b – Whatever is the influence of the environment, the nicotinism of the teenagers is accentuated with the age.
c – Regardless of the impact of their background, the incidence of teenage smoking increases with age
d – Notwithstanding the pressure of their milieu, the tobacco addiction of the teenagers becomes more marked with age

24 *[Ils sont 88 %] à se sentir investis d'une mission de prévention* (§6)

a – feel invested with a mission of prevention
b – feel duty-bound to discourage smoking
c – feel it is their task to deter patients from smoking
d – feel they have to prevent smoking

25 *s'ils estiment qu'ils doivent avoir une attitude exemplaire vis-à-vis des malades* (§6)

a – if they estimate they should have an exemplary attitude vis-à-vis the patients
b – while they recognise they should set a good example to their patients
c – in the event of their judging that their behaviour should be exemplary facing the patients
d – although they esteem that they ought to adopt a faultless behaviour in front of patients

2

Corrigés

Texte 1 La Route Payante	
1	C
2	C
3	A
4	D
5	C
6	D
7	D
8	A
9	B
10	B
11	D
12	B
13	D
14	B
15	D
16	C
17	D
18	C
19	D
20	D

Texte 2 M & S	
1	B
2	D
3	B
4	C
5	C
6	A
7	B
8	C
9	D
10	D
11	B
12	D
13	C
14	C
15	B
16	C
17	C
18	D
19	B
20	D
21	C
22	B
23	D
24	A
25	D

Texte 3 BNP	
1	B
2	A
3	B
4	A
5	B
6	B
7	C
8	D
9	D
10	B
11	D
12	B
13	D
14	C
15	D
16	C
17	C
18	C
19	D
20	B

Texte 4 Méthode Blair	
1	C
2	D
3	C
4	B
5	D
6	D
7	C
8	C
9	B
10	C
11	D
12	B
13	B
14	B
15	A
16	B
17	A
18	C
19	D
20	A
21	C
22	B
23	A
24	C
25	B
26	C
27	D
28	D
29	B
30	C

Texte 5 Chat Gras Garnier	
1	A
2	C
3	C
4	D
5	A
6	B
7	C
8	D
9	A
10	D
11	C
12	B
13	D
14	C
15	D
16	C
17	B
18	C
19	A
20	B
21	B
22	B
23	D
24	C
25	C

Texte 6 Apache	
1	D
2	D
3	C
4	C
5	A
6	C
7	D
8	D
9	C
10	B
11	A
12	D
13	C
14	D
15	B
16	C
17	D
18	B
19	D
20	C
21	B
22	C
23	C
24	D
25	B
26	D
27	C
28	C
29	D
30	C

Texte 7 Prime de maternité	
1	A
2	C
3	B
4	A
5	D
6	C
7	B
8	C
9	C
10	D
11	D
12	D
13	C
14	B
15	B
16	D
17	B
18	C
19	C
20	B
21	D
22	A
23	B
24	C
25	D
26	C
27	D
28	C
29	B
30	A

Texte 8 Universités	
1	D
2	C
3	D
4	B
5	B
6	D
7	A
8	C
9	B
10	D
11	B
12	C
13	C
14	C
15	B
16	D
17	C
18	B
19	B
20	C
21	A
22	A
23	C
24	B
25	D
26	B
27	B
28	C
29	D
30	D

Texte 9 Polluant mais indispensable	
1	C
2	D
3	A
4	C
5	A
6	B
7	D
8	B
9	D
10	D
11	C
12	B
13	B
14	C
15	D
16	B
17	C
18	B
19	B
20	D

Texte 10 Abeilles chercheuses	
1	B
2	C
3	A
4	C
5	B
6	D
7	B
8	D
9	C
10	B
11	C
12	D
13	B
14	A
15	A
16	C
17	B
18	A
19	D
20	D

Texte 11 Oui pour la vie	
1	C
2	D
3	B
4	B
5	C
6	D
7	C
8	B
9	B
10	A
11	D
12	B
13	D
14	D
15	A
16	C
17	C
18	D
19	A
20	B

Texte 12 Foot en danger	
1	D
2	C
3	D
4	C
5	B
6	A
7	D
8	B
9	D
10	C
11	D
12	D
13	C
14	C
15	D
16	B
17	D
18	B
19	D
20	B
21	D
22	C
23	C
24	A
25	B

Texte 13 La City	
1	C
2	B
3	C
4	B
5	A
6	D
7	C
8	A
9	B
10	D
11	D
12	C
13	B
14	B
15	A
16	A
17	D
18	B
19	A
20	C

Texte 14 Seniors créateurs	
1	A
2	C
3	D
4	B
5	D
6	A
7	C
8	B
9	C
10	A
11	C
12	A
13	C
14	B
15	B
16	B
17	A
18	C
19	D
20	A
21	A
22	C
23	B
24	B
25	D

Texte 15 Réforme retraites	
1	B
2	C
3	C
4	B
5	A
6	C
7	D
8	C
9	D
10	A
11	C
12	B
13	A
14	A
15	C
16	C
17	B
18	D
19	C
20	D
21	C
22	D
23	D
24	A
25	B
26	D
27	C
28	C
29	D
30	A

Texte 16 La « cup of tea »	
1	A
2	D
3	C
4	A
5	B
6	D
7	C
8	A
9	C
10	A
11	C
12	D
13	B
14	A
15	C
16	B
17	B
18	D
19	A
20	C
21	D
22	B
23	C
24	A
25	B

Texte 17 PC pour Pauvres	
1	C
2	B
3	D
4	B
5	C
6	D
7	C
8	C
9	A
10	B
11	B
12	C
13	B
14	A
15	D
16	C
17	B
18	D
19	C
20	C
21	B
22	D
23	D
24	D
25	A
26	B
27	C
28	C
29	B
30	B

Texte 18 Le Kombilohn	
1	D
2	B
3	C
4	C
5	B
6	A
7	B
8	D
9	A
10	C
11	C
12	D
13	B
14	C
15	A
16	D
17	B
18	D
19	D
20	B

Texte 19 Les SMS	
1	A
2	C
3	D
4	B
5	X
6	C
7	B
8	D
9	B
10	A
11	C
12	C
13	B
14	C
15	B
16	D
17	B
18	A
19	D
20	A
21	B
22	C
23	B
24	B
25	A

Texte 20 Enfants Pauvres	
1	D
2	D
3	B
4	C
5	B
6	D
7	C
8	A
9	C
10	A
11	C
12	B
13	B
14	A
15	B
16	C
17	B
18	C
19	D
20	D

Texte 21 Taxe d'embouteillage	
1	D
2	D
3	C
4	A
5	D
6	A
7	A
8	B
9	C
10	B
11	B
12	D
13	C
14	D
15	A
16	B
17	D
18	C
19	A
20	A

Texte 22 Carrefour	
1	C
2	C
3	D
4	B
5	D
6	B
7	B
8	A
9	C
10	C
11	A
12	C
13	B
14	A
15	A
16	B
17	D
18	D
19	D
20	B
21	A
22	B
23	A
24	B
25	C
26	A
27	C
28	B
29	C
30	A

Texte 23 Barbour	
1	A
2	C
3	B
4	C
5	B
6	D
7	D
8	A
9	B
10	B
11	C
12	A
13	A
14	B
15	C
16	C
17	B
18	D
19	B
20	C
21	B
22	A
23	D
24	D
25	B
26	D
27	C
28	A
29	C
30	B
31	D
32	C
33	C
34	D
35	A
36	C
37	B
38	D
39	B
40	A
41	D
42	C
43	C
44	A
45	B

Texte 24 Les jeunes et le tabac	
1	D
2	A
3	C
4	B
5	C
6	D
7	B
8	C
9	C
10	B
11	C
12	B
13	A
14	C
15	B
16	D
17	C
18	D
19	A
20	A
21	A
22	D
23	C
24	B
25	B

3

'Fair copies'

How to read the 'fair copies' and the footnotes

While a translation must remain faithful to original text, this does not imply a word-for-word translation. Indeed priority must be given to the meaning and tone of the original, and, where necessary, this may imply a major departure from the original wording in order to reach the target – here an English-speaking audience. Often students do this quite naturally and unconsciously when working from English to French (i.e. 'unseen' translation), but are far more wary when working into the foreign language (i.e. 'prose' translation). The 'fair copies' here attempt to take full advantage of this freedom of expression. They are not presented as the only possible rendering but as a plausible, polished piece of work. If the undergraduate reader has queries either regarding the proposed translation or additional suggestions he or she may have, then they should seek confirmation and advice from their local English lecturer. Just as the multiple-choice questions deliberately left out more obvious possible solutions, so too these fair copies have left aside quite acceptable terms or phrases. The reader will notice that there is not always a direct correlation between the length of the text and the number of footnotes. Sometimes, what, at first sight, is a short, readable text gives rise to many possibilities, whereas an apparently complicated or specialised text is, in reality, much easier to deal with.

In the footnotes, words or expressions in ***bold italics*** are alternative suggestions in the context, often with very little to choose between the term in the translation and the alternatives. On occasions, some slight rephrasing may be necessary, but this is usually indicated.

Similarly, words or expressions in *italics alone* are additional useful vocabulary, not directly applicable in the context given, but worth remembering for future use. Occasionally also, italics may be used to draw a distinction between different dictionary terms (LDOCE = Longman Dictionary of Contemporary English; OED = Oxford English Dictionary).

However, asterisks before a term in ***italics* highlight a suggestion which is not possible for the reasons given. Generally speaking, these are terms which past students have put forward as translations and which, therefore, could again be suggested by students today. Qualifying certain errors as 'Blacklist errors' refers to the checklist of common mistakes to be found in the earlier volume of texts entitled "Thèmes Anglais : Communication d'Entreprise" (P.U.R 1997)

All commentaries are in English and the style is deliberately relaxed. Any opinions on linguistic usage, social facts or events, unless directly attributed to another source, are the personal reflections of the present author. From time to time, the reader may be directed to a website. The sites and pages indicated were all available at the time of writing.

Pay as you drive[1]

British motorists[2] could soon find themselves with a spy-in-the-car[3] which would enable[4] the government to charge[5] them on the basis of the kilometres clocked up and the routes used,[6] according to a government agency project made public[7] on Sunday.

This proposal is part of a plan from the Commission for Integrated Transport to reduce road traffic and the eternal[8] rush-hour traffic jams, especially in London. This plan is to be presented[9] to the government on Monday next.

Under this proposal, motorists would receive a monthly bill[10] worked out by a GPS system via[11] black boxes fixed on the dashboard of the vehicles.

The cost for those who use the most congested routes[12] at rush hours could amount to several hundred pounds. The charge would be at least 3p (6 eurocents) per mile and perhaps as high as 45p per mile in central London.[13]

"Roads are the only public utility that are free of charge,"[14] David Begg, chairman of the CFIT, declared. "Consequently, everyone wants to use the same routes at the same time, and this results in snarl-ups.[15] There has to be a better way of going about things", he added.

"We've reached a point where traffic jams represent a health hazard for more and more people.[16] We must keep that in mind" he went on.[17]

The Conservative Shadow Transport Secretary, Teresa May, stood out against the plan, declaring it would not dissuade motorists from using their cars.

"It's just one more attempt at a sort of stealth tax,[18] and I don't think it would work,"[19] she declared on BBC radio.

Notes

1 The British system for paying income tax – prélevé à la source – is known as Pay-As-You-Earn (PAYE)

2 The definite article ***the British motorists* would point to motorists already mentioned earlier in the text or perhaps specified by a following relative clause e.g. *the British motorists who take their car to France*. *'The'* is a weak form of *'those'*; consequently if your reference is all-inclusive i.e. if you refer to *all* British motorists, then the definite article cannot be used.

3 The common name for the compulsory tachometer in lorries and vans to check speeds and length of time driving is *spy-in-the-cab* while *spy-in-the-sky* refers to a military satellite. ***stool-pigeon* & *informer* belong to the jargon of the underworld, while ***spy-hole* is a hole in a door to allow you to see without being seen.

4 ***allow*** is possible here, but be aware that 'permettre' does not always translate as *permit* or *allow*, both of which carry a strong notion of permission from a third party. As here, *enable* is often a more judicious choice, and on occasions it is even possible not to translate 'permettre' at all.

5 Strictly speaking it is not a ***tax*.

6 ***charge them according to distance and routes*** is more concise and sufficiently clear. Obviously any repetition of *'according to'* in this and the next two sentences is to be avoided. Here it would be possible to say *"… and the routes used. So says a government agency project…"* In the next paragraph, 'selon' can be avoided altogether by reformulating the sentence and using *'a plan from the CIT'*.

7 ***published* implies a printed document – ***revealed to the public*** is possible.

8 = colloquialism, synonymous with ***endless, never-ending***. On the other hand, *interminable* belongs to a more formal register of language in English.

9 Distinguish carefully between 'devrait' = probability / intention and 'devrait' = advice / suggestion. The meaning here is the first and provides a good opportunity to use *'is to be'*; ***should* & ***ought to* would simply express the writer's opinion.

10 Keep ***invoice* for business use – the ordinary man-in-the-street receives a [phone / electricity, etc] *bill.*

11 ***by means of*** *black boxes*. The correct term on board an aircraft for a black box is a *flight recorder*. While dashboard is the correct term here, the other terms – *instrument panel, control panel* & *performance data* - are all possible translations in other contexts.

12 Remember that the English term route = 'itinéraire'. Compare the usages in the English text of *'routes'* and *'roads'*.

13 Since no sum has yet been fixed, it is not possible to say that ***it may go up to 45p* (or *increase to 45 p*).

14 ***free of* = débarrassé de, sans; ***free for* = libre, non occupé (a *free-for-all* is either a fight involving several persons or a situation where everyone is free to do as he/ she wishes).

15 ***bottle-necks, traffic jams***

16 Be careful to what you attribute 'de plus en plus' – it is not the verb, therefore adverbial terms are inappropriate.

17 Remember that after direct speech the correct structure is Subject followed by Verb – *he added, he said* - i.e. the normal statement form. Admittedly, journalists do tend to ignore this rule more and more.

18 a recognized compound term.

19 Although in the previous sentence *would* [not dissuade] is the obvious choice because of the indirect speech, here, even in a direct quote, *would* is preferable to *will* in this particular context. If Teresa May had said *'it will not work'*, then implicitly she would be accepting that the plan will be put into operation, but by saying *'it would not work'* she is casting greater doubt on the implementation of the project.

Marks & Spencer France

The Galeries Lafayette group has made an offer to buy out the chain of 18 department stores belonging to Marks & Spencer France and to safeguard the jobs of the 1,500-strong workforce,[1] as from January 1st 2002.

The 18 French stores of the British group Marks & Spencer had been looking for a "rescuer"[2] since March, ever since the parent company had brutally announced the closure of 38 stores in mainland Europe[3] in order to refocus its activities on the British market.

Without a white knight,[4] the French stores were due to close[5] on December 31st. "This scheme is subject to prior approval[6] by the works committee (CCE[7]) and the French trade unions represented in the company"[8] a spokesperson for Galeries Lafayette stated, stressing that its offer corresponded to the wishes expressed by Marks & Spencer.

The news had been given only a short time earlier by the management to the works committee.[9] No further information, in particular either as to[10] the price agreed or the future of the workforce[11] "will be disclosed[12] before the works committee meeting" Galeries Lafayette announced in an official statement on Tuesday.

For the French group, this investment, which will be financed by buying out M& S shares[13], constitutes "a major development project for the group, which is at present undertaking the refurbishing[14] of its stores and the revival of high street activity."[15]

In Belgium, where no-one has come up with a rescue package,[16] the 4 stores belonging to the chain, will close definitively on December 22nd, a spokesman announced on Tuesday. The negotiations with the contenders[17] in France had begun in July.

The new chairman of Marks & Spencer France, Alain Juillet,[18] appointed in early May to conclude the negotiations,[19] had stated that he wanted an all-in offer from a single buyer with keeping on all of the staff[20] part and parcel of the deal.[21]

Two French suitors[22] were originally interested in making a bid, Pinault-Printemps-Redoute (PPR) and Galeries Lafayette, both of which have a flagship store[23] on the Boulevard Haussmann, directly opposite the Paris branch of Marks & Spencer. PPR made only a part offer to buy 6 to 8 stores, including some in Spain, while Galeries Lafayette had put forward an all-inclusive bid for the whole business.[24] But at the beginning of October, PPR withdrew its offer, considering the price too high, thus leaving Galeries Lafayette in the front line.

Notes

1 *An M&S spokesman said that the company had "always been committed to securing continuous employment for its staff."* Note that *employment* & *work* are 'uncountable' nouns and, unlike their French equivalents, cannot be used with the indefinite article. *'Safeguard'* puts over the essential idea of the workforce not losing their jobs, and not simply being given help to find a job in another company.

2 Keep *'saviour'* for (semi-)religious or humorous contexts and *'saver'* for banking (= épargnant). Elsewhere, *rescue* is required e.g. *Lifeboat Rescue service* (SNSM). The Longman Dictionary (LDOCE) even confirms *rescue = to help an organization or business*

3 ***on the Continent***.

4 *white knight* is used particularly in business contexts. *Horseman* and *rider* are pretty well synonymous, and skill in riding a horse is known as *horsemanship*. Note the bibilical expression *The Four Horsemen of the Apocalypse.* In the 16th century, at the time of the English Civil War, the *Cavaliers* were the supporters of the monarchy (Charles I) against the Parliamentary Roundheads under Oliver Cromwell. Today *cavalier* is used principally as an adjective with a meaning somewhat similar to the French adjective, i.e. blasé, paying scant attention to rules and regulations – an example of this usage is given in a later footnote.

5 ***were to have closed.*** Both verbal expressions put over the idea of something already planned. ***should have closed* & ***ought to have been closed* simply express the point of view of the writer; ***might have to be closed* expresses the possibility of a compulsory closure.

6 ***This scheme is conditional on its being approved by...*** *Subject to* & *conditional on prior approval* are set expressions worth noting.

7 Generally speaking, the rule is to leave the abbreviation in the original language – or to spell it out in full in the foreign language – so as to allow the reader to recognise or familiarize himself with the term. For example, in France a *fixed period work contract* is easier understood if CDD is added in brackets

8 Beware of phrasing 'de M&S' in such a way as to suggest erroneously that M&S have their *in-house unions* – the unions do not belong to M&S, therefore a possessive structure is impossible.

9 This sentence refers to GL's offer, not to the original closure decision. It is worth remembering that the unions protested that they had first learned of the closure decision by an internal note posted on the notice board, and it was for this 'cavalier' attitude to French social practices that the French courts fined Luc Vandevelde some € 3,500 in 2005.

10 ***as regards***

11 ***what precisely will happen to the workforce / what job offers will be made to the workforce...*** In fact, the great majority of the 1,500 M&S employees opted to take a redundancy package rather than accept similar positions with GL.

12 ***will be made public...*** Beware of introducing a double negative here

13 « *[Les Galéries] souhaitent que [la reprise] se fasse par un rachat de titres de la structure Marks & Spencer France, ce qui éviterait aux Galeries de maintenir le contrat de travail des employés passés sous l'une de ses enseignes.* » (Le Monde 01.11.2001)

14 Two terms – *refurbishing* and *revival* - are preferable in English to translate two aspects of the French *'renouveau'*; however they are not interchangeable. On the one hand, the reason behind M&S's withdrawal from the French market is its strategy to *revive its fortunes in the UK.* This may involve *refurbishing,* i.e. modernising the presentation and redesigning the outlay of the stores, perhaps even going upmarket.

15 *high street* is the central shopping area of a town, where most of the main nationwide store chains can be found. Its use also includes the volume of trade and the money spent by shoppers; thus *high street spending, high street sales* etc. correspond roughly to the French 'consommation des ménages' [en hausse, en baisse].

16 ***where no candidates have come forward.***

17 *contenders* stresses the notion of fierce competition between the candidates (*a leading contender for the world title, for the presidency, etc*). A useful opportunity to point out the spelling of *negotiate / negotiation* and the mnemonic – in French you négo**C**ier over a **C**offee, while in English you nego**T**iate over a cup of **T**ea.

18 In newspaper business section articles, Juillet is referred to both as *managing director* and *chairman*, which is relatively unusual in a British company, but which corresponds to the French term PDG.

19 i.e. to bring them to a successful conclusion, not to be confused with ***to put an end to the negotiations* which would mean to break them off.

20 ***wanted a comprehensive bid covering a full guarantee of employment / he preferred to sell the whole business to a single purchaser, who would guarantee full employment / he favoured a sole purchaser for all of the stores, allowing a guarantee of jobs*** (this last being a direct quote from Juillet). Beware of the faux-ami; the French term 'global' = *overall, comprehensive*, whereas the English *global* = French 'mondial'.

21 a set expression – if something is *part and parcel* of a bigger whole, then it is an integral part, e.g. *"binge drinking is part and parcel of the student lifestyle"* (Independent, 17.03.05). Juillet refused to countenance job losses or redundancies, consequently ***hiring*, ***taking back* / ***resumption* are inappropriate. Only *keeping on* stresses the continuity.

22 Although the term is no longer used in romantic contexts, it is often met with in business contexts of mergers and take-overs, presumably because the same qualities of persuasion, negotiation and outright.'

23 = the biggest and best in the group (*magasin phare*).

24 Note that the meaning of 'reprise' here is not the same as in the previous paragraph.

BNP to charge for cash withdrawals

The bank's customers[1] will be charged € 5 for any cash withdrawal of less than € 150 from the teller desk.[2] Consumer associations are up in arms.[3]

A charge for cash withdrawals other than through ATMs[4] officially came into force last Friday at the BNP-Paribas bank, despite protests from consumer associations.[5] Customers of the bank, which justifies its decision on grounds of security, will henceforth[6] be charged € 5 for any withdrawal below € 150.

The aim of this highly controversial charge is "to free our counter staff so that they are more available for customer service and advice," Yves Martrenchar, group marketing manager, explained on France 3 television. It's also a question of making sure there is less ready cash in the branch offices to discourage robbers,[7] and thus improve security.

VULNERABILITY

The bank aims to cut out, as far as is feasible,[8] most of the withdrawals of petty sums[9] from the cash desk. Those customers who do not have[10] a credit card will be given a cash(line) card[11] free of charge.

In the opinion of Serge Maître, secretary general of the French Bank Customers' Association (Association française des usagers des banques) this measure threatens to work against the more vulnerable customers[12] to whom it will apply.[13] "It is[14] precisely those sections of the public who, either because of their age or out of a feeling of insecurity, were in the habit of not holding debit and credit cards who are now being forced to use the cash dispensers" he deplored in a television interview on France 3. "The bank is denying them free access to their money".

The BNP, which gave public warning of this measure as early as last October, at the time gave the assurance[15] that cash withdrawals would still be available free of charge in the event of[16] a branch office not having an ATM, or its being out of order,[17] or if the amount requested exceeded the debit card allowance, and also for customers unable to use the cash machine for reasons of disablement,[18] health or old age.[19]

Notes

1 Only one bank has taken this step, consequently ***bank customers* is incorrect.

2 *teller* carries the meaning of someone who counts – in banking contexts, some one who counts money, but at election time a person who is responsible for counting the votes cast for each candidate. Perhaps understandably, in Britain at least, it is often bank employees who are called on to count the votes.

3 Set expression (worth remembering). Apart from obvious adjectives such as *furious* or *angry*, note too colloquialisms such as *get / be hopping mad, hot under the collar, shirty* (not possible here, different usage : *don't get shirty with me* = prends pas ce ton avec moi !).

4 short for ***Automated Teller Machines***. See final footnote for further information.

5 *wrath* belongs to a more formal register of language e.g. *the wrath of God*, *The Grapes of Wrath* (Steinbeck).

6 ***from now on*** (but not ***from now on in*); ***hereafter* belongs to the legal or administrative registers of language – for example the BNP could have used it in announcing the introduction of this charge; *in the hereafter* = after death, in another world.

7 a *robber* steals by threatening to use force and *bank robber / bank robbery* are the commonly accepted terms; a *burglar* breaks into a house or property – he commits *burglary*.

8 ***to all intents and purposes, on an everyday basis***

9 = trivial. Clearly it is the French adjective which has been taken up in English; however the usages are not synonymous. e.g. *petty cash* = a small amount of money kept in an office or business to make small payments; *petty officer* = low-ranking naval officer; *petty crime* = theft of small sums of money, etc.

10 Beware of the classsic faux ami – to *dispose of* something = to get rid of.

11 ***a debit card***

12 A common use of the comparative adjective in order to avoid having to define 'vulnerability' in the absolute : *'more vulnerable'* = relative to other customers.

13 ***threatens to fail those customers it is aimed at // risks handicapping those customers the measure will affect / risks disadvantaging / risks making matters worse for those customers…*** ***fragile* is not used with this meaning in English. Where 'fragile' in French is synonymous with 'à risque', then *at risk* is an adequate equivalent. Both in France and in Britain, efforts have been made to ensure access to the banking system by all – France is inventing a 'service bancaire universel, Britain has had *basic banking* since 2000 as part of its *social inclusion* programme (*financial inclusion*).

14 The time scheme here is present, not past.

15 *Assure, reassure* and *assurance* have little to do with *insure* and *insurance*, except when, in British English, the topic under discussion is *life assurance*.

16 As a very rough guide to current usage, Google comes up with 46 million occurrences of *'in the event of'* and only 38 million occurrences of *'in case of'*. The first of the two is more flexible, inasmuch as it can be followed by a verbal noun (as in the text *'its not having'*) whereas the second of the two is more commonly found followed by a straightforward noun. The Plain English Guide recommends that both be replaced by *'if'*.

17 Note the structure used here : possessive adjective + verbal noun : *its being [out of order]*.

18 or ***disability*** *"a* disability *refers to the lack of some bodily function; a* handicap *refers to the relationship between the disability and the environment"* (source : website of St. Martin's College, Lancaster).

19 If you think French banks are a 'rip-off', then perhaps what happens in Britain will make you think twice. In 2000, the major banks led by Barclays, tried to charge a 'disloyalty fee' if you withdrew money from an ATM belonging to another bank. (This idea has since been taken up by some French banks.) British banks then backed down in the face of a storm of public protest, but sold off a number of their ATMs, usually situated in shopping centres, petrol stations, pubs, etc., to other operators who charge approximately £1.50, regardless of the sum withdrawn. This 'convenience business' is worth £140m a year to the operators. The only ATMs where you can withdraw money free of charge are those in front of your bank branch. One major bank estimated that by the end of 2005, more than half of all ATMs would charge for withdrawals.

The Blair Method[1] hiccups[2]

From health care to the single currency, the storm clouds are gathering[3] – 49 % pro-Blair as against 62 % last April. This slump in popularity is essentially due to failings in the NHS.

There are headlines the most popular Prime Minister[4] of the post-war era could well do without. *"Problems mount up for Labour"*[5] the usually pro-Labour Guardian proclaimed yesterday.[6] A poll this weekend confirmed[7] that Teflon Tony's[8] star is waning. In the space of nine short months, his hitherto untarnished[9] popularity has slipped from 62 % to 49 %. Not a bad score after two and a half years in power, all the more so as the Tories are nowhere to be seen,[10] but for the first time the voters declare themselves to be dissatisfied[11] with a PM who recently seemed unable to do anything wrong.[12]

Makeshift morgues.[13] The nasty Sydney flu bug which laid bare the deplorable state of the health service is the main reason for this disenchantment. For the past two weeks, the newspapers and TV bulletins have been full of woeful stories of cancer patients condemned to wait months for a life-saving operation because of over-stretched hospital resources,[14] of makeshift morgues and of doctors and nurses admitting their incapacity to provide adequate care.[15] Last Sunday, the PM, scenting danger,[16] gave an impromptu interview[17] on BBC. Blair appeared to be on the defensive, acknowledging that the NHS was itself sick and promising to bring it up to the standards of the French or German systems. The NHS, set up after the war by the Labour administration and intended to provide free medical care *"from the cradle to the grave"*,[18] is what is held dearest in the hearts of the British public.[19] They can't understand how Blair, after 18 years of Thatcherism, has not managed to halt the decline, even at the cost of increasing taxes.[20] As if, on the question of the NHS, the Blair technique[21] of promising much without alienating the more right-wing elements of his electoral base,[22] had come to an impasse.[23]

Cherie versus Tony. On the question of the euro, the PM, who never puts himself out on a limb, is faced with the same dilemma. Tony Blair has declared himself to be in favour of the single currency, but as he knows the idea to be unpopular, neither he nor his government has the courage to stand up for this ambitious project. The result is that yesterday's Guardian reported a poll showing that more voters than ever – 63 % - were against the single European currency.

Another worry for Blair is the choice of candidate for Mayor of London, a post which, despite all his efforts, is likely to go to Ken Livingstone, nicknamed "Red Ken" because of his dyed-in-the-wool socialism[24] which is everything that New Labour is not. But Livingstone is the favourite candidate, and Londoners want nothing to do with an outsider the PM wants to fob off on them.[25] And the final worry for Tony is on the home front – his wife Cherie, five months pregnant and legal advisor to the TUC, is standing out[26] against a measure her husband has introduced restricting maternity leave[27] and has taken the government to court on it.[28]

Notes

1 Take note of this structure with proper nouns – either *Blair's method* or *the Blair method*; similarly *the Bush administration, the Tesco guide to easier shopping* but where the possessive is an integral part of the proper noun, then it is kept, e.g. *the Macdonald's guide to healthier eating.*

2 Apart from the medical use ('hoqueter'), *hiccup* has a second meaning of *"a temporary or minor fault or setback"* (Oxford Dict.) and is thus particularly apposite here. If we try to reproduce the medical metaphor, ***catches cold, **sneezes* hardly fit the bill, but *The Blair method off colour / out of sorts / one degree under* just might. Taking the other meaning of 'grippée, reference to a *machine* rather than to a *method* is preferable : ***The well-oiled Blair machine falters / blips / seizes up / [is] no longer running smoothly.*** Alternatively, and closer to the true meaning: ***The Blair effect wearing off.*** Remember that in 'headlinese' verbal structures are kept to a mimimum in English.

3 Cf. Winston Churchill's chronicle of WWII *The Gathering Storm*. Other expressions denoting an approaching storm include *a storm is brewing* and *a storm is looming.*

4 In recent years, there has been a tendency, noticeable in *The Economist* among others, to drop the capitals from *prime minister, house of commons, house of lords, etc.* Whether this denotes a demystification of, or lack of consideration for the constitutional infrastructure is a matter of personal conjecture, all the more so as it is not evident with *White House, Congress,* etc., which does suggest that some see Britain as no more than the 51st state!

5 A special Guardian report around that date was entitled ***"Labour Rebellion Looms"***. The popular newspapers in Britain (as opposed to the quality newspapers) love short, snappy headlines – few words but huge typeface – i.e. *banner headlines* .

6 Some newspapers include *'daily'* in their title, e.g. Daily Mail, Daily Express, but not The Guardian, which therefore excludes writing ***the daily Guardian.* To say ***the daily newspaper The Guardian* is too cumbersome. The weekly digest of news for overseas readers is called *The Guardian Weekly*, but the best solution is to leave it out altogether. In order to use the term some dictionaries suggest, the structure must be actual headline followed by verb, e.g. ***'Problems mount up...' the headline in yesterday's Guardian ran.***

7 ***bore out***

8 During his first period of office, he acquired the nickname of *'Teflon Tony'* because *'nothing stuck to him'* – or, to use another common English expression, *[criticism] was like water off a duck's back.*

9 *Stainless* should be kept for *stainless steel*, or for a *stainless character.*

10 ***are completely out of the running, are totally outdistanced***

11 ***the electorate declares itself / expresses its dissatisfaction***

12 ***unable to put a foot wrong***

13 ***standby morgues*** – but the alliteration is lost. An opportunity to use *impromptu* is given later. In actual fact, refrigerated, cold-storage lorries were used as *overflow* to cope.

14 A term often employed in this kind of political debate is *under-funding* (of schools, universities and hospitals), i.e. they are not getting enough money.

15 Avoid suggesting that they themselves are under-qualified, e.g. ***said they were incapable of looking after / incompetent to look after the patients* – the stress is on inadequate resources.

16 a set expression – ***sensing danger*** is also possible. Although it is possible to say that someone *has a nose for the weather* or *feels a storm coming on*, there is no expression similar to the French.

17 ***unplanned, off-the-cuff***

18 This is the time-honoured phrase; it is the sort of expression that specialists of British life and culture can be expected to recognise. Each culture has such expressions, which form part and parcel of the learning package (e.g. de Gaulle's "*Je vous ai compris*", or "*responsable mais pas coupable*" in the French contaminated blood scandal during the 1990s).

19 It is not the NHS which is ***sensitive*, not even as a symbol. Rephrasing is necessary.

20 ***even if it means increasing taxes***

21 Note the spelling – do not confuse with *Technics*, which is a trade name of Panasonic. A possible objection to *technique* here is that this is the only occurrence in the body of the article of *'méthode'*, which figures in the headline.

22 ***of promising the earth while at the same time appeasing his right-wing***

23 ***had reached its limits***. Lots of colloquial expressions would perhaps fit in here : ***had come up against a brick wall, had come a cropper, was snookered.***

24 ***die-hard socialism***

25 ***that the PM wants to lumber them with***. In both cases, the expressions suggest a second-rate choice. In the event, the unfortunate official Labour candidate, Steve Dobson, came third behind the Conservative candidate.

26 ***who, acting as their lawyer, has taken up the cudgels on behalf of the TUC against a measure***

27 Apparently a reference to the Employment Relations Act 1999, which however extended maternity rights from 14 weeks to 18 weeks and introduced unpaid paternity leave. Indeed the media often wondered whether father-to-be Blair would take advantage of this provision.

28 You *lodge a [an official] complaint*, when you formally notify the [police] authorities of a problem; if the law has been broken, then the police *press charges* (but not a private individual or a lawyer). More often than not, you *protest* by marching in the street or outside the relevant building (a *protest march*).

Investor anger deprives "Fat Cat" Garnier of a golden parachute

"Let's steal the fat cats' cream!"[1] Up went the war cry from majority shareholders[2] who, on 19th May last, voted down[3] a right-royal[4] pay package to Frenchman JP Garnier.[5] True, the CEO of the world's second-largest pharmaceuticals firm, GSK, had awarded himself a £22m (€31m) golden parachute,[6] payable even in the event of severance as a result of mismanagement.[7] And that's over and above[8] his annual salary[9] of £6m. Yet his performance[10] at the helm of this multinational hardly merits such rewards, given that Garnier has been responsible[11] for shareholders losing a third of their investment.[12]

This slap in the face[13] is a first in the British business world[14] since the introduction of a law[15] obliging publicly-owned companies[16] to get shareholders' approval for pay packages to boardroom members.[17] "The shock waves of this decision will ripple far beyond GSK.[18] Legislation is now needed to tackle such outrageous corporate greed."[19] The general secretary of Amicus, the largest trade union[20] in the US-based group,[21] sees nothing wrong in awarding chief executives international-class salaries,[22] provided that their results also come up to scratch internationally.[23]

Fat cats' pay is not the only problem. But the fact that a country traditionally more aloof[24] as regards corporate affairs[25] and with more of a laissez-faire[26] economic philosophy than France should be prey to such reactions[27] says a lot[28] about how sharply the earnings gap[29] is felt in Britain.[30] Add to that the good old English habit[31] of decrying success,[32] people's increasingly low regard[33] for the Establishment,[34] and a popular press hungry for sensationalism,[35] and you have all the makings[36] of the full-blown "Garniergate" currently featuring in the business sections of all the newspapers.

"We are taking this vote very seriously": faced with this mass revolt,[37] the Group Chairman Sir Christopher Hogg promised to heed the message from his shareholders.[38]

Notes

1 ***Don't let the fat cats get their cream*** – what is essential here is a *soundbite,* i.e. a short, sharp 'catchy' expression, the sort that demonstrators can chant or display on their placards. Note that a verbal structure is also possible with *to cream off* [prélever] – ***Don't let the fat cats cream off any more!***

2 ***institutional investors*** would be appropriate here (French = les 'zinzins') to mark them out from *individual shareholders* or *small shareholders.*

3 ***voted against / voted out / refused to accept***

4 Note that in such metaphorical contexts, the adjective becomes *right royal.* Alternatively ***a princely sum.*** A few months earlier, an attempt to double Garnier's annual salary from £ 6m to £ 12m was foiled by institutional investors.

5 ***the French J-P Garnier* has a totally different meaning: e.g. *J-P Raffarin is the French Tony Blair* or *'Loft Story' is the French 'Big Brother'* – this latter idea can also be expressed by a structure such as *the Eiffel Tower is to France what Big Ben is to England.* Apart from that, it is rather disconcerting to find a confusion between adjective 'French' and noun 'Frenchman' in student scripts!

6 This is the term most commonly met with at the moment in this context. Elsewhere *golden handshake* or even *golden good-bye* are used. When, as a student, you leave your work placement, you may be given *a going-away present.*

7 ***even if he is sacked / dismissed / forced out of the company for mismanagement,*** but not ***made redundant.*

8 ***And that's on top of / without mentioning***

9 an individual earns a ***salary*** or *wages* from his employer, and in the case of a chief executive it is certainly not the latter term which applies.

10 Surely ***his*** performance is more natural and more explicit than *the* performance.

11 He didn't really ***make them lose* which implies he had some authority over them and they did what he told them to do – he merely *caused them to lose.*

12 ***shareholders seeing their investment shrink by a third***

13 ***come-uppance*** = one's deserved fate or punishment (OED) and ***backlash*** = a strong adverse reaction are two other possibilities, which are worth remembering.

14 ***British business circles***. ***Premiere* is only used in the context of the first public performance of a theatre play or cinema film.

15 *legislation* is an uncountable noun therefore ***a legislation* is incorrect – ***a law*** is required. There is an opportunity later on to use *legislation.* Keep *legislation* to refer either to a collective package of laws, e.g. civil rights legislation, or, as later, to the overall, indefinite concept of parliamentary action – e.g. *France wishes to introduce legislation on visible signs of religious belief.*

16 This is the definition of a ***public limited company (plc),*** one which has *gone public,* i.e. has sold shares to the general public and is *quoted ON the Stock Exchange,* whence therefore ***quoted companies.***

17 i.e. members of the *Board of Directors* (**board directors**), not to be confused with *top executives* or *managers.*

18 ***The impact goes far beyond GSK***. However, it cannot ***overtake,* which is what a car or a runner does to another car/runner. Or rather, curiously, if you *were* to say *'this decision overtakes GSK'* it would mean quite the opposite – i.e. that GSK has been caught up (rattrapé) by the effects of a decision taken elsewhere!

19 This last expression was actually used by Derek Simpson, joint general secretary of Amicus. Alternatives include ***to cap such gross abuses, to limit such shameless rewards for failure***

20 ***syndicate,* although it refers to an organisation of powerful people, does not have the same meaning as in French, e.g. *the Mafia is a syndicate of crime.*

21 Beware of suggesting that the union is based in the USA (e.g. ** *the biggest group union, which is headquartered…*); this would be illogical – does the French CGT or CFDT operate in Britain? (*"Amicus is the UK's largest manufacturing, technical & skilled persons' union. With over 1.2m members in the private & public sectors, we are a major industrial force."* Visit www.amicustheunion.org for further confirmation.) That being said, GSK is also actually *"Headquartered in the UK and with operations based in the US"* according to their website www.gsk.com.

22 ***considers it quite normal that the CEO get / should get / gets*** – all three forms of the verb are possible in this instance!

23 ***provided their results are up to international standards / bear international comparison / match the salary / merit the sum.***

24 What precise characteristic of an aristocrat is being referred to? The meaning proposed here is "deliberately not becoming involved in something" (LDOCE).

25 Beware of the faux-ami – *social problems* are "problèmes de société". The French adjective can be variously translated as *industrial [relations, action]*, *labour [relations]*, *corporate [affairs]*, … *in the workplace*.

26 ***with a less interventionist approach to economic affairs / a more liberally-minded attitude***. Not ***economical.*

27 To put over the idea of 'théâtre': ***the fact that this should be happening in a country traditionally*** etc. It is not possible in this context to use the verb '***stage*' which is synonymous with *organize*.

28 ***That this should be happening in country like Britain… gives a good insight into how…***

29 ***revenue* is used for businesses and the state, not for private citizens – the *Inland Revenue* is the taxman.

30 ***how acute the salary differentials are felt / how much in the public eye the topic of the earnings gap is / how much prominence is given to the topic of salary scales***. These structures are easier to manipulate and to understand in English than ***the acuity of the question of differences of salaries*, where the repetition of '*of*' is inelegant.

31 Sign of the times – reading Tolkien leads some students to confuse *habit* with the *Hobbits*!

32 ***belittling / pooh-pooh-ing / disparaging / trivializing / playing down success.*** Colloquially, ***knocking success***, but inappropriate in this style of text.

33 ***the declining respect of public opinion towards*** Note the structure *decline IN* (and earlier *approach TO*). The 'opinion' is 'public opinion' and therefore '*people*' or '*the general public*'.

34 = *the group in a society exercising authority or influence, and seen as resisting change* (OED) – with a capital 'E', it is the term generally used in Britain equivalent to 'les corps constitutes, les institutions'.

35 ***eye-catching headlines,***– the term ***tout* is not possible, first and foremost because it is either a verb or a noun, but not an adjective; secondly because a *[ticket] tout* is a person who buys tickets for a sporting event or a concert and tries to sell them above their face value; the verbal form is closer to the French meaning – to persuade someone to buy the goods or services on offer, but not in the same contexts, e.g. *door-to-door salesmen or tradesmen go round houses touting for business; a taxi driver is not allowed to slowly drive around the streets touting for business.* What newspapers want is to sell more copies, so ***juicy titbits of news to increase circulation***.

36 ***ingredients***

37 ***given / in view of the size of the revolt.*** ***in front of* should only be used to situate objects in space, (geographically) e.g. standing in front of the building, spend hours sitting in front of (the) television, Schumacher is in front of Coulthard on the fifth lap.

38 to implement / to put into effect the recommendation of the shareholders. But not ***to apply the message* which is meaningless. In another statement, GSK chairman Sir Christopher Hogg said: "The board clearly registers shareholders' particular sensitivity to termination payments."

APACHE

They're under twelve[1], they know what they want and their parents will go to any lengths[2] to get a smile out of them.[3] Result: a new market.[4]

At the end of[5] the secret tunnel where parents may not venture,[6] there is a sweetie factory[7] and a pocket money shop,[8] play areas[9] to learn how to make toothpaste[10] or model hot-air balloons,[11] shelves laden with toys and books,[12] kids' bedroom furniture, and so on. Somewhere between[13] a toy shop, an all-round store[14] and an amusement park,[15] the new Apache chain of stores[16] are a kid's dream ......[17] dreamt up by a kid.[18]

During the first eight years of his life, each child gets almost FrF1,800 a year in toys alone.[19] The 5.2 million four- to ten-year-olds share a total of over FrF4 billion in pocket money,[20] and their spending power[21] goes on increasing. Half of the BNP's junior account-holders[22] are under 12 years old and have on average FrF2,000 on their account. What's even more incredible is that according to the head of the Children's Institute (IDE)[23] which has been monitoring youth consumer behaviour[24] for over 25 years now,[25] 43% of annual household expenditure is directly or indirectly influenced by the children in the family.[26]

For more than 15 years now marketing men have been making inroads into the teenage market, by dint of designer labels.[27] But the tiny tots market was new territory.[28] As Christophe Parot puts it[29] "Mail order firms were[30] the first to cater for this segment with a wide yet select range of goods[31] suited to every age from toddlers upwards.[32]

Today[33] even the superstores,[34] which until recently targeted the middle-aged housewife,[35] are now opening up to youngsters. "The store seen as an outlet for the mass selling of toys[36] is a thing of the past. We have to make shopping a game[37] to project a different, more grown-up view of the child in his mother's eyes"[38] Joel-Yves Le Bigot stresses.

Notes

1 ***They're less than twelve years old / of age.*** Note that English often uses the structure *under-10s, under-12s, etc.* notably where French uses "benjamin, minime, ..."(sports and other activities). A minor – but preferable – adaptation of the text would give ***They're not yet twelve, but they already know what they want and their parents ..***

2 ***are ready to do anything.*** However, ***will stop at nothing* implies ruthlessness and this is not the connotation here and ***ready for anything* means "paré à toute éventualité"

3 ***Take some twelve year olds who know what they want, parents ready for any sacrifice to get a smile out of them, and what do you have : a new niche market.*** The translation ***make them smile* is not totally appropriate in this context, as there is an opposition between

the idea of a smile freely given by a happy child and the constraint implied by the structure *make some-one do sth.*

4 The whole paragraph would sound better if we said ***Take a generation of twelve-year-olds who know what they want and whose parents are prepared to indulge their every whim and what do you have : a new niche market !***

5 ***behind the tunnel* is meaningless.

6 ***tunnel that only children may enter / where grown-ups are not admitted / where no grown-up dare go*** – In this context, *may* is sufficient to put over the idea of *allowed to go.* ***forbidden to (adults)* is not an English structure, only *some-one is forbidden to do something / you forbid some-one to do something*

7 ***a confectionery factory / a candy factory.*** *Candy* is the American term for sweets – in British English *candy* is a form of processed sugar, as in *candyfloss* (= barbe à papa). However it is not a ***candy store* because sweets are being made but not sold. Beware of the term ***plant* – certainly it can be used as a synonym of *factory*, but it also refers to vegetation, and in the expression *plant hire* it refers to "engins de travaux publics (sous contrat)".

8 Traditionally *a tuck shop* was a sweet and bakery shop close to a school where schoolchildren used to buy cakes and sweets for a mid-afternoon break (= goûter)

9 ***workshops*** – however this term refers equally to the adult world of factories, so that something less austere is perhaps required here; both refer to the location, while ***classes*** would put over the notion of learning (outside school)

10 Certainly not *how to **manufacture* toothpaste! Note the faux-ami *elaborate*, which in English means to give details about something. And to avoid all ambiguity – since the purpose is more one of education rather than an apprenticeship, it might even be preferable to say ***learn how toothpaste is made.***

11 **balloons* on its own would be ambiguous – the sport is known as *ballooning*..

12 ***shelves of toys / filled with toys*** but not ***toy shelves* and certainly not ***toy departments*. Apart from the repetition to be avoided here, it would have been possible to say *toy hot-air balloons.*

13 ***a cross between***.

14 *a general store* usually implies simply a kind of *grocer's shop* while *a department store* translates into French as "grand magasin". *Store* is now used to suggest a bigger retailing area – everything from the French "grand magasin" to "hypermarché" (which has never taken on in GB or USA). Although the text merely talks of "magasin", evidently here the reference is to a *toyshop.*

15 ***an amusement arcade*** is where *slot machines* and *video games* are to be found. *A funfair* suggests *helter-skelters, roundabouts, Big Dippers, etc.* A *theme park* would apply to Disneyland or Asterix park. ***Half store, half leisure park, the new Apache complex...***

16 Or simply the ***new Apache store*** if there is only one.

17 Here is an excellent example of the distinction between French and English usages of "..." (points de suspension) of which there are two in the French text – in the first case, English prefers an expression to round off the list (*and so on, and suchlike, etc.*), while in the second, the purpose is precisely to "suspend" the sentence, i.e. to temporarily halt the reader in his flow so as to emphasise and insist on the idea or the play on words.

18 ***Apache is a kid's dream come true; ... is all a child could dream of – the brainchild of a child.*** In the last suggestion, the repetition of *child* emphasises the term *brainchild.* On the other hand, ***a childhood dream* is inappropriate, as you can only achieve a childhood dream (= rêve d'enfance) when you are older.

19 A baby can't possibly **earn* it, especially if you say **earn in toys* ! – A waiter may *earn* more *in tips* than in salary! Thus *earn in toys* would come to mean that the youngster was paid not in money but in toys! **gets for toys* = he is given money with which to buy whatever toys he likes; *gets in toys* = the toys are bought by parents (which is more plausible). If you prefer the structure ***he gets FF 1,800 worth of toys,*** then *alone* is redundant in the sentence. ***Parents spend / fork out*** *FrF 1,800 per year in toys.*

20 They certainly do not **share among themselves* or **share with each other* which implies that someone hands them the money and leaves them in charge of dividing it up! Note that *between them* implies only two persons involved; more than that requires *among them*

21 ***disposable income*** = for an individual, what is left after all his unavoidable expenses – tax, national insurance, rent, food – have been taken into account; for the country the total money available for spending on consumer goods; ***purchasing power*** = a similar notion, often used to compare currencies - what a worker can buy with the equivalent of one hour's work in different countries, or how much a particular item costs in several countries, e.g. the Economist introduced some 20 years ago the Big Mac Index, comparing the cost of a Big Mac (identical product par excellence) in different countries.

22 **a minor client* would mean an unimportant client! Most banks give a specific name to their marketing of this segment (e.g. *Rainbow account-holders, Smart 2 Save customers, Route 15 accounts*); however you can refer generally to ***this youth clientele*** or ***young clients***, or even use the marketing men's term for this age group – ***tweenage customers***
There is absolutely no justification in translating BNP into English. BNP is the registered trade name of that bank, and cannot be changed.

23 Normally he is ***Chairman***, and would be referred to as such, had his name appeared. However, given the style of the text and the fact that he is not the focus of the sentence, *head* is sufficient. Next, given that it is highly unlikely that he alone is responsible for the research, ***which*** is required in preference to *who.*

24 Like ***furnitures* earlier and ***spendings* later, ***behaviours* does not exist in general English - only the uncountable singular forms ***furniture & behaviour.*** You could alternatively talk of ***consumer attitudes / consumer trends***.

25 ***analysing / scrutinising the behaviour of consumers in short trousers*** is a word-for-word translation but doesn't go down very well in English – which might just say ***consumers in pigtails***. Terms such as *teenyboppers* and *bobbysoxers* are terribly dated today – the market has become much more sophisticated and it is therefore less possible to use such condescending terms to refer to young consumers. The diminutive term *kiddie / kiddies* would be appropriate for the under-7s.

26 ***by the under-18s in the family*** comes to the same thing. ***The children in a family have their say – directly or indirectly – as regards 43% of the household budget.*** Note the French conditional tense usage to suggest an unconfirmed report or a point of view other than that of the journalist – this usage (***would be*) is totally impossible in English. The source of the information is clearly expressed in English in the mention of the IDE, and this is enough. Often newspaper journalists or television newscasters will express this idea with *according to reports coming in from Nicaragua,... it has been reported that..., sources close to the Prime Minister state that...*

27 *By dint of* is usually to be found in structures with *"+ing"*, meaning precisely *by force of.* The meaning here is not that manufacturers have been *flooding* the market or *bombarding* it with *brand names* (i.e. more and more of them), but that they have exploited this market by *imposing* or insisting on particular *brands* or *designer labels (Nike, Reebok, etc.)* ***Well-known brand names* is less likely as a translation, as it would suggest that marketing men were assisted in this marketing strategy by famous brands, rather than the idea of imposing the value of any brand. Note in this context the use of *well-known & recognisable* (brands) – rather than the overworked *famous*. Such well-known brands are sometimes referred to as *household names.* The play on words in French ("labourer / défricher") is not so easy to put over – *ploughing the terrain / had lain fallow* is a possibility.

28 ***hadn't yet explored the tiny tots' market.*** Alternatively, ***Marketing men have been stalking the teenage market for 15 years, but had not until recently thought of the under-10s as potential prey***.

29 You are not restricted to using ***according to*** on every single occasion.

30 ***The mail order sector was the first...***

31 Note not **selected!* The adjectives *choice* & *select* are used like the French expression "de choix", while *prime* = "de premier choix". The French text is deceptive in its use of "et + à la fois". The contrast in meaning comes over better in English with *yet* (= mais en même temps, et néanmoins). Note that this use of "à la fois" can only be translated by *at one and the same time.*

32 **since* is not acceptable as a translation of "depuis" – ***from*** *the time they are out of nappies.*

33 **nowadays* is too wide in scope – useful for a direct comparison with a previous period in time, preferably several decades ago.

34 The French term *hypermarket* has been translated into English, but not the concept. GB and America still separate out, to a larger extent than in France, food shopping from consumer durables. *Superstore* is the usual term.

35 Distinguish between "ménagère" & "femme de ménage" – the former is *housewife*, the latter is *a cleaning lady, a charlady* (out-of-date), or in homes *a house help.*

36 Grammatically there is nothing wrong with *toy sales factory*, but it doesn't stress sufficiently the essential idea of mass selling of any item – the sales strategy being described here is a turning away from the *"pile them high, sell them cheap"* strategy of superstores (bulk buying, low prices) towards a more subtle strategy.

37 ***create a playful / relaxed atmosphere***. The sentence implies that the new marketing strategy is to actively involve the child in shopping for all kinds of goods, rather than considering that the only department that interests him is the toy department, and that his mother will park him there while she does the food shopping, perhaps in return for the purchase of a small toy to keep him quiet.

38 ***To make mothers see their children as more sophisticated and money-conscious***. The term "valoriser" needs explanation, as obviously *any* child has a 'value' in his mother's eyes. The other three suggestions mean precisely that a mother loves her child very much (although he may be a little hooligan to every onlooker).

Labour Law: Is a male employee entitled to a maternity grant[1] from his employer?

Case history:[2] female employees[3] with Renault[4] who go on maternity leave receive an ex-gratia payment[5] of FrF 7,500.

A male employee, whose wife was expecting their child, put in a claim[6] under this arrangement,[7] on the basis of[8] the EU principle of equal treatment for men and women as regards working conditions, training and pay,[9] but the company rejected it outright.[10] The employee took his case to[11] the industrial tribunal[12] in Le Havre, and it eventually came before the European Court of Justice (ECJ),[13] which found against the employee.[14]

Our legal expert's commentary:[15] In this case, the argument put forward by the Renault employee was simple. He contended[16] that, while the granting of maternity leave was justified on grounds of health, the same did not hold true[17] of the granting of a sum of money, since the birth of the child was as much the affair of the father as of the mother. By not following this reasoning,[18] the employer was guilty of unjustified discrimination in breach of EU texts.[19]

The ECJ did not follow this line of thinking. On the contrary, the judges held[20] that the payment of a gratuity[21] to expectant mothers in the company did not go against the principle of equal treatment between men and women. To their mind, the principle of equal pay[22] presupposes that employees are in comparable situations.

This is not the case during maternity leave. During this period, the female employee is at a disadvantage career-wise,[23] since her contract with the company is in abeyance,[24] and she misses out on opportunities for promotion or performance-related pay increases. Male employees, on the other hand,[25] do not suffer from such hitches[26] in their careers. The Court therefore held[27] that male employees are not entitled to financial compensation awarded by a company to mothers-to-be.

It is worthwhile pointing out[28] that in an earlier decision, the ECJ took the opposite stance on a question of retirement. In its opinion, determining different retirement ages for men and women runs counter to the sex equality provisions.

Notes

1 *maternity benefit* is given by the welfare state.

2 ***The facts***

3 ***expectant mothers / mothers-to-be working for Renault.*** In this first instance however, it is perhaps preferable to make reference to their status of 'employee', and keep '*expectant* *mother'* for later in the article. There is no need to say ***who become pregnant* since the meaning is expressed adequately in *'who go on maternity leave'*.

4 The possessive case is impossible here, as the link with the original M. Renault has long since disappeared – it no longer belongs to one man. Admittedly, some companies and stores have incorporated the possessive into their trade-name (e.g. Kellog's, MacDonald's), but that is not the case here.

5 Very aptly, one dictionary defines this as a "payment that is made as a gift, and not as a legal duty" (LDOCE) – it is what students may hope for at the end of a work placement. Although for the sake of simplicity, Renault will probably give *a fixed sum* or *set sum* to each employee in this situation, the emphasis has to be on the notion of gift rather than any obligation, and this is best put over by *ex-gratia*.

6 Note the difference between English and French as regards the use of tenses. The facts in this paragraph refer to a *past* situation and are therefore normally expressed in the simple past; *receive* remains in the present, as it refers to a general rule in the Renault company, which is not limited in time.

7 he is not in a position to ***demand,* while ***profit from* in this context is synonymous with gaining an unfair (financial) advantage.

8 ***by reference to / referring to.***

9 ***Equality of opportunity in the workplace*** would cover all these aspects and would even be an apt translation for the "projet de loi pour l'égalité des chances" which so agitated French public opinion in early 2006. Many job adverts in Britain now contain the assurance that *"we are an Equal Opportunities employer"*. The relevant European provisions are to be found in the directives on Equal Pay (75/117), Equal Treatment (75/207), Pregnant Workers (92/85). For update see also http://europa.eu.int/eur-lex/en/com/pdf/ 2000/en_500PC0334.pdf (PDF file)

10 Avoid whenever possible the 'telegraphic' style of the French sentence here. Rather than a sentence without a verb, join up two sentences.

11 ***lodged his complaint with...***

12 aka ***employment tribunal***

13 ***Court of Justice of the European Communities*** In line with Eurospeak practice, a compromise term is the one which is closest to a word-for-word translation into most EU languages. However, British sources – especially the media – refer to the ***European Court of Justice.*** Visit http://curia.eu.int.

14 ***held against the employee / came out against the employee / dismissed the appeal.*** Compare these legal terms with *rejected his demand* used earlier. ** *found [him] guilty* is not possible as the employee was not on trial accused of a crime. The next paragraph shows a use of *guilty*. If you *find fault with someone,* you simply blame them or criticize them, which is not the case here.

15 In Britain, there are two professions which answer to the term 'avocat': the *solicitor* corresponds roughly to a "notaire" in France but the only way an individual citizen can gain access to a *barrister* – who will plead the case in court – is by going through a solicitor. However, in the present context, the writer may be a journalist specialising in legal matters; in any case he/she is not acting as either a solicitor or a barrister here. *Lawyer* is an overall term encompassing "notaire, avocat, conseiller juridique, juriste" depending on the context. An **attorney* operates in the American legal system, except for the office of *Attorney General*, who is the British government's lawyer. *Power of attorney* in England corresponds to the notion of "procuration" in France.

16 ***asserted / claimed*** – these three verbs all convey the message that the writer is distancing himself from the point of view held by the other person.

17 ***the same was not true / the same could not be said*** – note this use of *same* as a pronoun, not as an adjective i.e. there is no need to add *[the same] thing.*

18 ***while not* in this sentence would be synonymous with *although the employer did not*; what is required here is the causal meaning *because he did not ... For ignoring this reasoning* can also be rephrased *because he did not ...* but in the context of a motive behind a punishment or fine, but this is not the case here.

19 ***incompatible with.*** *Breach* is a generally-recognised legal term, as in, for example, *breach of contract* (rupture de contrat) or *breach of the peace* (atteinte à l'ordre public).

20 ***magistrate*, although referring to a kind of judge, has a far more limited meaning in English, and there is reason to believe that the *magistrates' courts* in Britain inspired to a certain extent the recent introduction in France of 'juges de proximité'. That being said, 'Eurospeak' is leading to the use of the term *magistrate* with a pan-European connotation.

21 More commonly and more precisely, a *gratuity* is a *tip* given to someone in return for a service (waiter, porter, etc), but inasmuch as it is *freely* given, then it is not totally out of place here. Moreover, it avoids repetition of *"payment of an ex-gratia payment"*.

22 ***equal pay for equal work*** is what is often heard – the difference between 'traitement' in the previous sentence and 'rémunération' here has to be made clear. Clearly the former term is far broader in scope.

23 'Professionnel' is a notorious *faux-ami*. several terms are used in English: *occupational* hazard (risque professionnel ou du métier); *vocational* training = formation professionnelle; *business* expenses = frais professionnels, etc.

24 ***interrupted / suspended*** – her contract is not ***held up*, but her career advancement is! More colloquially, her contract (and her career) are *put on hold* (= en attente). In criminal law, *a suspended sentence* = avec sursis.

25 It would be sufficient to say ***Men do not...*** This is because English is a stressed-based language, and, both in spoken and written form, emphasis is only given to syllables and words carrying new meaning. Consequently there is no need to add pronouns as the French language has to do.

26 = temporary obstacles.

27 Another occurrence of the legal term meaning *came to the conclusion, decided*. An amusing *faux-ami* might be the term *upheld* in English and 'debouté' in French, because the common link between 'up' and 'debout' might lead to considering the two terms to have the same meaning, whereas in fact *"the Court of Appeal upheld the decision of the lower court"* means it *confirmed* the earlier decision. The French term is best translated by *to dismiss [the case or the appeal]*.

28 ***it is interesting to note that***

France exhorts students in Europe to stand out against privatisation[1]

Paris (AFP)[2] On Saturday France urged students throughout Europe to stand out against the threat of privatisation which is hanging over education[3] in the EU, defending above all the principle of free education for all,[4] with the long-term goal of[5] an "Educational & Cultural Maastricht".[6]

"How come we can move mountains[7] in order to set up the single currency and open up markets[8] and yet not put the same energy into supporting language-learning[9] and student exchanges?" Jack Lang, the French Minister of Education,[10] asked[11] on Saturday whilst declaring himself in favour of a "Maastricht for Education" which he called an "achievable utopia".

The Minister, who was addressing[12] some 300 student union delegates[13] from almost thirty European countries meeting together in Paris[14] until Sunday for the inaugural European Student Forum,[15] acknowledged however that the issue was a "major struggle"[16] that was "only just beginning."

"If state-funded education is a value shared by all your organisations,[17] then your message must come over loud and clear"[18] Jean-Luc Mélenchon, minister for vocational training, added, calling upon the students to speak with a common voice[19] in their dealings with the European authorities.[20]

"The idea that education is something that can be bought and sold[21] outrages me[22] as it does Jack Lang,[23] but it is one that is gaining in popularity throughout the world,"[24] Mr. Mélenchon[25] stressed, while Mr. Lang underlined the fact that within the EU itself "two or three countries, such as GB, the Netherlands or Germany, are lukewarm on both the individual state's role in education and that of the EU.[26]

UNEF-ID, the biggest[27] French student union, for its part pointed out that today "there are more students than farmers in Europe, but the EU spends € 41 billion on agriculture[28] as against only a few hundred million euro on education."

Nevertheless, before achieving[29] the harmonisation of curricula and a Europe-wide degree – which may never see the light of day given[30] the strong hostility and the internal wranglings within each country – France will hasten the European cultural melting-pot[31] by developing student mobility.

At the present time, 120,000 EU students each year obtain Erasmus grants to take part in exchanges. "Not enough"[32] in the opinion of Jack Lang, who aims to have a five-year student mobility plan adopted by the EU Council of Ministers,[33] for which he is counting on the support of the students to counter the opposition of certain member states.

The French plan should make it possible to increase the proportion of "mobility" to 20 % of students (it currently stands at 5 %)[34] by doubling the number of Erasmus grants,[35] currently worth € 120 per month over a seven-month period.

The Minister of Education also expressed his support for direct participation of students in the European institutions, and took note of the suggestion[36] of a Student European Parliament to heighten[37] public awareness of the threat to the university systems in Europe from the "forces of opposition and conservatism".[38]

Notes

1 ***France: Say No to Privatisation*** would be typical British newspaper "*headlinese*".

2 There is no justification in changing the registered name of the Agency - Check this out by visiting its website where it presents itself thus: "*Agence France-Presse is the world's leading news and photo agency. AFP is the world's oldest established news agency, founded in 1835 by Charles-Louis Havas, the father of global journalism*" (http://www.afp.com/english/afp/).

3 ***hanging over the education systems.*** Beware of suggesting that there is *only one system* in the EU (some may think that is the aim of harmonisation, but as the text says, we are not there yet.) A *threat* is merely virtual, and, like the sword of Damocles, only *hangs over your head.* An argument which "*carries weight*" also "pèse" ... but that is not the meaning here. Likewise a difficult unresolved problem may "*weigh heavily on your mind*", ... but not here.

4 ***the state financing of education.*** Remember that the French term "public" can often be translated by *state* – often used adjectivally (*state education* as opposed to *the independent sector* in GB, or a *state university* in the USA).

5 ***to aim ultimately for...*** **to end with* is ambiguous – it can be synonymous with *to put an end to*, which is exactly the opposite of what is required here. Similarly ***to end up with* should only be used in negative connotations (e.g. *anyone who drinks the tap water here will end up with gastroenteritis).*

6 ***a Maastricht agreement for Education and Culture***

7 ***How can we be capable of moving heaven and earth when it's a question of setting up the single currency...*** The word-for-word translation ***For what reasons* is unjustified here. Distinguish between the uses of *what* and *which* in questions: ***For which reasons...?* requires Lang to then list possible reasons and ask his audience to choose from among the list. *For what reasons...?* suggests that the speaker cannot think of any acceptable reasons and would be appropriate if the Minister was expecting his audience to respond with some reasons.
The 1st person plural is more appropriate since both the Minister and his audience belong to the EU, and are thus directly involved in the events. As for the modal auxiliary, *can't we / shouldn't we (find the energy)* are preferable, expressing ability or encouragement, whereas ***wouldn't* , being a form of *will* ("volonté") suggests that the determination is NOT present, and this contradicts the meaning of the sentence. Furthermore, since *the single market* and *the single currency have* been put in place, the conditional mood is inappropriate.

8 'Eurospeak' talks equally of ***the single currency*** and ***the single market.*** There is little excuse for not being familiar with the former of the two - it is a major issue in British politics.

9 ***multilingualism*** (note spelling), ***language skills***

10 ***Jack Lang, French Education Minister*** is more concise and journalistic.

11 After a quotation, avoid inversion of verb and subject wherever possible. If Jack Lang had ***asked himself*, then no words would have been pronounced, since everything would have remained in his head; if he had ***wondered* (or even more improbably ***mused*), then again in his head he would have formulated the question, but would have been unable to provide a satisfactory answer (to himself). In truth, in this instance, he pronounced a rhetorical question – he more likely than not ***asked of his audience***.

12 The use of the continuous past is appropriate here to show that the quotation is an extract from his speech. Similarly, the continuous present is required later: ***who are meeting***.

13 ***trade union* is impossible here although the dictionary may suggest it for normal use. The English delegates would be from the *National Union of Students* (visit the website http://www.nusonline.co.uk/) On British campuses, *student union* also refers to the building where students can socialise together. A *syndicate* in English has nothing to do with workers' rights – certainly the term refers to a grouping of individuals ... perhaps to play a single ticket on the National Lottery !

14 Beware of punctuation if you have used a past participle to translate "réunis" *(assembled / gathered, etc.)*! A comma in front of "*assembled*" would almost automatically make "*the Minister, who...,*" the subject of the verb (= the Minister [who was speaking... countries] gathered...). A present participle is preferable as in ***gathering, meeting***.

15 ***Conference*** perhaps, but not **Assizes* whose use in English is purely restricted to that of a court of justice. Admittedly, the Norman French origin was similar to that used here in modern French.

16 ***it was about (a fight)* doesn't mean anything – say simply ***it was a major struggle***. Not **fight*, which is purely physical. *Struggle* suggests difficulty (and possibly incomplete success, even failure) e.g. *the struggle for existence, the struggle for (trade) union recognition (in the workplace) the struggle to make ends meet.*

17 ***(a value) common to all of you*** - but avoided in the text above because of the repetition within the same sentence. ***free access to education* is totally different, implying non-selective admission to university studies.

18 ***then it is in your own best interest that this be known and understood***

19 i.e. in the sense of *a single voice, united*, which is the meaning here. Very informally, *Mélenchon called upon them* ***to get their act together***, which the Oxford Dictionary explains as "to become properly organised". Check the Blacklist for ways of expressing the French "face à" – here ***to face up to Brussels*** would be adequate.

20 ***Brussels / the EU institutions / Eurocrats*** – these are the "instances" being referred to.

21 ***that education is for sale / can be bartered / is nothing more than a commercial commodity / is a merchandise.*** *goods* doesn't exist in the singular, therefore ***a good* is impossible.

22 ***appals me, horrifies me, is abhorrent to me***

23 Here is an opportunity to use the auxiliary in English, rather than repeat the verb as in French

24 ***at the scale of (the world)* is a "gallicism" whose over-use is to be avoided in English wherever possible - keep it for statistics, when it is possible to multiply the results of a *small-scale* survey. Here the expression simply means ***in many countries***.

25 Never write ***Mister.*

26 ***are opposed to state intervention in education policies both domestically and for the whole of Europe.*** More informally, **take a hands-off approach to education both at home and for Europe.** The term ***strong* needs interpretation - what it means here is the fact of decisions being imposed by central government, i.e. London, Berlin or Brussels. Beware of confusing *policies* and ***politics* in this context, and beware also of a double negative: ***are* not *favourable* neither ... nor

27 Classic Blacklist mistake! ***First* is chronological. Here you could say ***principal / main / foremost,*** etc.

28 *spending* and *expenditure* are collective terms, and have NO plural form *(**spendings, **expenditures).*

29 ***without waiting for (harmonisation)*** would perhaps be a more precise translation of the underlying meaning of 'avant de parvenir'.

30 ***so outspoken is the opposition and the division on the subject within each country.*** Note the relatively complicated structure and word order that are required – which is why the easy way out is the structure with *given*.

31 ***France intends to foster better European understanding through greater mobility / to bring about a cultural melting-pot.*** Or to borrow directly from the EU commission presentation of Socrates: ***... to enhance the European dimension ...*** An auxiliary that expresses more determination than **would like to* is needed to translate 'souhaite' – an expression of *will* or *intention* is required.
A British politician, in front of such an international audience of young students, might well have said something along the lines of ***[We] will do everything [we] can to get all you young students to intermingle / to make sure you get to know one another better.*** Terms such as **integration,* **blending* would not fit in here.

32 "***Too few***" – referring to student numbers or number of grants.

33 This structure – *aims to have adopted* – is possible because the speech was made during the French presidency of the EU. Consequently, Lang was in a position to give leadership. Logically, the plan will last five years, not the mobility of each student! Note that in Eurospeak, the term *Council of Ministers* refers to the meeting of counterparts from all EU states, e.g. Ministers of Education, and that what the French system considers a "conseil des ministres" would correspond to a *summit of heads of state.* It is therefore incorrect on both scores to translate the term here by **Cabinet.*

34 **by 20 %* is totally wrong. If 120,000 students = 5 % of the student population, then *increasing BY 20 %* = 120,000 x 120 % = 144,000; whereas *increasing TO* 20 % = 120,000 / 5 % x 20 % = 480,000 students – and *that* is far more eye-catching (and for Jack Lang, vote-catching !!).

35 Beware of any structure which would suggest that the individual student would get more money! *(*by doubling the amount of Erasmus grants* or **by doubling the grants which amount at present to…).*

36 Example of what the French call "la langue de bois" since the term covers a wide variety of reactions, but, since Lang has no decision-making powers in this field, it is best to steer clear of ***adopt* / ***decide*. Something less definite is required: ***he took on board the suggestion / he approved of the idea / said he would give consideration to the idea***

37 ***increase***

38 ***opposition strength of dyed-in-the-wool traditionalists / of die-hard reactionaries***

A necessary evil[1]

In the 1960s with superstores sprouting up everywhere,[2] the plastic checkout carrier bag[3] quickly came to symbolise[4] the new throwaway, consumer society.[5] Today, more than 14 billion[6] are produced in France for a public that hasn't got a good word for them[7] and yet cannot do without them.[8] How long before we get the environmentally-friendly bag?[9]

Transparent[10] except for the shop name[11] printed in washable ink,[12] it is biodegradable, photo-degradable and water-soluble.[13] "It" is the environmentally-friendly supermarket carrier bag. When incinerated, it burns without trace. When dumped[14] in the countryside by an inconsiderate rambler[15] or deposited on the ocean by a gust of wind,[16] it disintegrates within a couple of months, leaving behind nothing more than a few molecules of carbon and hydrogen. Industrialists have the know-how and technology to produce this "wonder bag", but its production costs are rated too high by retailers, and so it stays where it is – on the drawing-board.[17]

Ever since it first came on the scene[18] some forty years ago, the plastic checkout carrier bag has been frowned on.[19] In 1963 Carrefour opened the first superstore in France at Sainte-Geneviève-des-Bois in the département of the Essonne. It very quickly became apparent[20] that plain brown paper grocery bags were inadequate.[21] Something with handles and cheaper to produce was needed. "Plastic cut the production costs of grocery bags by three"[22] according to[23] Daniel Valeri, head[24] of Alplast, the second largest manufacturer in France of plastic carrier bags.[25] Today, the cost stands at around 6cts a bag. In the USA, the first plastic bags made their appearance in the mid-70s, while in France their popularity came[26] with the expansion of the major retailing chains.[27] Supplanting fabric shopping bag, wicker basket and string bag,[28] the plastic carrier bag became synonymous with[29] this new throwaway, consumer society, handed out freely and free of charge,[30] and thrown away without a second thought.[31] Each year, shopkeepers[32] go through some 14 billion.[33]

Over its forty years of existence,[34] the checkout carrier bag has also lost weight. The lightest among them is only 8 microns thick as against 40-50 in the 1970s; consequently,[35] producing them uses up less oil.

Notes

1 ***Pollute and be damned !*** by analogy with the adage of the popular press *Publish and be damned* (= "on publie l'article, tant pis pour les conséquences / tant pis si l'on nous jette l'anathème").

2 ***with the advent of major retailers / the expansion of supermarkets***. Apart from the fact that it is not a suitable translation for the French "grande distribution", the term *mass marketing*

is now out-of-date and in total contradiction with the marketing philosophy of "le client est roi" (do you personally want to be treated simply as "one of the masses" or as "a very special customer"?). Beware of the French term "distribution" – "grande" or otherwise, with this meaning it is *retailing*. Thus here ***major retail chains*** would be a suitable translation. However, in paragraph 3 of the text 'distribué' has a different meaning and could be translated by 'distributed'

3 We should really perhaps refer to ***polythene*** *bags*, The *check-out* is where you pay for your groceries, and ***supermarket check-out bag*** would be a translation of the French term, except that the expression is not common in English. A ***cashpoint* is a *cash dispenser* (= guichet automatique bancaire / GAB). There is however a connection with superstores inasmuch as chains such as Safeway and Tesco offer customers paying for groceries with a credit card the possibility of withdrawing cash – *cash-back* – as if £ 50 was simply another item on their shopping list. Given that some British banks charge customers a commission if they withdraw money from another bank's cashpoints (the so-called *disloyalty fee*), superstores are likely to become more popular as sources of ready cash.

4 ***became the symbol of***

5 Putting the adjectives in this order makes the expression less ambiguous than *the new consumer, throw-away society* (where the reader might be tempted to consider "consumer" as a noun rather than an adjective). Note that ***consumption* is NOT used in this sense (See Blacklist). ***our buy-it-and-throw-it-away society / our consumer society and of its wasteful ways / our wasteful consumer society*** (a slightly narrower interpretation), but ***wasting*, ***wastable*, ***of waste* or other such concoctions are not possible here. Lots of products today are *disposable* (nappies, paper plates and cups, handkerchiefs, etc.) or *non-returnable* (bottles, etc.) – this is the meaning here: a *one-off* use.

6 Care is needed when expressing figures – *14 billion* **of them** (i.e. *of* + a pronoun) is possible as is *14 billion* **of these bags** but not ***14 billion of bags* – figures are to be considered as (invariable) adjectives.

7 The complete expression is *(a society that) does* ***not have a good word to say in their favour***.

8 ***that dislikes them /that complains /*** **moans** ***about them ...*** **disparage*, **decry* belong to a formal register of language and do not fit into this context of items such as plastic bags. You could sum up the whole idea expressed with the two verbs in French by saying ***that sees them as a necessary evil*** as in the title.

9 In other contexts (highly unlikely here) "*when is it for?*" could be used.

10 ***see-through*** is often used for clothes, but could be used here with the idea of deliberately showing (off) one's purchases to total strangers.

11 ***shop's name, retailer's name***

12 ***water-based***

13 ***It disintegrates organically and in ordinary daylight, and dissolves in water*** is perhaps "more English" and to be preferred over the Latin and Greek-based adjectives (remember George Orwell). It is worth noting the advice on usage given by the 'Grand Dictionnaire Terminologique' : « *miscible : se dit de deux liquides ou plus qui peuvent se mêler en formant un mélange homogène. Il ne faut pas confondre* 'miscible' *et* 'soluble', *qui se dit d'un corps solide ou gazeux qui peut se dissoudre dans un liquide ou un solvant en formant un mélange homogène.* » (www.granddictionnaire.com).

14 ***thrown away / left lying*** – not ***forgotten*, precisely because the gesture is deliberate!

15 ***thoughtless***. Unfortunately it is not possible to introduce here the term *litter*, which refers to waste paper left lying about, and the sort of person guilty of such behaviour is popularly called a *litter lout*. Check the advice often to be found on *wrappings* and tin cans: "*Keep Britain tidy. Dispose of litter properly*".

16 Although one well-known dictionary suggests ***gale*, note that this term refers specifically to a Force 8 or 9 wind on the Beaufort scale lasting a certain time; ***blast* is also too strong (cp. blast furnace); what is meant here is simply a sudden rush of wind, i.e. a *gust of wind*, which need only be strong enough to send a plastic bag flying. A *breath of wind* would not be enough.

17 Note the English equivalent for an idea that never gets any further than the R&D department.

18 ***From the very outset, the plastic bag ...*** A ghost *makes an apparition*, while a famous personality *makes an appearance* (at a ceremony).

19 ***has been disapproved of / has not had a good public image / has had a bad press.*** Logically, "*its (bad reputation)*" is inappropriate since it did not already have a bad reputation when it was first introduced – it had first to acquire this and has had to ***live it down*** ever since. Not really possible here, but worth noting is the popular, fairly recent, expression *he/she/it's (not) flavour of the month*" (= (ne pas) avoir la cote, être en vogue, être la coqueluche du moment) which comes from the marketing of flavoured ice-creams.

20 This is not the same as saying ***it appeared* or **it seemed* – these expressions refer to a first impression which turns out not to be true; consequently they are used to draw attention to this opposition between reality and aspect.

21 ***very quickly standard / ordinary brown paper bags turned out to be useless / proved not to be suited to new requirements.*** ***maladjusted* refers to the psychological inability to fit into society, to cope with problems and personal relationships – ***ill-adapted*** is what is meant here. Unfortunately, although *kraft* is to be found in the dictionary, the term belongs to the specialised vocabulary of paper manufacturers (as does, to a lesser extent, *manila),* and not to general English, which refers simply to ***brown paper***. Besides which, *Kraft* is a household name for foods and most English speakers would immediately think of processed cheese slices (which are disparagingly referred to as ... plastic cheese!).
Since the next sentence refers to the need for bags with handles, there is little advantage to be gained by including in this sentence "*without handles*" – the idea is implicit in the reference to the grocery bags still to be seen today in American films. ***handless* is not recognised by many dictionaries, but in any case would mean "without hands" and by extension "clumsy with one's hands, incapable of manual tasks" (maladroit); *handleless*, although it exists, is a clumsy construction.

22 not **cuts costs by a third*! That would be much less of a saving. Rephrasing clarifies the meaning, since production costs (of bags) existed even for paper bags.

23 **specify* is a faux-ami – *DV states* or even would be adequate. See an example of the correct use in footnote 27 below.

24 This avoids giving him a job title – he may very well be ***managing director*** (MD) or ***chief executive*** (CEO) or anything else!

25 Beware of suggesting that DV is N° 2 in France (***Alplast's manager, DV, N° 2 in France)*. Nor is "*number two in the field*" very explicit – what field of activity?

26 It is not a good idea to have bags "**exploding*" at check-outs!

27 It would not be inaccurate in the context to specify ***the major food retailing chains***.

28 In each case here, the material is mentioned to balance the sentence, although this is not so in the original French. A *shopper* here is the standard shopping bag (not the person using it): ***Ousting traditional shopping bags, baskets or nets***.

29 ***became the mark of / the emblem of our consumer society.*** The simple past is preferable to the present perfect because *new* makes it clear that we are talking of an earlier period than now.

30 deliberate contrasting of the two ideas in the French text, making use of the similar terms in English. ***Freely available free of charge*** is also possible. *Gratis* is only used in the informal set expression *free, gratis and for nothing.*

31 Surely if you have a true psychological *complex* or *hang-up* about throwing away plastic bags, then you don't do it ! Avoid psychological terms here. As for ***uninhibited(ly), no inhibitions*, this is perhaps true when you sunbathe in the nude on a public beach, but not for the mere act of throwing away a plastic bag. ***You get them for nothing, you get as many as you want, and then you get rid of them, in total peace of mind.***

32 ***tradesman* today is closer in meaning to "artisan", so inappropriate here.

33 Here *go through* = use up; the emphasis is on how many bags they need to buy in order to make them available to customers.

34 ***In its forty years***

35 Two interpretations of "dès lors" - *from then on* implies a major innovation in manufacturing, which unfortunately, is not borne out by any information given in the text. Since the whole text revolves around the idea of industrial pollution and wastage, then it seems more logical to consider the *consequence* of the thinner bag.

Sniffer bees[1]

American scientists working for the Pentagon[2] are looking for a way to train bees[3] to detect[4] traces of explosives[5] with the long-term aim of sniffing out bombs,[6] the NYT claimed in its Monday edition.[7]

The research project, which started up three years ago, is in its early days yet but a first stage has been reached.[8] Bees were first of all[9] taught to help locate landmines, now they are being trained to identify a truck[10] carrying minute traces of explosive.

The bee's sense of smell[11] is 99 % reliable,[12] or so says the Air Force research laboratory in Texas, pointing to recent tests.[13]

As a result, swarms of bees could be positioned near security check areas and, in the long term, bees could also be used to warn of biological or chemical attacks, the scientists hope.

The scientists are looking to equipping bees[14] in the more distant future with transmitters the size of a grain of rice.[15] In this way their movements could be tracked,[16] the paper adds. As a reward – when the bees do what is expected of them[17] – researchers from the University of Montana, also working on the project,[18] give them sugar.

Pentagon officials[19] are aware that these experiments[20] could raise a few eyebrows or even a titter,[21] but they are convinced that they can produce results.

Over the past five years, the Pentagon has spent $25m on this and other similar projects involving animals.[22]

Notes

1 ***explosive-seeking bees***. *Sniffer dogs* is the recognised term for dogs trained to detect drugs or explosives. In the middle of the 1970s, Elf (now Total-Elf) was involved in a financial scam involving "avions renifleurs" – planes which could ***sniff out*** oilfields – note the postposition which is absolutely necessary for the meaning. ***explosive researcher bees* means there is a risk of the bees exploding; moreover it is unlikely that they are capable of doing any research. Although in military terminology *a homing missile* ('à tête chercheuse') will ***home in on*** its target, and although bees are being trained to do the same thing, there is nevertheless the risk of confusion with the meaning in *homing pigeon,* which is one trained to return to the same spot (home), and which was used in former times by armies to carry messages.

2 ***at the request of (the Pentagon)* is inappropriate here – did the Pentagon say "please?" – a term implying a stronger link is required: ***on orders from / by order of*** *the Pentagon* (e.g. for the researchers at the Air Force research lab.), ***under contract to*** *the Pentagon* (e.g. for the outside researchers from Montana University).

3 Certainly you find *performing animals* in a circus, but they have to be ***trained*** or ***taught*** (2nd paragraph) before they can *perform.* Lions and other big cats may have to be *tamed,* but surely not bees!

4 Care has to be taken in the choice of verb to translate « repérer » – *to locate* insists on *where* something is, such as landmines which are buried; *to spot* implies *visual* recognition; *to detect* suggests the presence (or absence) of explosives.

5 ***American researchers have undertaken work commissioned by the Pentagon on a method to train bees to identify traces of explosives.*** Beware of using the term as an adjective, i.e. ***explosive traces* as the expression is ambiguous. Even worse is ***explosive tracks* – *tracks* are the patterns that tyres / shoes make on the ground!

6 ***allow to detect bombs* – wrong structure, wrong choice of verb! Normally you *allow S.O. to do sth,* the direct object (being the person who obtains the permission) is indispensable, unless the structure is *allow something to happen*. Thus either *allow the police to detect bombs* or *allow bombs to be detected* where the passive form eliminates the person or persons. However, with a similar structure, a much better choice of verb is ***to enable*** *(s.o. to do sth / sth to happen)* which is more often than not the meaning of the French term "permettre" – or more simply ***make it possible to detect bombs***. Finally note that in some contexts there is even no need to translate "permettre".

7 ***affirm* = assert strongly – which one only does if there is a risk of contradiction. ***confirm* would be possible if it were the Pentagon reacting to a scoop in the NYT – but not ***confirmed Monday* which means that 'Monday' was the information that was confirmed.

8 ***overcome* an obstacle in figurative language, certainly, but ***reach*** or ***complete*** a ***stage*** or ***a milestone*** or ***a turning-point.*** Beware, these terms are not for use in all contexts; *milestone* is a significant point, while *turning-point* suggests that what happens afterwards is plain sailing or at least not fraught with the same difficulties. The project cannot be "***still at its initial stage (starting-point)*" AND "*complete a first stage*" – this is a contradiction in terms; this can be overcome in English by using the plural : *is still in its initial stages*, which allows some leeway.

9 ***at first* implies a change which intervenes later; thus here, *at first bees … taught … landmines, now … trucks* suggests that, for the Pentagon, the danger used to come from landmines, but now comes from trucks, and so there is a dramatic about-turn in the programme to take account of this – all implied in the expression "*at first*". Alternatives possible here include ***to begin with, as a first step***.

10 Usually a *heavy goods vehicle* is a *truck* in the USA, and a *lorry* in GB – though both are possible. Since this project is being conducted in the USA, then the American term is appropriate.

11 The five senses are the *sense of sight, of smell, of taste, of touch and of hearing*. *Olfactory sense* is used as often in English as you say "*l'olfaction*" in French, i.e. far less often than you say "*le sens de l'odorat*" – for which the English say *the sense of smell.* If you prefer to use the plural 'bees', then the possessive is expressed simply by the apostrophe : ***Bees' sense of smell***.

12 Apart from the above, rather than "accurate to more than 99 %", English would probably borrow a term from mathematics such as: ***is accurate to within 1 %*** or ***is less than 1 % out*** – or ***is almost totally 'spot-on' / is accurate in more than 99 cases out of 100***.

13 Clearly it is not possible to use **according to* twice within the space of two lines.

14 ***envisage equipping bees***

15 ***no bigger than a grain of rice*** – the expression has to negate the idea of size, since the emphasis is on how small it is.

16 Avoid all references to ***follow every (foot) step / follow their tracks*!! Bees don't leave their footprints behind them.

17 Introduced as a transition between two different ideas in the same paragraph. Take the opportunity to examine this expression and its structure.

18 Visit http://beekeeper.dbs.umt.edu/bees/.

19 ***Pentagon spokesmen.*** It is unlikely to be ***people in charge of the Pentagon*, since they are the Chiefs of Staff and the Defense Secretary. The distinction being made here is between the '*responsables*' who are part of the permanent staff, and the researchers who have been brought into the Pentagon from outside.

20 ***experiences* does not refer to scientific activities.

21 ***could lay them open to criticism and leg-pulling / could mean they will be criticised and made fun of / may provoke disbelief and taking the mickey / may spark off expressions of incredulity and ridicule***

22 ***implicate* … in a crime.

Saying "I Do" to Life Together[1]

Young couples today[2] set up house[3] gradually, in stages: to begin with, each goes on living at their own place,[4] and then they move in together.[5]

Things only start getting serious[6] when they start buying household appliances. Not so much a cooker or a fridge,[7] which are associated with eating,[8] and where the notion of pleasure outweighs[9] that of commitment.[10]

A washing-machine, on the other hand, plays a key role, because washing your smalls[11] implies intimacy and sharing.[12] Financial considerations apart;[13] holding back from buying a washing-machine[14] is in a way not being willing to take the plunge.[15] Conversely, acquiring one is the first step towards togetherness[16] and confirms[17] the building of the love-nest – no more trips to the launderette or taking the dirty washing back home.[18] This appliance is in reality[19] a stepping-stone[20] – from being a young couple starting out in life, they put down their roots[21] and are ready to plan their future life together.[22]

Notes

1 ***I Do*** is the sacrosanct answer in the wedding ceremony to the question *"Do you take this man / woman to be your lawful wedded husband / wife?"* and is thus the equivalent here of 'Oui'. A headline or a title is an opportunity to give free rein to inventiveness : ***When a Hotpoint points the way to Happiness / Happiness is a Hotpoint / When a washing-machine means "I love you" / Tumbling into True Love*** etc., etc., – Hotpoint is a registered trade mark, and *tumble* is a play on words : *fall in love* plus a reference to a *tumble-washer*.

2 ***Today's young couples*** - note the possible use of the possessive form with expressions of time. Avoid the question mark which is more typical of French speech than of English usage; however, if you interpret the question mark as meaning that this is a reply to a question (e.g. "what about young couples?"), then ***As for young couples, they...***; or ***Turning to young couples...***

3 ***set themselves up / come together***. Later on in the text, there will be an opportunity to use *settle down*, which is often confused with *set up* (= s'installer). This latter verb insists on the start, the beginning of something, while *settle* suggests the end to movement. It is absolutely essential to distinguish between *house* and *home* and to use the former at this point in the text, as this is the basis of the writer's argument: without the clear starting-point given by a marriage, at what point (stage) does merely 'living together' become 'a stable relationship'. For once, the popular expression *"home is where the heart is"* puts over this nicety very well.

4 Note the use of the politically correct *their* to avoid the distinction *his/her*. ***living on their own*** is also correct, since in the context it is highly unlikely they are already living with some-one else; ***living apart*** suggests they used to live together and that they have since separated and **living at home** means they have not yet left their parents.

5 ***move in under the same roof***

6 ***Commitment comes with the buying of household electricals / electrical goods.*** However, it is not possible to use commitment twice in the same sentence – see footnote below.

7 Distinguish between the uses of *imply* & *implicate*; the latter suggests an attempt to involve a person in something wrong. Neither term is suitable here, where 'impliquer' is very close to the

idea of ... commitment (!), of being tied down or bound (see next footnote). Since this has already been expressed at the beginning of the paragraph, it is preferable to avoid repetition by leaving out the verbal structure altogether. However, *imply* will be used a little later.

8 *linked with / to*. However, ***bound* is inappropriate here, as it suggests a *tight bond*, e.g. a legal contract is *a binding agreement* – something you can't get out of easily.

9 ***blurs*** (= rendre flou, moins clair, moins visible), ***cancels out, blanks out*** would retain the image of the French term, ***overrides***, like ***outweighs***, introduces a hierarchy.

10 Note the use of *that* (i.e. the notion) and not **the one of commitment*. Obviously it is not possible to use *commitment* twice in the space of two lines : "contrainte" can also be interpreted here as an obligation: either (a) "la corvée de faire de la cuisine = the ***chore of cooking*** (cf. *household chores* = tâches ménagères), or could also be (b) l'acquisition de l'appareil = ***the basic need***.

11 ***your clothes*** – *smalls* refers to underwear, etc. and so, obviously, it is most definitely intimate! ***linen* as a translation of "linge" is inappropriate since nowadays hardly any of our clothes are made of this material. Note *en passant* the English expression *to wash one's dirty linen in public* is the direct equivalent of "laver son linge sale en public". Note also here the use of the impersonal *your* – remember that *you/your* can on occasions be used to translate "on" & "son".

12 ***communal/collective* are inappropriate for two people only. *Cleanliness* = propreté - hygiène. The French sociological jargon means no more and no less than *sharing*. For the purists among you who are still not happy, and who insist on equally incomprehensible jargon then how about *implies organizing the indivisibility of the combined cooperative responsibility for cleanliness* – which is totally meaningless for the average English speaker.

13 ***Money problems aside / Apart from questions of cost, not wanting to buy a washing-machine...***

14 ***not wanting to buy; being reluctant to buy suggests a reluctance to take the plunge***

15 ***in a way a sign that you're not ready to settle down***

16 The argument to the effect that the writer, with the expression "machine conjugale", is drawing a parallel with *washing-machine* ... does not hold water (i.e. stand up to examination) since the French text refers consistently to "lave-linge" and not to "machine à laver".
Furthermore, even if French dictionaries do equate "conjugal" with "matrimonial", the original Latin meaning is "to join" or "to bring together"; consequently, in this context, the writer has deliberately chosen the adjective for its original meaning and we should avoid terms such as "marriage": *Togetherness* in the text above does precisely that (in addition to enriching students' English vocabulary) while the most obvious, acceptable term here would be ***partnership,*** which is both how modern heterosexual couples refer to their relationship (*partner* = 'compagne, compagnon') and the name of the Act of Parliament – the *Civil Partnership Act 2004* – granting same-sex couples the same rights as (heterosexual) married couples. Finally, to satisfy those who want a 'mechanical' reference in the English translation equivalent to the French term 'machine', then *acquiring a washing-machine puts in motion the whole process of setting up house together* would fit the bill.

17 ***demonstrates, establishes, affirms***

18 The use of the single word *home* puts over nicely the underlying notion that as long as a young person continues to "*bring his/her washing back to mummy and daddy*" then he/she is not ready to settle down as an independent, fully-fledged adult. The American term ***laundromat*** is also possible. The Stephen Frears' film *My Beautiful Laundrette* is not the usual spelling.

19 As "en fait" introduces the final paragraph, you can translate it as ***in fact / indeed / to sum up / in short***.

20 ***a milestone***, i.e. an important point in their lives; ***a turning-point***. *A **go-between* refers to a person, as in the L.P. Hartley novel *The Go-Between* and J. Losey film which was distributed in France as "Le Messager" (1971).

21 ***settle down***

22 ***they settle down, ready to make plans for their future life together*** - there are many opportunities to use the expression *settle down*, you simply have to avoid too much repetition.

Football : Danger on the wings[1]

By raising the stakes too high,[2] has professional football killed the goose that laid the golden eggs – its beloved television? The escalation of broadcasting rights is implicated in the bankruptcy of Kirchmedia,[3] the subsidiary of the Kirch group which went into liquidation on Monday 8th April, a liquidation that comes hard on the heels of[4] that of ITV Digital, a British digital pay channel. The German group had undertaken to pay € 1.5 billion over four years to the German Football Association and the Bundesliga clubs.[5] ITV Digital had bought for several million euro the broadcasting rights to the English League 2nd, 3rd & 4th Divisions for three years. Today both companies have been bled white.[6] The hoped-for revenue never materialised.

Too much football kills televised football.[7] As a result of broadcasting boring encounters[8] and of paying outrageous sums simply to ensure that such and such a competition would not fall into the hands of a rival operator[9], these TV companies got their fingers burnt[10] and brought about their own downfall. Turned into an everyday item by the media moguls,[11] football has become a run-of-the-mill affair.[12] The electric atmosphere of the European Cup matches has been dissipated in the second-rate games with which the viewer is bombarded[13] throughout the year. France seems to be one of those least hit by the low spirits spreading throughout Europe's televisions: in Italy and Spain the digital channels are on the brink of financial ruin.

The footballing world is aware that it is likely to be the first victim of the upheaval in broadcasting[14] which has begun. In England, the Division Two, Three & Four clubs teetering on the brink of bankruptcy as a result of the liquidation of ITV Digital can be counted in their dozens.[15] The official receivers are currently negotiating with the English Football League[16] to bring down from €300m to €83m the fee to retain broadcast rights. In Germany and in France the budgets of the smaller clubs in the higher divisions are more than 50 % dependent on the income from television. In the case of Sankt Pauli, at present bottom of the German league, its budget is funded for 69 % by the television rights.

Only the top clubs have been capable of seeing which way the wind is blowing[17] and of making other sources of revenue a priority. The spiralling players' wage bills[18] nevertheless place them in difficulty, so much so that more and more chairmen are coming out in favour of capping the wage bill. They were also the first to claim the right of each individual club to negotiate its own television rights. But it's a cruel world – in Italy over half the top clubs have not managed to sell their rights. Market forces favour big clubs over minnows.[19] Professional football, which for so long wanted to be judged by these forces,[20] is learning that they crush the weak.

Notes

1 Deliberate re-working of the sporting expression *on the wing* (sur l'aile) with *'in the wings'* (dans les coulisses, prêt à surgir) ***from the wings*** would be equally possible.

2 Only commercial companies can try to ***outbid each other*, not the football authorities – they are in a position of strength and can pit one rival company against another.

3 Broadcasting rights are probably not the only reason for the bankruptcy, which is why they are not ***responsible for* … (note spelling).

4 ***less than a fortnight after***

5 This is the same distinction as in other countries between the Football League, in charge of the championship (here the Bundesliga) and the national association, in charge at international level (Deutscher Fussball Bund).

6 This is the past form of the verb *to bleed* – the passive voice indicates that the television companies are not totally responsible for this financial bloodletting. ***wan* describes a pale or tired complexion, while ***bloodless* is more often used in contexts implying absence of killing (*the regime was overturned in a bloodless revolution*) – *moneyless* would be more appropriate.

7 Admittedly this is what the French text says, though it would be more logical to put it the other way round and say that ***too much televised football kills off the sport in all its forms***.

8 ***matches*** is more commonly used.

9 the 'bouquet' refers to a collection of programmes – *a channel package* – and this would not fit in here.

10 = to suffer the unpleasant results of something that you have done. Although the myth of Icarus is known, it has not given rise to a familiar expression in English. However there is the expression *to clip somebody's wings* = to restrict someone's freedom, activities, or power.

11 It is advisable to avoid confusing the issue by a reference to ***supermarkets* here!

12 Alternatively, ***turned into a mundane TV staple by the media , football has become humdrum***.

13 ***showered / that rain down on the viewer*** would keep the water image, but fit in less well.

14 ***sea change / reshaping / revamping***

15 Somewhere between thirty and fifty English D2,3 & 4 clubs are at present threatened with bankruptcy because the revenue from broadcasting rights goes essentially to the Premier Division clubs, with the 'leftovers' going to some First Division clubs. The Premier League's current £1,024 billion deal with B Sky B runs over the course of three seasons from August 2004. Note, *en passant*, that in England there is both a Premier Division *and* a First Division; D1 clubs therefore are not the top clubs.

16 The French text makes it clear that the situation referred to is that in England by the use of the English term ('Football League'), but it becomes less clear when the whole sentence is in English.

17 ***have been able to have the foresight to find other sources of revenue***

18 In Britain at least, commentators continue to talk in terms of *weekly wages*, even though the figures are astronomical "*Chelsea's wage bill of £ 115m in 2003/04 is "almost certainly" the highest in world football, according to an annual financial review by Deloitte.*"(BBC News Online, 8th June 2005).

19 A *minnow* is a small fresh-water fish, but the expression is often used to refer to small or minor companies or persons. Similarly the expression *small fry* ('menu fretin') refers to unimportant people.

20 The major English Premier Division clubs are publicly owned companies quoted on the London Stock Exchange. Manchester United was recently bought out and is 100 % owned by a single American shareholder.

The City : an investment haven for terrorists[1]

A French Parliamentary report[2] made public on Wednesday castigates[3] London's Square Mile[4] as an *"investment haven for terrorist organizations"* and identifies the Channel Islands as *"veritable money-laundering plants[5] for the proceeds of organised crime."* The world's largest financial centre[6] is *"highly attractive to money-launderers"*[7] mainly[8] by virtue of its *"lax legislation[9] on investment trust funds which guarantees[10] total anonymity to the true beneficiaries of the funds and the flagrant want of regulation of certain financial services"*[11] the French Parliamentary financial crime committee[12] underlines.[13]

This "State within the State,"[14] where some[15] € 3,800 billion worth of assets are invested,[16] *"flaunts[17] a disdainful disregard for the risk of money-laundering"* according to[18] this report drawn up by the French Socialist MP[19] Arnaud Montebourg under the title *"The City of London, Gibraltar and Crown Dependencies: offshore sanctuaries for dirty money."* At this particular time, when we have just been given a *"bitter demonstration"* of how organizations linked to Osama bin Laden *"have taken full advantage of[20] the financial freedom available"*, the report goes on, it comes as *"no surprise to note[21] the importance[22] for underworld organisations bent on terrorism[23] of London's Square Mile and the offshore territories"*.

The report also points the finger of accusation at the Channel Islands of Jersey and Guernsey.[24] The fiscal and banking strategies of their authorities[25] *"with the tacit encouragement, if not[26] the explicit[27] backing of the United Kingdom"* have turned these territories to all intents and purposes into "the black holes[28] of world finance".

The French parliamentarians further condemn *"the lack of official cooperation not only for financial fraud but for all kinds of crimes and offences, notably extraditions."* The Home Office, the report complains, *"persists in[29] its habit of putting spokes in the wheels of judicial investigations in other European countries, thus handicapping, if not totally paralysing,[30] the war against money-laundering"*. It also notes that although the Blair government decided in 1997 to be more "pro-active" in reinforcing its financial provisions, by first and foremost setting up a watchdog – the Financial Services Authority – *"but four years on, Britain's track record in the anti-laundering war is lacklustre"*[31].

Notes

1 ***haven*** is used with the same meaning as in *tax haven* (= paradis fiscal). ***Centre*** can be used later. Saying that ***the City is a safe place for terrorists* gives a totally wrong meaning.

2 An enquiry is *undertaken / carried out,* while a report is ***drawn up / compiled.*** *To draft a report* is similar, but the term suggests an unfinished piece of work (*draft* = Fr. brouillon, premier jet) See footnote further on regarding **deputy*.

3 Only the police can ***charge* someone with an offence – the report ***points the finger of accusation at / accuses*** *(the City)* ***of + -ing / alleges that the City is an investment haven / lays the allegation of money-laundering at the door of the City***.

4 Term often used to refer to The City. However, it has nothing to do with the coincidental fact that the French term "place", used as a street name, can be translated as "*square*".

5 **factory* sounds inappropriate in English both because of the origins of the term and the connotations it carries. ***Powerhouse*** is an original choice. Note the structure ***laundering money FROM crime***.

6 ***the stronghold of world finance*** was a term used in the report. ***Money market*** is also a judicious choice. The superlative adjective requires ***the biggest IN the world***.

7 Not ***laundrymen*, which refers exclusively to workers in a laundry. There are three different translations of the French term blanchir': to *whiten* is literally to make (more) white; then minimalist interior decorators may *whitewash* the walls of a room and, with a figurative meaning, the Hutton enquiry in Britain was recently said to *whitewash* the Blair government over Iraq. Finally the usage here requires *launder*, which is now becoming less common as a term for the ordinary washing of clothes.

8 **among others* is incorrect here – *among other reasons* would be the expression, but it does not put over the meaning of the French text.

9 ***permissive* means *tolerant*, especially in sexual matters cf. *the permissive society,* which was the name given to Britain during the second half of the Sixties - the age of the Beatles, the mini-skirt, Swinging London, acts legalising (i.e. *permitting*) abortion, homosexuality, divorce, etc.

10 ***ensures*** but not ***insures*. Similarly while the noun *warranty* is synonymous with *guarantee*, the verb *to warrant* is not; it means *to be worthy of (attention), to attest to* . Nor is ***vouch for* possible.

11 In the context it would be equally true to interpret « de » as ***vigilance by certain financiers*** (= de la part de) as well as ***control over certain financial service operators.*** Note the use of *want* = lack, absence (also the adjective *wanting* and the adage *waste not, want not* = il ne faut pas gaspiller afin de ne pas être en manque).

12 ***fact-finding mission.*** The noun phrase should be as concise as possible, otherwise the verb which follows *(underlines)* gets lost – avoid stringing words one after the other as in ***fact-finding mission of the French National Assembly about the laundering of money* – the sentence is too long-winded.

13 The simple present tense is required when quoting a written document e.g. *the Bible says that*

14 The set expression *a law unto itself /himself / herself, etc (*= n'en faire qu'à sa tête*)*, though interesting, is not appropriate in this context. Clearly the report is suggesting that the City does not operate within the normal legal framework of the British state.

15 ***nigh on / nearly / around***

16 ***to be found.*** Also, ***deposits*** could replace *assets,* or ***deposited*** could replace the verb. ***Stacked, **stocked, **amassed, **piled up* all suggest a huge pile of banknotes, as in Fort Knox. In a different context it is possible to say that some-one *has stacks of money* and that he *is filthy rich* (which does not imply illegal activities). ***accrue* is not possible here - interest *accrues* on savings, i.e. it is added and accumulates on the invested sum, while only a miser ***hoards*. If by "s'accumuler" you interpret a gradual building-up, then perhaps, with tongue in cheek, you could say "*- some 3,800 billion have (over the years) found their way here*" Beware also of confusing the singular and plural uses of "avoir" – a *credit note* corresponds to the singular, but ***assets*** or ***holdings*** is necessary for the meaning of the plural form.

17 ***displays / puts on / shows / feigns .*** Beware of misunderstanding the French adjective "superbe" which is here used with the same meaning as the old-fashioned and rather literary noun; ***haughty, superior*** would be other possible translations. Alternatively, the whole phrase could read ***pays scant regard to the risk of money laundering*** or ***cocks a snoot at the risk***.

18 This neatly avoids the problem of the English sentence structure, which requires the verb to follow the subject (unlike French). An alternative solution would be to avoid translating the participle "rédigé" thus: "***... money-laundering***" ***states socialist MP Arnaud Montebourg in his report entitled... / states socialist MP Montebourg, author of the report entitled...***

19 Once the French context has been made known, ***député*** (in French) would be acceptable here. However, beware of using a term such as *deputy* from the very outset, as it has a totally different meaning in English (= adjoint, remplaçant). Indeed, there is little justification in using ***deputy* – either you keep the French term or anglicise it as ***M.P.*** An *MEP* is a *"député européen"*.

20 ***used to their best advantage, made full use of***

21 Not ***notice* which implies (a) visual observation and (b) chance observation. It might sound more English to say ***It comes as no surprise to learn of the importance ...***

22 ***significance***

23 ***organisations with terrorist intent***

24 It is plausible to suggest that some French readers may need reminding that Jersey and Guernsey are also known as the Channel Islands, but it is hardly necessary for English readers. However, there is no justification either for the brackets or the dots (points de suspension) in English.

25 Remember that each of these Channel Islands is self-governing; the parliament is known as the States of Jersey / Guernsey.

26 ***and on occasions even the ... / when it isn't the out-and-out backing***

27 ***clear, unqualified*** (= total).

28 Advisable to keep the astronomical image. In order to avoid repetition of the adjective *veritable*, it is possible to use an adverb or adverbial expression. Thus ***have truly turned these territories into the black holes of world finance / have turned them into nothing more nor less than the black holes***. However, adjectives such as ***authentic*, ***genuine*, etc. are inappropriate in this context. ***worldwide finance* is the wrong meaning – ***the world of finance / the world's financial community*** are acceptable. Finally, the definite article is required with *black holes* to put over the idea that they are the biggest, most pernicious, etc.

29 The verb *persists* contains the notion of obstinacy. Remember the distinction in meaning between the two structures *go on to do something* as opposed to *go on doing something*.

30 ***pursues its tradition of obstructionism, thus hampering and even totally frustrating the battle against money-laundering***. *Struggle* is not always appropriate, as it emphasises the difficulty, the effort involved – and possibly the ultimate failure. Here it is too negative, suggesting that there is little point in doing anything.

31 ***is sadly lacking***. A freer interpretation would give: ***The British contribution to the anti-laundering war over the past four years has been modest***.

British business: Enterprising Elders[1]

In Britain the number of new businesses[2] set up[3] by those in their late middle-age[4] in fact grew by 23% last year. According to a report by[5] Barclays Bank Research Unit, 23,600[6] businesses were registered by British entrepreneurs[7] in the 55-64 age bracket[8], although year-on-year the number of company start-ups[9] in Britain is falling.

Overall, half of all new business start-ups were by the over-50s – secretarial services,[10] piano tuition,[11] interior decorating,[12] marketing consultancies[13] retailing[14] etc.[15] Changes in the welfare system,[16] plus longer life expectancy,[17] are encouraging the mature fringe of the workforce[18] to find new things to do,[19] especially those who have not managed to save enough[20] through a pension fund scheme,[21] Mike Davis, manager of the small business section[22] at Barclays, explains.

Who then are these[23] new-style businessmen? Some have been made redundant[24] by a shake-out in their firm[25] and have had to find a means to earn a living[26] until they are able to draw their pension.[27] But quite a lot of them, of their own free will, have switched from employee status to being self-employed.[28] In this way they can work fewer hours – 36 on average – and take longer holidays[29] – four to six weeks[30] – than their younger counterparts.[31] The turnover[32] of such businesses is moderate,[33] running at an annual € 110,000 as opposed to an average of € 220,000 for all businesses.[34]

Such business ventures are usually small, and run from home,[35] which is made all the easier by the fact that[36] these elderly entrepreneurs[37] are anything but afraid of[38] new technology. They more often than not use a computer and a fax and they even access the Internet.[39]

Notes

1 A number of alternative amusing headlines spring to mind : ***Founding Fathers / Golden Oldies / Age Concerns.*** The first of these is a play on words by reference to the early history of America. *Age Concern* is a charity which pays particular attention to the needs of the elderly, but here used as a play on words with *concern* carrying the meaning of *company* or *firm. Golden Oldies* are the songs or films from days gone by which remain popular favourites.

2 **society* is closer in meaning to the French "association de type 1901" where the purpose is cultural but excluding money-making or commercial activities – e.g. *debating society* – Consequently, the term is totally inappropriate in this context. The very name *company* suggests that more than one person is concerned, whereas here these are mostly one-man (or one-woman) affairs; however, the term is necessary in the next sentence referring to the total number declared at ... Companies House (http://www.companies-house.gov.uk).

3 **founded* and **established* should be kept for reference to companies that have stood the test of time, i.e. that are still going strong after 50-100 years of existence. The most usual verb for *start-ups* is *to set up a company;* but using the noun obviates the need for a verb: ***the number of company start-ups by middle-aged people increased by 23%*** - Note in the next sentence the use of *registered* - this refers to the obligatory administrative formality, but it is also the indicator used by government statisticians to reach the conclusion that there were some 50,000 new companies last year.

4 ***the elderly***. The context is that of people who may have been *pensioned off* by their employer but who have not yet reached retirement age. Consequently terms such as ***retired people / **pensioners / **senior citizens* are inappropriate. These terms are only used for the over-65s, and the context makes it clear that the people here are younger. Indeed the French writer is not flattering for his "*elders and betters*", as few 55 year-olds would appreciate being considered as being "*over the hill / one foot in the grave*" – 55 hardly qualifies as "troisième âge". Many of them will still have their *elderly* parents. Remember that the term "seniors" in this context is a *French* neologism by sociologists and admen. In certain cases in Britain you become a *senior* when you move from primary school to secondary school at the age of 11, while sportsmen and women become *seniors* at the age of 18. *Middle-age* is defined as being "*the period of life between 40-60, when you are no longer young, but are not yet old*" (Longman Dictionary Contemporary English).

5 ***As reported by*** Barclay's. ***a report OF Barclays* would mean that Barclay's was the *object* of the report, and not the author/source. You can *conduct* or *carry out* a study (on which you report), but you can't ***lead* a study. Though correct, ***a Barclay's Bank Research Unit report*** is an overloaded, cumbersome structure.

6 ***twenty-three thousand six hundred companies***... en toutes lettres. Be careful when expressing figures – here and later on in the text. However, there is no particular reason to write out figures such as this, except on a cheque, a commercial contract or in a legal document.

7 Beware the French *enterprise* may be an *undertaking* in English, but an *entrepreneur* cannot be an ***undertaker* (= croque-mort, pompes funèbres). The Thatcherite 1980s were the time of the *entrepreneurial revolution* when people who had been made redundant and saw no probability of finding another job were encouraged to *"take their future into their own hands"*, *"take responsability for themselves"*, *"take the initiative"* and... set themselves up in their own business

8 ***British 55-64 year-olds*** – NEITHER ***by British aged 55-64* NOR ***55-64 year-old(s) British!...* *The British* exists as a generic plural, but ***a British, **five British, etc.* do not. Consequently, *British* here being an adjective, a noun is required : *55-64 year-old British citizens / entrepreneurs* – the use here of *people* shows a distinct lack of vocabulary, as clearly only *people*, not *animals* or *insects* are likely to set up a company! Similarly ***by over fifty British people* has a totally different meaning = 'par plus de 50 Britanniques'.

9 ***the average of creation of companies* is a barbarism – i.e. a word-for-word translation that means absolutely nothing in English. In this structure "*average*" appears as an adjective requiring a noun (e.g. *the average number of new companies*). Alternatively, translate this notion of "moyenne" ***... although generally speaking the number of company start-ups is declining.*** You can only *average* out by comparison of one set of figures with another, therefore *from one year to the next*. Note the noun *a start-up* referring precisely to the "creation" of a company. Distinguish clearly between *find, found, found* (Irregular verb meaning "trouver") = *found, founded, founded* (Regular verb meaning "fonder") = *fund; funded, funded* (Regular verb meaning "financer"). These companies are not ***floated*, which means that shares in the company are sold on the Stock Exchange to the public.

10 Keep in mind that this list gives examples of *types of business activity*, not of jobs.

11 ***piano lessons*** is possible, but *tuition* here has the advantage of keeping the term in harmony with the detached, general, less concrete terms used for the other types of business.

12 ***home improvements.*** By definition, ***DIY* (Do-It-Yourself) is totally inappropriate. The context here is that of businesses and professional tradesmen – precisely the kind of people "bricoleurs" do *NOT* turn to. The interpretation ***housework* is highly implausible as doing it for a living requires the sort of vitality that the over-50s cannot always demonstrate. As for ***homework,* no comment!!

13 The type of business would be a ***consultancy***, and the type of work carried out a *market study.* A *business consultancy* allows these middle-aged executives to put all their life-long experience and skills at the service of firms who call on such outside help. Note that ***researches* doesn't exist in English.

14 in preference to *shops* – same justification as for the other terms. ***Small businesses*** is possible, but not ***businesses* on its own, as all the examples given here from secretarial services onwards are different kinds of *business*.

15 The "points de suspension" are a feature of French writing, and would not be used in this context in English! Depending on circumstances, expressions such as ***and so on / and such like*** / *to name but a few / X, Y, Z spring to mind / X, Y, Z are typical examples / for example* ... etc. (*sic* !).

16 ***the benefits system*** – rather than the knee-jerk automatic translation ***social system* which means nothing at all in English – remember that French uses the same term "*social*" for two totally different concepts in English (a *sociologist* is not an *economist).* Note too that *development* generally has a positive connotation and is therefore inappropriate here, since the deep-down meaning is that the welfare system is becoming *less* generous – otherwise these people wouldn't need to find new things to do.

17 ***plus the fact that people are living longer*** – note the rather unexpected use of the present progressive with 'live' to denote that society is undergoing a change at present; the simple present is also acceptable.

18 Not ***the eldest section of the population* – what about the over 75s??. Despite what the text may say, this is not **the oldest section of the population* – a 54-year-old is not the same as a 75-year-old ... unless you are also willing to concede that a 22-year-old (student?) is the same as a two-year-old baby. Throughout the text, the comparative form of adjectives is preferable to the superlative. Here the superlative is possible provided you make it clear that the term 'population' refers to 'la population active,' since 55-64 year-olds are at the top end of the workforce.

19 ***are prompting / are spurring them to / start a new career / to look for new occupations.*** ***incite* is only used in contexts of a person deliberately encouraging others to fight or argue, or to racial hatred, murder, etc. Here ***prompt, cause, encourage*** are other possibilities, but ***exhort,* ***urge* imply a human agent. The context implies that ***encouraging*** is synonymous with ***compelling / obliging them... Occupations*** but not ***hobbies,* ***leisure activities* in this context – it's anything but leisure!

20 ***put enough aside*** is often used in this context; ***those who have not built up a nest-egg*** is more colourful. **hoard* is pejorative, it is what a miser does; **amass* similarly has negative connotations. Interest *accrues* on savings in a bank account, but the usage is unsuitable here.

21 ***by means of a pension scheme***.

22 ***SME department*** – although the *small and medium-sized enterprise (SME)* is a recent addition to English terminology, more often than not *small business(es)* is the familiar term used.

23 ***those* is totally inappropriate since the text is about to describe them – consequently, as in the distinction in French between "celui-ci" and "celui-là" the notion of proximity / separation is emphasised.

Who are this new breed of entrepreneur? Obviously ***firms' creators* is impossible – as would be ***firm creators* – choose ***company creators,*** if you wish, where there is no ambiguity in the meaning. ***Who are these new-age / born-again Founding Fathers*** is very tongue-in-the-cheek, but you could get away with it here.

24 ***pensioned off*** but certainly not ***fired* or ***dismissed.* Furthermore, the structure *fired / dismissed FOR* indicates the *misconduct* given as the reason for a dismissal, e.g. *he was dismissed / fired for using the company phone for personal calls.* In the present context *as a result of* would put over "du fait de".

25 ***a company shake-out / corporate reorganisation / downsizing / restructuring***

26 or more simply ***have had to earn a living / have had to get by*** The meaning requires you to insist on the financial support needed but ***subsist* is inappropriate here – it is the minimal level of existence – closer to the French RMI – and it is unlikely people would give up gainful employment for that.

27 ***until they reach retirement age*** – which is still 65 for men in Britain, and 60 for women, but not for long. Already, the retirement age for women is being put up to 65, and the Turner Report (November 2005) recommended raising *the pensionable age* (the age at which a person becomes entitled to a state pension) to 66 by 2030, to 67 by 2040 and to 68 by 2050 – i.e. 68 for youngsters at present aged 23 and under – in other words, your counterparts in England.

28 ***to being their own boss / from working for some-one else to working for themselves.*** The 1980s were a period of growth in the self-employed sector in Britain as it became clear that mass lay-offs could not be offset by rare recruitment of labour by existing companies or businesses. Setting oneself up in business was the only alternative to unemployment. ***freelance* is not the same thing, and is not the meaning here; although the Inland Revenue (*the taxman*) may consider that *to work freelance* is equivalent to being *self-employed*, a *freelance* (or *freelancer*) offers his services to several companies, and does not set himself up in business. Think of the origin of the term – in medieval times, a mercenary who sold his military skills (and weapon – his lance) to anyone who paid him, and who was not loyal to one single employer (cf. French 'pigiste'). Note the spelling of *independent*. Even self-employed, he remains the *wage-earner* in the family!

29 This is not exactly the same thing in this context as to *go (off) on holiday* which more often than not implies travelling. *Take a holiday* can be compared with *take a day off, take a break*, i.e. simply an interruption of work.

30 This is a superb illustration of ... 'l'exception française' where the 35-hour working week has become the norm, and where paid annual holidays stretch to 5 weeks. Britain works more hours than any other European country, and 4 weeks' holiday (20 days) only became the legal minimum as late as 1999, as a result of a European directive. However, the 'loophole' is that public holidays such as Easter Monday can be included in these 20 days. This same directive also limited to 48 hours the maximum working week throughout the EU, and Britain implemented this provision, but in 1999 an amendment allowed employers to go beyond this ceiling if he got written consent from the employee to work longer hours. At that time, around 1998, the average UK worker worked 43 hours a week. This *'opt-out'* from the EU directive was still in place in 2005, and France, though opposed to it in principle, has made use of it, principally for hospital medical staff *'on call'* for up to 70 hours a week

31 ***rivals* and ***competitors* are inappropriate, as the context is not that of business competition – despite the French term – but of the different components of the working population – the suggestion is that people start out as employees, then when they reach their fifties, they voluntarily decide to quit their jobs and become self-employed in order to have more free time – they are not in competition with other employees. If you talk of *younger competitors*, then the only context can be that of young company owners, and not of all employed persons, but there again, there is no real competition, since the mature start-ups are not trying to develop and extend their activities, but simply ensure an income for a number of years.

32 ***the figure* is insufficient - nor is it a translation. The French usage is an abbreviation for "chiffre d'affaires" but ***figure* is not part of the English term. As for ***salary*, a little thought should make it obvious that anyone earning that sort of money doesn't have to worry too much about his retirement pension!

33 ***unpretentious*** – this is an unusual use of the term, but quite acceptable here.

34 **global* means *world-wide,* which is surely not meant here – the context is restricted to Britain (Eng. *globalisation* = Fr. mondialisation) Note that it is necessary to repeat the currency sign (£, FF, €, etc.) with the figure.

35 *To run a company* is far more natural in English than to *administer.*

36 ***which is all the easier as*** – Note the structure with *as* – NOT ***than* or ***that* (cf. *all the more so as* = "d'autant plus que"). 'Confortable' has nothing to do with the over-50s being less mobile or in need of their home comforts – it refers to the new-style of *working from home*. Technology is taking everyone in that direction, it just so happens that these entrepreneurs do not rent offices in town, but use their homes as business premises.

37 ***contractor* is the dictionary translation for "entrepreneur en bâtiment" – it is short for *building contractor*.

38 ***they are not averse to using***. Even if the dictionary suggests the noun *technophobe* (although the Microsoft Word word-checker has just refused it!), it is a fairly recent addition (as is its opposite *techno-geek*). Try to express it in your own words.

39 using a computer is common as is too a fax and the Internet. An opportunity to use the 'reprise par auxiliaire' (here 'is' refers to the verbal noun 'using' therefore singular) – ***they frequently use a computer as they do a fax and the Internet***. Remember too that – for the time being at least – English refers to ***the*** Internet.

Chirac kicks off[1] the pensions debate

On Monday Jacques Chirac started the ball rolling on the pensions debate, one of the most sensitive issues facing Prime Minister Raffarin's government, requiring[2] it to put forward its recommendations before the summer.

"The government will engage discussions with both sides of industry and come to the appropriate conclusions before the summer break, President Chirac stated to an audience of some 1,500 representatives from trade unions, management and the voluntary sector[3] during a reception to mark the New Year.

The head of state reiterated his faith[4] in the contributory pension scheme, calling it "a pact between the generations". But he felt it necessary to supplement it by a personal retirement savings plan[5], which nevertheless should[6] only be looked on as a top-up scheme. "It was," he said "a question of making available to the whole of the population[7] what was the prerogative of the privileged few, referring to the advantages that public sector employees now enjoy.

Although one of the major difficulties in pensions reform lay in adjusting[8] the 'qualifying years' in the public sector to those in the private sector, Jacques Chirac insisted on the absolute necessity of "a fair deal for all."

While standing by the idea of retirement at the age of 60, he stressed that it was also necessary to "allow everyone the freedom and opportunity of going on working if they so wished."

For the head of state, early retirement was a waste of manpower and economic potential.[9] "Let us put an end to this waste," he urged his audience, "by calling on both sides of industry to tackle the problem head on[10] and commit themselves sincerely to keeping the over-50s in work.

Jacques Chirac expressed his confidence in winning people over to this viewpoint. "The task is daunting, but it[11] is not insurmountable," he said.

He laid out the approach the government should take, through consultation and, over and above negotiation between the two sides of industry, through forthright discussion. All solutions "should be looked at carefully with an open mind. Nothing is predetermined. Everyone must be allowed to have his say."

"The pensions debate is a reaffirmation of our belief in social inclusion."[12] It is not a question of lining up one section of the community against another,[13] the workforce against pensioners, the public sector against the private sector, employees against the self-employed" Chirac insisted, hinting at the failure of the Juppé government's initiative in 1995.

"If everyone agrees to do their bit,[14] then you will see that the indispensable changes[15] are within our reach"[16] he added.

Initial reactions were on the whole favourable. "It's a roadmap[17] which suits us well at the CFDT" secretary-general François Chérèque commented. "He promises us negotiations, so let's negotiate."

OK to working out "new and different methods" but only "if they lead to real improvements in the workplace"[18] Bernard Thibault, secretary-general of the CGT union, declared.

"Mr. Chirac has stated quite clearly the guidelines: fairness, freedom and a guaranteed pension", MEDEF boss Ernest-Antoine Seillière commented.

Jacques Chirac also insisted on the need to make France competitive once again to ensure its continuing appeal for investors.[19] Continuing to reduce income tax rates and NI contributions,[20] limiting public expenditure, reforming public services, doing away with red tape, these are the measures he put forward to restore 'confidence'.[21]

Notes

1 Why not keep the sporting image both here and in the first sentence.

2 ***by requiring*** would also be possible, expressing how President Chirac 'kicked off the debate' *require* here puts over the hierarchy between presidency and government, where the former has the power to *oblige* the latter. *Ask* is often used for requests between people of equal status.

3 One major dictionary suggests the "***lifeblood of the country*", and another "***the resources of the nation*" but neither expression in English corresponds to the French usage here (equivalent to 'acteurs socio-économiques') for which there is no single generally-recognised term; it is preferable to make use of the clue which follows. The *voluntary sector* covers activities "to the benefit of the community" which come under the legal heading of *charities*. (See Charity Commission www.charity-commission.gov.uk). Expressions such as the above in the dictionaries should be kept for contexts such as "*Volunteers are the lifeblood of sport in this country and the recruitment of them is an essential part of a successful Games." Sebastian Coe, chairman of London 2012 Olympic challenge, said*" or "*MG Rover is the lifeblood of the West Midlands car industry*".

4 ***belief in / restated his firm intention to maintain the***

5 what in Britain is referred to as ***a stakeholder pension***. The government in Britain is worried that people are not saving enough for their retirement and is currently thinking of making it compulsory to put money aside to complement the state pension, which is among the lowest in Europe according to the OECD. The Turner Commission made such an official recommendation in its report in late November 2005, urging that a National Pension Savings Scheme (NPSS) be set up.

6 ***should*** rather than ***can*** since he is not stating a fact but giving advice and suggesting that it cannot replace the state pension.

7 ***a question of letting everyone in on what was the prerogative of the few / letting everyone benefit from what up to now has been the prerogative of the few***

8 ***evening out the differences between***

9 ***a waste in both human and economic terms***

10 ***to grasp the nettle***

11 There is no particular need to introduce the notion of a *wall* in English, as both adjectives here can be used with *task*.

12 ***is yet another battle in the struggle against social exclusion.*** French politicians refer more often than their English counterparts to the notion of *'solidarité'*, which can sometimes be translated as *'community spirit'*.

13 ***the French one against the other***

14 A whole plethora of expressions would fit in here ***If all sides are all willing to do their fair share / If everyone agrees to pull their weight / If there's a bit of give and take from***

all concerned / If everyone mucks in (too informal for a President), or with a slightly different emphasis: ***If we are truly determined to ensure a fair deal for everyone / to ensure fair and equal treatment for all***. All of these expressions could be useful in later life!

15 A reminder that *******evolution* should be kept for Darwinism. Depending on the context, *changes, developments, improvements, rise, weakening, worsening of the situation, decline etc* are all possibilities.

16 ***are within the realms of possibility / are achievable***

17 the term used by President Bush in the context of a Middle East peace plan. A ***blueprint*** is a suitable alternative.

18 There is no harm in referring simply to *the workers*, given the political stance of the CGT union: ***only if they represent real progress for the workers***.

19 ***to ensure that once again France will be able to compete effectively in international markets / will be able to attract stable inward investment***

20 ***bringing down income tax and NI contributions even further*** However if you are writing about the French system for British expatriates setting up house in France, then *Social Security contributions* would be appropriate; however to the average 'Brit', *social security* refers to the benefits handed out by the state, rather than the revenue from the workforce.

21 ***the feel-good factor*** is the journalese term in the British context.

Storm in a tea-cup? [1]

Could it be[2] that the legendary[3] 'cuppa' is no longer to the taste[4] of British tea-drinkers?[5] Going by[6] a report published on June 16th by the London market analyst Datamonitor, Her Britannic Majesty's subjects[7] now prefer herbal and fruit teas. "*Herbal teas used to be*[8] *part of the hippy scene.*[9] *But nowadays such beverages are more popular than tea with people who put their health first*"[10] analyst John Band emphasizes.

According to the author of this report, which is based on the analysis[11] of supermarket sales in the drinks sector, fashion trends and subtle marketing[12] account for the surge of interest in[13] mint-, camomile- and blackcurrant-flavoured teas among the ordinary population. So does this mark the end to the ritual[14] of pouring water that is just coming to the boil[15] into a teapot that has been brought to the kettle (and not the other way round).[16] Not to mention savouring and daintily sipping the brew in appreciative silence,[17] with the pinkie turned upwards, which is the height of good etiquette.[18]

"*Stuff and Nonsense !*"[19] William Gorman, head of the Tea Council, retorts "*What about all the tea drunk in teashops,*[20] *restaurants or even on planes.*" For this staunch defender of the national drink, infusions are a vulgar mixture of fruit, herbs and spices. Nothing in common with the plant known as "Camellia sinensis,"[21] that noble leaf that wards off[22] heart disease and even plays a role in cancer prevention.[23]

The Tea Council[24] is striking back[25] by starting up the Tea Guild,[26] handing out Michelin-style stars, helping young designers come up with the shape of the teapot to come.[27] In the workplace,[28] the traditional tea break[29] is under threat, but the City is wakening up to the *power tea,* a counter-point to the lunch of the same name.[30] Like the Queen, pop stars such as Boy George,[31] Robbie Williams or top model Kate Moss take their supply of Twining's tea on tour with them.[32]

A new website, nicecupofteaandasitdown.com, given over entirely to the delights of a cuppa and a plain biscuit[33] is a great hit with the in-crowd.

Notes

1 *A storm in a tea-cup* is a set expression equivalent to the French expression 'tempête dans un verre d'eau.' An equally acceptable headline would be ***Storm brewing over the traditional 'cuppa'*** – an opportunity to use the adjective ***traditional*** correctly for once**.** The play on words is possible thanks to the multiple uses of ***brew*** : *to brew a cup of tea, a storm is brewing* (= couver, se préparer) as well as, obviously, *a brewer brews beer in a brewery.* Check other uses in an English-English dictionary.

2 Unlike French, English does not use the conditional tense to put over this type of hearsay or reported speech, so some form of set expression has to be introduced and the sentence turned round somehow: ***Rumour has it that*** … ***It would seem that***.

3 ***legendary*** is somewhat more original than the classic and overworked ***famous;* ***traditional*** would be correct here (see usage later), and ***renowned*** is yet another possibility; even ***nice*** would be preferable to **famous* ! Later on, the French text introduces the two terms used by the British, so why not use one of them here – ***cuppa***.

4 The French text gets away with (= réussit) the play on words by using both languages, thus avoiding an obvious repetition. However the effect is lost somewhat if you simply repeat the English expression, which is why it is worth trying to find another way round it. An alternative translation ***Could it be that the legendary 'cuppa' is no longer flavour of the month in Britain ?*** provides another play on words, since herbal teas are '*flavoured*' and the expression *flavour of the month* = to be in fashion, to be in favour (= avoir la cote, 'être la coqueluche du moment' [Collins-Robert]).

5 'Les Britanniques' – obviously they are British, but which category of the British population ? By adding a term such as *tea-drinkers,* the sentence becomes much clearer. On top of that, the use of the term *tea* is still correct, since we learn that this category is abandoning traditional tea in favour of 'tisane' – which translates as *herbal tea.*

6 ***Judging by, If we are to believe*** – two more alternatives to the classic *according to.* Note that in French the conditional ('serait') is used by the speaker/writer to mark himself off from the source of the affirmation. However, in English usage, and particularly in this case, there is no doubt about the truth of the affirmation and therefore the present indicative should be used (and not ***would,* ***should*). Normally, then; it is sufficient in English to make a reference to the source by a phrase such as *according to.* In this instance, then you can run the two sentences together and say ***The British cuppa is no longer in favour with British tea-drinkers, if we are to believe the findings of a report published by Datmonitor***.

7 *Britannic* is to be used exclusively in this set expression, which figures on the inside front page of British passports, where "*Her Britannic Majesty [...] requests and requires all those whom it may concern to allow the bearer to pass freely without let or hindrance and to afford the bearer such assistance and protection as may be necessary.*" It was also the name given to a sister ship of *Titanic*, and sank after striking a German mine during WWI. More importantly, however, take note that no 'Brit' would ever pronounce this expression, which should be considered as exclusively part of 'la langue de Molière.' (Nor indeed is there any direct equivalent for 'la langue de Shakespeare'.)

8 Again, the French text offers the opportunity for you to show your mettle – i.e. that you recognise how the English language normally puts over this meaning.

9 More accurately, John Band is apparently quoted as saying "***Fruit teas were once looked down on as a drink for New Age puritans, but they have gradually acquired mainstream credibility as a healthier alternative to tea or coffee,***" (*The Telegraph*).

10 ***health-conscious, concerned about their health***

11 The singular form is preferable – regardless of how many supermarkets were visited for this study, the results were all put together to form one *analysis.* Keep the plural for situations where different people each reach their own conclusions.

12 ***skilful / clever marketing***

13 ***the trend towards ... among the general population / the population at large.*** Remember there are alternatives to the adjective *mass* (which should be avoided where possible) – *the* ***wholesale*** *move towards, the* ***widespread*** *interest in* being two of the easiest to use. See also above the use of ***mainstream***.

14 A simpler structure would be to say ***So is this the end of the ritual***.

15 ***hardly* is inappropriate in this context – it is a translation of 'à peine' and both the English and French terms contain the idea of difficulty ('peine') – e.g. *your exam paper is so poor that it is hardly worth 05/20* (= on a du mal à lui attribuer cinq sur vingt") ***simmer* means to allow to boil gently for a period of time after the liquid has reached boiling point, and is inappropriate here.

16 http://www.atsrilanka.com/tea.htm Beware here of misinterpreting the end of the sentence – the tea ritual implies that no time is wasted between the water reached the required temperature and its being poured over the tealeaves – the teapot has to be alongside the kettle at the crucial moment, otherwise the water comes off the boil and the flavour is lost.

17 i.e. concentrating on savouring the taste. A different interpretation – le thé est sacré – would lead to ***a holy silence***.

18 ***the last word in refinement***. But *"The other theory dates back to the middle ages when the gentry, or upper classes ate with only three fingers and the commoners ate with all five. To extend one's pinkie was an indication of arrogance, an inflated self-importance and was really rather rude. So despite the fact that children often play "tea party" and drink with their pinkies raised, it really isn't a considerate gesture and should be eliminated."* (http://www.seedsofknowledge.com/etiquette.html)

19 Any number of expressions are available from the archaic to the vulgar – in between these extremes you could say *Fiddlesticks!, Fiddle-faddle! Codswallop* ! but more probably simply ***What a load of rubbish*** !

20 Surely it is rather inappropriate in this context to talk of ... 'cafés' – there are *coffee-shops* and *tea-shops* (far less pretentious than 'salons de thé').

21 ***that goes under the scientific name of 'C.S.'*** *In 1959 after several centuries of botanical debate, a decision was made under the International Code of Nomenclature. The current and correct name for the tea plant is Camellia sinensis (L.) O.Kuntze. "Camellia" comes from a Moravian Jesuit named Kamel (1661-1706) who studied the plants of Asia. The epithet "sinensis" is from Linneaus and the (L.) refers to him* (http://www.darjeelingtea.net).
***so-called* suggests that the leaf has no right to be called by this name. If, for example, you say *"the so-called student, Ann Onymous, was not in class today"* the sentence implies clearly that she does not behave like a student, she claims to be a student but since she never attends class then she is simply a waster (= 'touriste'). Note that this type of expression can be dealt with by means of a compound adjective; e.g. *curiously-sounding, foreign-sounding, tongue-twisting, highly-evocative, pleasantly-named, aptly-named* (as in footnote on 'biscuit' at the end of the text).

22 ***staves off***. Several words which in French begin with a 'g' or 'gu' have an English form beginning 'w' (e.g. Guillaume / William). Here ***ward*** is close to the French 'garder' (this may explain why French people pronounce the name of the English daily newspaper as the 'gwardian') – here, then, to ***ward off*** is synonymous with to ***guard against.*** Pay particular attention to the structures you use : to ***prevent heart disease*** (i.e. a direct object) but ***provide protection against heart disease,*** while to *protect some-one from heart disease* requires a direct object (some-one) plus a postposition, and so is more difficult to introduce here.

23 *"Tea is one of the single best cancer fighters you can put in your body," according to Mitchell Gaynor, MD, director of medical oncology at the world-renowned Strong Cancer Prevention Center in New York City" & "Drinking black tea may lower the risk of heart disease because it prevents blood from clumping and forming clots. In a recent study, researchers found that while drinking black tea, the participants had lower levels of the blood protein associated with coagulation."* Better Nutrition, Jan 2002 (http://www.teamuse.com/article_030501.html).

24 www.teacouncil.co.uk Clearly, since you are addressing English speakers, there is no need to explain what the Tea Council is, as the French journalist is obliged to do.

25 The present tense is preferable here simply to make clearer the allusion to the 'Star Wars' episode *"The Empire Strikes Back"*

26 This is a far more natural structure in English than the French structure – use a simple Subject + Verb + Direct Object rather than the abstract noun and then the colon. Note the spelling of the English term *connoisseur*

27 http://www.tea.co.uk/mcot/auction.htm

28 ***in the companies* – the presence of the definite article would imply that you have previously defined (referred to) particular companies; the meaning here is broader- a generic term for where people work is required. The primary meaning of ***enterprise* is an initiative, an undertaking

29 It used to be said – and is still perhaps true today – that executives and top managers took a *coffee break* while only the lower staffs had a *tea break*.

30 "Remember the opening scene in *The Player*, where a smarmy agent played by Tim Robbins cuts a movie deal while sipping a cappuccino ? It was shot at the Ivy, otherwise known as home of the **power lunch** – and breakfast and dinner." (http://www.eonline.com/Features/Features/Robertson/ivy.html)

31 Note the distinction in usage between *like* and *such as* as translations of 'comme'.

32 Any true tea-lover will scorn ***'tea-bags'* in favour of loose tea, which use whole tea-leaves rather than the powdery dregs to be found in teabags and which adulterate the taste of the tea. Here is a good example of how a sloppy translation can put over entirely the wrong message. The 'sachets' in question must be boxes of tea.

33 Normally in English there is no need to add a translation for 'sec' – *biscuit* is sufficient. Here the reference is to a particular kind of biscuit with neither filling nor chocolate topping – precisely what is called a ***tea biscuit***, the best known make being the apty-named ***Rich Tea*** (which is not however 'low-fat').

Government to rent out computers to the poor[1]

London, 28th Oct[2] (AFP): Families in Britain[3] who cannot afford to buy a computer[4] will get the chance to rent one cheaply[5] and thus avoid[6] missing out on[7] the "knowledge revolution" and the Internet, the government declared on Thursday.

"We will pioneer a system[8] under which[9] the least well-off[10] will be able to lease computers and software in the new century,[11] the way[12] public libraries have loaned books[13] in the century just ending"[14] Chancellor Gordon Brown[15] announced at an Internet conference in London.[16]

The scheme will[17] enable up to 100,000 low-paid families[18] to get into IT[19] and onto the Internet[20] from home[21] between now and the end of 2004.[22]

The rental charge has not yet been fixed[23] but the government hopes it could be as low as[24] £5 a month ($8 or €7,5).[25]

The Opposition criticises the scheme[26] because it fudges the issue[27] of connection costs. A recent study showed that a net surfer[28] who spends one hour a day on the web[29] adds £30 to his monthly telephone bill.[30]

"There is little point in giving people[31] a cheap bit of kit[32] if they find themselves with an enormous phone bill[33] at the end of the month," Alan Duncan, Tory technology spokesman,[34] asserted.

Mr. Brown claimed[35] that the strengthening of competition in this sector, helped by government measures, would continue to bring prices down.

The Minister is counting[36] on businesses, local authorities and community associations[37] to donate second-hand computers which will be refurbished[38] and made Internet-compatible[39] with government aid.[40]

"As[41] we enter the new Millennium, we have to ensure that no-one is left out of the "IT revolution"[42] Gordon Brown declared. The Blair government[43] aims to avoid[44] "inequality in access to computers leading to inequality in life."[45]

Notes

1 ***intends to / aims to*** – ***wants to* - and even more so ***wishes to* – suggest that it is not completely within their power to achieve the aim – *want* would be more appropriate in the second last paragraph of the text: *the government* wants *businesses and local authorities to hand over old computers* ... Remember that *the poor* is invariable, as are most adjectival nouns (notable exceptions being colours: *The Blacks, the Whites* referring to ethnic communities, and *the Reds* for the communists)

2 Note the correct way of writing the date, although more and more newspapers content themselves with e.g. *28 Oct*. Under no circumstances do you write **the 28 of October*.

3 Although *the British families* is grammatically correct, there is no real justification for the definite article, since the 'definition' comes with the relative clause which follows (*who can't afford... etc*). Furthermore, in some contexts especial care must be taken with national adjectives : *British* *families* could be interpreted as referring to those who have British nationality, whereas *families in Britain* covers all residents regardless of origins.

4 Good opportunity to use the verb *afford a computer* (no need to express *to buy*): ***who do not have the financial means to buy / who do not have the wherewithal / whose finances do not allow them to buy***.

5 ***for a modest charge, at a reasonable price***

6 or ***(so as) to avoid*** – in the text above the structure implies *and will avoid*, whereas the second implies *will get to chance to avoid / will be able to avoid*. The first is more affirmative in its objectives.

7 ***avoid being left out of the knowledge revolution / avoid (letting) the revolution passing them by***. Note *miss out ON* – but *left out OF.* Note structure *avoid + -ING* See also *avoid sth leading to sth.* later in the text.

8 it is illogical to say ***we will launch* – that is precisely what he is doing with this announcement. Often governments will initiate a scheme and then, once it has *'got off the ground'* will expect it to finance itself – the term used in this instance is *'to kick-start'* (as on a motor-cycle); however it is not part of a minister's register of language.

9 ***a scheme by which the least well-off.. / a scheme whereby the least well-off... / a scheme which will enable the least well-off.*** Since the criterion will be purely and simply economic, i.e. the income level of the family, then adjectives which refer openly to a financial situation are to be preferred to ***disadvantaged or underprivileged*** which are not necessarily financial. However ***destitute* is far too strong, implying homelessness and hunger. Note the term *means-tested,* equivalent to the French notion of "critères sociaux".

10 ***poorer families, the poorer sections of the community.*** Note the use of the comparative adjective here and the superlative in the text. You can talk of *the poor* but ***the poorer / the poorest* are not used as adjectival nouns on their own, and must be accompanied by a noun phrase (here *poorer families, the poorer sections of the community, the poorest amongst us*).

11 ***A system which will allow the least well-off*** – Note structure *allow someone* not ***allow to someone.*

12 ***just as, in the same way as***

13 Known as *a lending library* (= bibliothèque de prêt). While the verbs *lend* and *loan* are to a large extent interchangeable, note that the noun form is *a loan:* e.g. *a bank loan, the painting is on loan to the Louvre from the New York Metropolitan Museum;* a *loan shark* = 'usurier'.

14 What he actually said in his statement was "*the way local libraries have loaned books in the* last *century*". However, his use of the Present Perfect here is misleading; normally you would expect the simple past ("*the way they* loaned *books in the last century*"), but Chancellor Brown is placing himself at the very end of *this* century (and so he uses the Present Perfect) but with one foot already in the new Millenium (so he talks of *last* century). Do not confuse *past & passed*: you can say *centuries have* passed *since Britain was a People's Republic, but over the* past *century democracy has thrived.*

15 Although in EU terms ('*Eurospeak*') he is the British *Minister of Finance*, here it is appropriate to give him his British title of ***Chancellor***.

16 **a conference on the Internet* would probably suggest that he was communicating via the Internet.

17 ***should / is intended to / aims to*** but not **must.* Remember that *must* is simply an encouragement to oneself *(I must get up earlier in the morning)* or a piece of advice to others *(You must learn your English irregular verbs)* and the remedy lies in the hands of the person concerned. Consequently, using *must* here is simply an expression of wishful thinking.

18 ***badly-off, poorly-off, needy***

19 *IT* = *Information Technology*. Although *informatics* appears in some dictionaries – but only since 1990 – it is not a generally accepted term (see the 'avant-propos'); **data processing* is out of date, and can only be used as a translation of "traitement des données"; *computer science* refers to the academic subject area at school and university level as does *computing.*

20 ***to gain access to computers and to surf the web***

21 Note use of preposition *from home.* ***abode* is used in set expressions – *Mr X, of no fixed abode* = 'sans domicile fixe'.

22 ***… home by the end of 2004.*** New technology now allows more and more employees to *work from home* – they are becoming *home-workers* and presumably what they do is … *homework*. The danger, however, is to spend too much time doing *housework* and not enough on *homework*!

23 ***The hire charge has not yet been decided / set.*** Note the use of the Present Perfect here. ***rent* applies particularly to land and accommodation; *rental* is appropriate for TVs, cars, and why not computers.

24 **reduce / decrease* etc. imply that a higher price has already been fixed; **until* can only be used with expressions of time, not of quantity.

25 No justification in writing **pounds/dollars* nor in placing the sign after the figure, whatever may be possible in French.

26 Note the structure: ***reproaches the government with leaving aside*** – nor is it possible to *reproach* a concept or an object, only humans can be *reproached with doing something*.

27 ***it leaves aside / it says nothing about / it fails to tackle / it fails to address / it pays scant attention to / it side-steps the issue of / it ignores the problem of***

28 ***Internet user***

29 ***who logs on for one hour a day.*** Distinguish between the uses of *during* & *for* – here ***for one hour*** is required, whereas earlier libraries *during this past century* have lent books. *For* describes the whole period (starting point and finishing point) while *during* often implies *at some point during the period* but not all the time.

30 ***sees his bill go up by £30***

31 ***What's the use of giving / It's no use giving...***

32 ***some cheap hardware / equipment***. These terms are invariable (i.e. ****equipments / hardwares / softwares* are wrong) and consequently *a few* cannot be used here since it requires a plural.

33 ***if they are going to be landed with a whopping bill***

34 ***Shadow Minister for Technology.*** Beware of ***technological questions*: it's not the questions that are technological.

35 **assure* requires a direct object *(assure somebody that…)* – ***asserted / declared / affirmed***.

36 ***is relying on***

37 **clubs* would be inappropriate here; a *club* focuses on being the centre-point for its members, whereas the emphasis for ***voluntary organisations / charities*** is on *social aid* and helping others.

38 ***upgraded, reconditioned, overhauled, given a new lease of life, updated***

39 ***Internet-ready***

40 used rather than *help* to imply ***financial assistance***. Avoid **with the help of the government* as this sounds as if Cabinet ministers themselves are actually going to roll up their sleeves, get out their screwdrivers and strip down the computers!

41 **whereas* puts over the wrong meaning here – it is used to introduce an opposition between two ideas, and can sometimes be considered as a synonym of *although*, e.g. *Whereas the EU Commission has decreed that the embargo on British beef should be lifted, the French government has decided to maintain it.* See also use in an earlier footnote.

42 IT = Information Technology (pronounced 'aie-tee'). This is what is taught in schools to make pupils *computer-literate* or *IT-literate*. Sometimes, 'Communication' is tagged on to the course, so that it becomes CIT or ICT. This challenge is often referred to as ***the digital divide*** (cf. French 'fracture'), and the sentence could be rephrased ***we have to ensure that no-one is left on the wrong side of the digital divide***. Another priority for the future is to prepare *the learning society* through investment in education and *lifelong learning.* More prosaically Gordon Brown actually said *"the computer revolution."*

43 ***Tony Blair's government*** – but you can't use both *the* and the possessive *Blair's* – it's either-or; not both.

44 *avoid* requires a structure with + ing *(avoid leading).* Here a complication arises out of the use of a quotation after *avoid*; normally the words in inverted commas should be a word-for-word quotation, so that if Brown did not use the term *'avoid'* then it is unlikely he used the –ing form. Consequently, *leading* should be presented in square brackets – [leading] – to indicate that the word is not a direct quotation. Alternatively, in order to respect the exact words Brown used, it would be possible to say *avoid creating a situation where "… leads to …"* or *avoid allowing "inequality … to lead to …"*, depending on the original expression.

45 He could have said *inequalities of job opportunities,* but the text above quotes him verbatim. Never failing to produce a memorable 'sound-bite', he also said *"Inequality in computer learning will mean inequality in earning tomorrow"*, playing on the assonance of *learning* and *earning*. The full text is available on the Treasury website – Press release 171/99 at http://www.hm-treasury.gov.uk./newsroom_and_speeches/press/1999/press_171_99.cfm.

Germany pays the unemployed to work

Government sweetener[1] *to persuade*[2] *those out of work to accept low-paid jobs.*[3]

In response to[4] the worsening unemployment figures, which are once again set to top the 4m mark this month,[5] G Schröder has come up with[6] a scheme he hopes will do miracles[7] – the Kombilohn or "combined pay" – under which any jobseeker who accepts a low-paid job at[8] less than € 900[9] a month will be subsidised.[10] For up to three years,[11] the State will take over responsibility for part of the national insurance contributions[12] that these new members of the workforce would normally pay. Thus a single person[13] can claw back[14] up to € 67 per month, plus € 77 for each dependant.[15] "*In this way workers take home a larger share of their gross earnings*"[16] Chancellor Schröder explained yesterday "*and so it's more worthwhile their accepting a job.*"[17]

The Kombilohn is a softly-softly[18] approach to tackling one of the problems that lie at the heart[19] of the German labour market, which is to persuade the unemployed to go back to work when both the generous benefits and the length of entitlement[20] afford[21] jobseekers just as high a standard of living as if they were working.[22] In the west of the country, according to the Jobcentres[23], two-thirds of those out of work are poorly-skilled[24] and/or the long-term unemployed whose only hope is a low-paid job, and who therefore don't go out of their way[25] to look for one.

However, in the view of most experts,[26] the Kombilohn, which has been tried out in many guises for a number of years in Germany, is neither new nor efficient.[27] "*A scheme where part of the aid went to employers to encourage*[28] *them to create new jobs would be preferable*" Klaus Zimmerman, head of the Berlin Economic Research Institute (DIW) suggests. "*It would also be more worthwhile bringing down the employers' contributions that weigh heavily on low-paid jobs, as the Jospin government did in France in 1997,*" Thomas Hueck, for his part, argues. "*But that wouldn't come cheap,*[29] *we're talking about between € 1bn - € 2bn. Plus the fact that*[30] *the unions, Schröder's electoral base,*[31] *are hostile to the idea, because they are afraid it might lead to the introduction of a low-paid workforce that would be with us for a long time to come.*"[32]

Notes

1 ***incentive, inducement, carrot, backhander***. If you work exceptionally well, then your employer may give you a *bonus*, extra money which you could perhaps use to pay your insurance *premium.* Here a **grant** would be the appropriate official term.

2 ***to encourage the jobless back into poorly-paid jobs.*** A direct object is required in English with *encourage / persuade /* . If you ***incite* some-one then beware – they become angry and will stir up trouble (= fomenter la révolte).

3 An individual worker – any one of us - may claim he is *badly-paid*, i.e. insufficiently, but the standard economic term is *low-paid*, which is also used as a collective adjectival noun (*the low-paid*), very roughly equivalent to the French use of "smicards" The opposite, however, is *well-paid*. ***Employment* is an abstract concept and cannot be used in the plural; a ***placement* is what a student does in a company as part of a university course of studies in order to gain practical experience of the working world.

4 When you are *faced with* a problem, you have to *face up to* the situation (or *cope with* it) by finding solutions, as here. ***Faced with*** is possible if structured correctly: e.g. ***Faced with worsening unemployment figures, Schröder has come up with..*** ***in front of* should be kept for locating items such as buildings – e.g. *the school is in front of the station.*

5 *once again* would be sufficient to put over the idea of "remontée"; remember the structure *the increase IN unemployment.*

6 Do not misinterpret the 're' in 'ressorti' as ***once again*, which is meaningless in this context. If Schröder has already tried out this scheme, then he must know whether or not it will work! True, later in the text, other commentators are of the opinion that variations on the theme have already been tried out - at regional government level (Mainz, Kassel, Magdeburg among others) - but not at federal level, not by Schröder, so he, as subject of the verb here, cannot be 'accused' of doing this ***once again.*

7 All sorts of images are possible here, provided you do not mix your metaphors (e.g. a 'weapon' cannot also be a 'drug'): ***a scheme he hopes will turn up trumps / he hopes will prove to be a panacea / He has produced a rabbit out of the hat that will hopefully put an end to the problem / he is waving a magic wand to put an end to the problem / is wielding an arm he hopes will be a way out of the difficulty / he has come up with a hoped-for wonder cure***.

8 Note the standard structure *(a job)* ***at*** *a salary of (£).*

9 Should you or should you not add an 's' to form the plural of "euro"? The problem is more easily solved if you get into the habit of using the symbol … and then wait for common usage to guide you.

10 There is a cultural gap here, since in Britain, low-paid workers are paid *weekly,* not monthly, and they do not get a *salary* but ***wages***, whence the need to avoid the use of either term.

11 This structure is sufficient to express the notion of a limited period. Grammatically speaking, there is nothing wrong with "*during a period limited to three years*" except that the connotation expressed by 'limited' is negative, whereas the Kombilohn is intended to encourage, to stimulate – a much more positive image.

12 Or quite simply ***the State will pay part of the employee's contributions.*** Although the French text uses two different terms (here and §3), in GB *National Insurance Contributions* (NICs) are paid by both employee and employer. ***social security* refers to what the state provides, i.e. the term covers all the benefits handed out by the state, including maternity, housing or sickness benefit, and even old-age pensions. Consequently, although such benefits are financed by NICs, the distinction has to be made between the two.

13 ***bachelor,* ***spinster,* ***old maid* !!! … are all unsuitable here, and are, in any case, outmoded. Very few unmarried girls "spin" wool today, waiting for Mr. Right to come along ! Moreover, these terms have the disadvantage of referring to male or female, whereas a neutral term is required here. ***unmarried* is also inappropriate in this context – the adjective in current popular usage – *single* – also happens to be the correct administrative term (e.g. *single-parent family*).

14 = recover money paid out from a source such as taxation (Oxford Dictionary).

15 ***dependent child.*** Note the difference in spelling between the noun (above in the text) and the adjective (here in the footnote).

16 ***that way their take-home pay is more*** - *take-home pay* is the generally recognised everyday term for « salaire net », i.e. after all deductions, since in GB the PAYE scheme *(Pay-As-You-Earn)* deducts income tax at source.

17 In the text above the apparently curious structure firstly makes use of a verbal noun *'accepting'* (plus a possessive adjective *'their'*) which is the subject of the verb 'is' (worthwhile); secondly *'it'* announces the inversion of subject and verb – i.e. it refers to 'accepting'. Strange to say; that structure is more naturally English than ***their accepting a job is more worthwhile* which nevertheless means exactly the same thing. More simply you could say ***it's more worth their while to accept a job***.

18 = cautious, discreet (Oxford Concise Dictionary).

19 ***one of the fundamental / deep-rooted difficulties.*** For some totally inexplicable reason, students using the structure "*one of the ...*" regularly forget to put the noun which follows in the plural (thus they write ***one of the fundamental problem*) – and this can occur up to 20 % of the time ! Note too that the French term *'problème''* can often be translated more accurately by *issue* which means an important topic for discussion rather than a major difficulty.

20 More simply, ***the length of time they can claim / they can remain on benefit.*** Alternatively, ***the high level and duration of benefits ensure them an equally good standard of living***.

21 ***guarantee.*** Although *warrant* can on occasions be synonymous with *guarantee*, its primary meaning is *to authorize* or *to justify*.

22 ***when they can live just as well for a long time (for a lengthy period) on the high state hand-outs.***

23 ***national employment agencies***

24 The generally-accepted term is *unskilled.* Not all trades require a diploma, so expressions such as *with few qualifications* are inexact, as this implies some form of academic training sanctioned by a diploma.

25 ***make little effort to find work.*** Note use of singular in English. Given current attitudes in Britain, an expression such as ***who are too lazy to get off their backsides to look for a job*** would probably be used.

26 You can't talk in English of ***a large part of people / experts* (= une grande portion de personnes!!) The expression can only be used with an uncountable noun.

27 ***effective*** – Both English adjectives are possible here: *efficient* = "productive with minimum waste" while *effective* = "having the desired effect".

28 ***induce***

29 ***that would cost a lot***. Note the set expression used above.

30 ***On top of that***

31 Certainly, the unions support Schröder :.. for the time being. But it is necessary to put the emphasis here on the political impact of the 'Kombilohn' on the federal elections due to take place a few months later (mid-2002) – i.e. disaffection, discontent, and a weakening of this electorate which is indispensable to Schröder's victory.

32 ***might lead to a long-lasting situation of a low pay sector / because they fear the long-term creation of an extensive low-wage sector***

Text Messaging : War of Words

UFC-Que Choisir, the French equivalent of *Which* magazine[1] has called for a boycott of text messaging on Sunday 9th May,[2] so much has it become a moneyspinner[3] for Orange, SFR and Bouygues.

What started out as a simple teenage fashion fad has gradually spread[4] over the past two years to all sections of society. What with reality show polls, weather forecasts and all the rest, texting[5] is growing by 35 % a year.

According to the consumers' association, the 11 billion text messages sent this year will generate a turnover of €1.4 b, and a profit of over a billion euros,[6] in other word a profit margin of over 80 %.

These text messages, whose cost to the operator is only[7] 2.21 eurocents are charged[8] on average 15 eurocents to French users[9] as against 5 eurocents to Danes.

This wide gap[10] shows just how enormously high are the profits made by the operators,[11] and not only in France.

A study from CDC-Ixis shows that the return on investment by mobile telephone operators – most of whom have paid a fortune[12] for the UMTS 3rd Generation licences – is often as high as 150 %[13].

Their profit margin ranges from 14 % for Bouygues, the fourth largest operator in Europe, to 34 % for the leading world operator Vodaphone which sells them at 18 eurocent to British callers[14].

For some time now, this gap has been raising suspicions among national watchdogs,[15] with the result that two months ago Vodaphone announced unilaterally[16] a reduction of 15 % in the cost excluding VAT as from September.

Apart from text messages, another hot potato is 'roaming' – the charge[17] the caller pays to make a call from abroad[18] – which is also well above the real cost of the connexion.

The arrival on the scene in the near future of virtual operators (MVNOs)[19] who will buy minutes in their millions[20] from the regular operators will also be to the benefit of consumers.[21]

Notes

1 This is the name of the equivalent magazine in Britain (www.which.net) It is worth remembering that when you translate into another language, certain references have to be made clear for your new audience – if they don't understand the article in French, it's unlikely they will recognize the likes of UFC or 'Que Choisir'.

2 The meaning changes according to the placing of this expression of time: either *Que Choisir* put out an announcement on Sunday (placed at the beginning of the sentence as in the French text), or called for a boycott to be held on Sunday 9th May. Aimed at private individuals who used their phone at weekends rather than corporate users of mobile phones, the latter is more likely, whence the displacement of the adverbial expression of time.

3 ***to protest against the way it has become a moneyspinner***

4 ***been spreading***

5 It has also become a verb – *text me* or even *sms me* (pronounced ess-emm-ess).

6 Should we write and say *euro* or *euros* and *cent* or *cents*? In … Eurospeak, i.e. the language spoken in Brussels, it should be the former (see for example http://europa.eu.int/comm/economy_finance/euro/faqs/spelling_en.pdf). However, taking a cue from Ireland, which is the only Eurozone country to use English as one of the national languages, then *"Elsewhere, and especially in documents intended for the general public, use the natural plural with 's' for both terms"*(http://www.evertype.com/standards/euro/todayfm.html) Naturally the British would be in favour of anything that reduces the power of the Berlaymont.

7 ***which only cost the operator / whose cost is a mere 2.21 cents***

8 ***billed***

9 If anyone quibbles about the translation of 'abonnés', then certainly owners of mobile phones use them regularly (***regular customers***) and they have signed a contract (***subscribers***) but before either of those terms perhaps simply ***customers***.

10 ***price range***

11 Note the inversion which avoids placing the unstressed verb 'are at the end of the phrase. In any case, there is a difference in structure compared to French: *how high the profits are.*

12 ***have paid a lot*** ***paid dearly* is inappropriate in this context and should be kept for non-monetary situations = in a way that involves a lot of suffering, damage, trouble etc. The Present Perfect *have paid* highlights the link between past and future – the licences have been bought, but the service is not yet in operation (at the time of writing).Note too the expression *they paid through the nose* implying that the price was excessively high.

13 ***reaches 150%***

14 ***which charges British callers 18 eurocents***

15 ***regulators*** is less colourful. With the advent of privatisation of state monopolies and free competition, Offices such as Oftel and Ofgas were set up. While the term *watchdog* is applied by journalists to these agencies, it is also applied to the Which magazine (see footnote 1) – *the consumer watchdog* – which is not an official regulator.

16 ***off its own bat***

17 ***price***

18 ***make an international call***

19 *Mobile Virtual Network Operators* 'piggy-back' on physical networks established by SFR, Bouygues or Orange to offer a new variety of services. Debitel became the first virtual operator in France.

20 Note this set use of millions with a final 's'.

21 ***will work in favour of consumers***

In London, one child in two in poverty

If Charles Dickens were alive today,[1] he would certainly find plenty to write about.[2] He would need look no further than[3] the shock findings[4] of a survey[5] handed over[6] to the Mayor of London on the eve of International Children's Rights Day, showing that 53 % of the capital's children live below the poverty threshold.[7] In other words, the wealthiest, the most affluent, the most expensive of European capitals[8] shelters in its bosom,[9] alongside its many £ sterling millionaires,[10] more than 300,000 officially "poor" children.

They are not to be found in the far-flung outskirts[11] but right in the heart of "Inner London",[12] with a population nigh on 3 million[13] and the highest per capita income in the whole of Europe.[14]

They live in the most run-down[15] parts of the boroughs[16] of Hackney, Lambeth, Southwark, or Tower Hamlets, just an Underground ride away from[17] the most upmarket parts – Chelsea or Kensington – where property prices go through the roof.[18]

What is also surprising is that, proportionally speaking,[19] child poverty hits harder in the heart of London than in any other area of the country.[20] In UK, poverty officially starts at[21] 60 % of the income of the average household – and the report handed over to the Mayor is based on the official statistics of the Department of Work & Pensions. In order to compare like with like,[22] it only takes into account income net of tax,[23] NI contributions and housing costs,[24] which vary[25] greatly from one region to the next. At 73 %, child poverty in London is greatest among the ethnic Pakistani & Bangladeshi communities. The very low national unemployment rate – just a little over 3 % – hides tremendous regional differences. Every year, 150,000 new residents settle in London.[26]

The great majority of them either have[27] an unskilled[28] job or none at all.[29] In real terms,[30] incomes of male manual workers[31] in London have risen by only 9 % in the past 10 years,[32] those of female manual workers by 12 %. Inner London, with one of the highest unemployment rates, is one of the country's "black spots".[33] Children in poverty belong to families where one or both parents are out of work.[34] And to cap it all, tuberculosis is three to eight times as common[35] in London as elsewhere in the country.[36] Which[37] would certainly come as no surprise to Dickens.[38]

Notes

1 There is no justification in English for the construction "***Charles Dickens, if he were alive today*" – there is no need for both name and pronoun.

2 ***find plenty inspiration for his literary talents / his literary muse would be inspired by a reading of the findings ... / he would find the wherewithal for new novels in the findings...***

3 ***he could quite justifiably get worked up / get angry / he would find reason to be angry if he read***. A 'literary' expression here would be: ***he could vent his ire on***.

4 Journalese, for effect – ***one of the highly unexpected / the totally unforeseen / the surprising findings in a survey...***

5 an ***investigation* is what the police conduct, an ***inquest* what the coroner conducts (to investigate an unnatural death).

6 ***submitted* implies a request for correction or approval; *presented to* is possible.

7 ***poverty line*** is also used.

8 ***the most costly capital in Europe*** – repetition of definite article merely for dramatic effect. Note too *'in Europe'* – ***the most well-off capital of Europe* implies that London is the capital city of the whole of Europe. In actual fact, recent surveys show that the cost of living in Oslo rivals with that of London, though the cost of housing in London rose a dramatic 30 % in a single year (2002) according to the mortgage bank Halifax.

9 ***accommodate* (note spelling) does not put over the right idea in this context; alongside the meaning of *providing lodgings* (which is not true here), it also expresses the idea of doing someone a service or of compromising – the adjective *accommodating* = conciliating. ***harbour* is only appropriate in contexts such as *"Saddam Hussein is accused by George Bush of harbouring terrorists"*. Where ***shelter*** has a positive connotation of providing help to those in need, *harbour* has a negative connotation of aiding and abetting criminals. However, anyone can *harbour doubts*, i.e. distrust, not believe what he has been told or has heard about a person or from that person.

10 It is tempting to use the set expression ***rubbing shoulders with*** *(the millionaires in £ sterling terms)*, but obviously the two worlds do not meet – which is precisely why ***next to* is not possible either ! Remember that *next* is a form of superlative (like *nearest*), consequently, in this context the two worlds would be too close the one to the other !! These terms all tend to imply some possibility of (physical) contact. So too can ***alongside***, but in addition this latter term suggests two facts or object running parallel; it is therefore useful for contexts where arguments are weighed up or where comparisons are made.
Note that ***sterling millionaires* would give a wrong meaning, since the adjective describes a person of worth ("valeur"), a reliable person.
Why detail *millionaires in £ sterling* – simply because, given the exchange rates, it has always been relatively easier (sic !!) to 'accumulate' a million francs, dollars or euros than a million pounds. Before the neo-liberal wave of Thatcherism, it used to be a fact that, with a few exceptions, the salary range in GB in the 1960s and 1970s was 1:6 compared to 1:12 in France. Nowadays, however, people talk of *six-figure salaries* or *telephone number salaries*. Top bosses – who earn such huge salaries – are referred to derogatively as *fat cats*.

11 ***distant / far-off / remote / outlying***. Despite what dictionaries or journalists may say, in this context, ***suburbs* is inappropriate except from the purely topographical point of view (location). The connotation of *suburbs, suburban,* and *suburbanite* is that of well-to-do middle-class families living in desirable, affluent areas with trees and gardens (*'leafy suburbs'*), where the children may well go to independent, fee-paying schools – quite the opposite of the children living in poverty – indeed the towns around London are generally known as *the stockbroker belt*. Consequently, to say that the poor children do not live in the *suburbs* is a truism. Remember too that 'banlieue' may translate as *commuter area, dormitory town* (and *commuter* for 'banlieusard'). Where French uses 'banlieue' as a euphemism – as during the recent troubles in the 'banlieues difficiles' throughout France – Britain still often refers to *inner-city problems* even though the *inner-city slums* have long disappeared and their populations rehoused in *housing schemes, overspill areas* or *council estates* (= logements sociaux), terms which now all carry this negative connotation implied in 'banlieue' e.g. *"International courier firm DHL has suspended deliveries to some of the UK's inner-city areas because of thuggish behaviour by gangs of youths."* (BBC Online 19.06.2005). In many cases, such as Glasgow, which had some of the worst housing in Europe, the inner-city slums (Glasgow Gorbals) were demolished and *high-rise flats* or *tower blocks* built in their place on the same spot (New Gorbals), so that the population did remain pretty much in the city centre.

12 ***downtown London* is a transatlantic usage, not used either in or about Britain – an Internet search via Google for the expression *'downtown London'* did come up with results … all referring to London, Ontario, Canada!

13 ***counts* is not English, *have* is required in this context – ***which has a population of 3m***.

14 ***highest income per head of population***

15 ***dilapidated***

16 Do not fall into the trap of trying to translate *'subdivisions administratives'*, when in fact it is the journalist who has had to find a term in French to express *boroughs*!

17 Note the more common expression to express such a short distance : ***a stone's throw away from***.

18 A set expression which is particularly apposite here.

19 ***in relative terms***

20 The comparative ***harder*** is required because London is being compared to all the other regions, i.e. London versus the rest of the country = a comparison between two realities. The superlative would have been possible if the sentence stopped before *than:* ***hits hardest in the heart of London***. Full stop.

21 ***is officially defined as being 60% of the average household's income***.

22 *out of a spirit of even-handedness / of fairness* would do as a translation of the French, but is far less likely than the correct economic expression given in the text. Note, however, that the expression *"to be fair"* would be misleading (= "soyons juste, rendons-lui justice, il faut quand même dire, il faut admettre"). Note also that *equity* is more commonly used in English today with the financial meaning of *shares in a company*.

23 singular in English because it is short for *income tax*, which is what is meant here. Local tax – in the form of *council tax* – could perhaps be included in *housing costs*

24 ***rent*** would also be possible here since poor families are unlikely to own their home (but see previous footnote). It is also possible to say *income after tax, NI … – contributions* are what every employee and employer pays to the state, *social security payments* (or *benefits*) are what some sections of the population receive from the state.

25 Obviously income tax and NI contributions are the same for everyone in the country – only housing is different, whence the use of the plural with ***costs***.

26 ***London welcomes 150,000 newcomers***

27 Note that the journalist here adopts the English usage of the plural verb where French normally demands an agreement with the singular 'majorité'. To***hold down a job* is inappropriate here, as it stresses the idea of *coping with the demands* and *giving satisfaction.*

28 it would be the worker, not the job, who might (or might not) be *qualified.* However, in English the terms ***skilled / unskilled*** are used to refer both to labour (workers) and to jobs.

29 ***when they have even that / when they are not out of work altogether***

30 ***After inflation***

31 *blue-collar / white-collar workers* is rather old-fashioned nowadays. Useful to recognise the term, but normally should be avoided.

32 Note that *over* can also be used here to translate 'depuis': *over the past 10 years.*

33 ***Inner London suffers from one of the highest unemployment rates of all the sub-regions in the country***.

34 ***where unemployment affects either or both parents***

35 ***prevalent***

36 ***as in the rest of the country***

37 To understand the difference between the two usages of 'ce qui', compare the usage of *which* here with that of *what* at the beginning of the previous paragraph.

38 On child poverty, see for example « New Labour's Poverty Trap » (Guardian 03.02.2003) or the report on child poverty in Britain and Germany by the Anglo-German Foundation for the Study of Industrial Society: http://www.agf.org.uk/pubs/pdfs/1278web.pdf.

Congestion charge[1]: 30 % fewer cars[2] in Central London[3]

Traffic in central London has fallen by 30 % since the congestion charge was introduced in February 2003, according to the British capital's mayor, Ken Livingstone, during his presentation of the first annual report on the introduction of the highly-controversial[4] electronic toll.[5]

The primary purpose of this charge of £ 5 per day[6] (approximately € 7.50) – to do away with the habitual London traffic jams[7] – has been met, with the incidence of snarl-ups down by 30 %.

At the same time, the number of private cars[8] entering the city centre is also down by 30 %. Even taking into account[9] an increase in the use of taxi-cabs and buses, with many commuters opting to use public transport[10], overall traffic is down by 18 %.

Going by[11] the figures presented by the Mayor of London, bus and taxi traffic has gone up by 20 % in the 20 sq. km area[12] covered by the congestion charge[13], with an extra 29,000 bus passengers during the morning rush hour[14] between 7am and 10am.

Refuting[15] the idea that the congestion charge is having[16] a negative impact on London's economy, Ken Livingstone claimed that, on the contrary, it had improved both the flow of traffic in the city centre,[17] a welcome[18] effect worth some £50m for businesses based in central London.

At £ 68m, the actual revenue generated[19] from the charge is below the £ 130m originally forecast, but Livingstone attributed this to a better-than-anticipated effect of dissuasion.[20]

On average,[21] every day some 110,000 car drivers pay[22] this charge to enter the city centre,[23] and every month 165,000 fines are handed out to dodgers.[24]

Notes

1 The terms ***tax* and *duty* should be kept for compulsory contributions to state or local authority revenue that everyone is liable to pay. They do not apply to such situations.

2 ***less* is only possible with an uncountable noun.

3 ***Inner London Congestion down by 30%***. Blood *circulates* in your veins, but not traffic on the roads. Blood ends up where it started (your heart), i.e. it goes round in a circle, but hopefully traffic moves from point A to point B. The noun expression *cars in circulation* would be interpreted as le "parc automobile" i.e. the total number of cars registered in Britain!

4 ***highly-debatable***

5 ***his presentation of the report on the first year's operation of the toll***

6 ***daily £5 charge.*** Do not confuse *daily* with ***everyday* – both may translate as 'quotidien' but the latter term carries the meaning of *ordinary, common-or-garden,* and does not refer to time.

7 ***to reduce the familiar / customary / infamous / constant snarl-ups in the city centre***. ***traditional* is inappropriate in this context, as it generally has a positive connotation – *the traditional Christmas (or Thanksgiving) turkey.*

8 ***particular cars* would mean that only specific cars were singled out to pay, not all cars.

9 It is illogical to say ***thanks to a rise [...] there is a fall* – ***despite a rise*** is the meaning.

10 Although the distinctive red London buses still remain, and the provision of services is coordinated by Transport for London (TfL), nevertheless the different routes are now run by a number of private bus operators such as Arriva, Stagecoach, London United – to name but three. This has been the case since the mid-1980s.

11 as an alternative to *according to.*

12 ***20 km^2 area.*** The banking and financial centre of London – *the City* – is also referred to as *London's square mile.*

13 ***in the designated 20 sq. mile area -*** without the need to translate the following expression, which can then be used elsewhere.

14 ***peak period***. – Using a term from the report : ***bus patronage was up by over 7% in the year to March 2004***.

15 ***Dismissing the notion*** but not ***denying the fact* which suggests that 'the fact' is true but Livingstone does not admit it.

16 ***has had***

17 ***eased the flow of traffic / allowed traffic to flow more smoothly / move more smoothly***

18 ***positive***

19 the *benefits* of this congestion charge are less pollution, less noise, fewer accidents, etc. – but that is not what is meant here. Nor is it likely that the sum of £68m is pure ***profit.* If that were the case, then Londoners would demand a reduction in the daily charge – and quite rightly so ! Besides which, the term *profit* does not appear in the report. Secondly, surely it is incoherent to use 'escompté' and 'prévu' in the same phrase – the *forecast* earnings can't be less than they were *forecast*, only the way things turn out – ***actual earnings*** – can change forecasts.

20 Beware of the faux-ami ***preview* which is most commonly found with reference to new films meaning to see in advance before anyone else.

21 ***Generally speaking, some 100,000 motorists / An average of 110,000 car users / On a typical weekday, ...*** – opportunities to vary the classic *on average.*

22 ***to acquit* = to free someone of a criminal charge; similarly *to get off* and *to be discharged* – all three are used in court contexts; ***to acquit oneself of a task / duty* = to do it well.

23 The plural form of the verb is required even if you say ***an average of 110,000 drivers [pay the charge]***.

24 ***fraudsters / non-payers / those who cheat. "The Artful Dodger"*** was the nickname of a character in "Oliver Twist" by Dickens, and it has since come to refer to anyone involved in crafty or criminal practices – cf. *fare dodger* on London Underground or *tax dodger* for income tax.

Positive Thinking Carrefour-style[1]

"Carrefour, je positive !" *This corporate byword,*[2] *adopted in 1988, sums up*[3] *for customers Carrefour's total approach to the art of retailing and the resolute commitment of all its employees*[4] *to improving our service to shoppers and anticipating new consumer trends.*[5] *Although sometimes decried by purists of the French language, this new coinage has nevertheless found its way into the dictionary.*[6]

Marcel Fournier was born in Savoy in 1914,[7] the eldest in a family of ten children, and in due time took over the Fournier family haberdashery business[8] started up five generations previously in 1822[9] in the centre of Annecy.[10] A classic example of the long-established small-time business that seems set to go on unchanging for ever and ever.[11]

However, an enterprising[12] and ambitious young man, with a family to support,[13] he was not content to sit back and let the business run itself.[14] "Nothing ventured, nothing gained"[15] – without investment no business, however well-established, could survive,[16] and thus within a mere 20 years not only did he transform the original corner shop into a major 1000m^2 department store[17], but he also opened a second shop in nearby Annemasse.

The early Fifties was a period of economic growth[18] and of post-war technological expansion[19] – man-made fabrics, plastics and consumer durables such as washing machines, fridges and television had already started making their appearance on the market, with lots of other new ideas in the offing.[20] Everything was there for the asking and retailing was ready to take off, provided consumers could afford to satisfy their newly discovered taste for luxury.[21] Modern retailing techniques – buying in bulk and selling at a discount[22] – were on their way.

This period also marks the beginning of urban sprawl, and though car ownership was as yet restricted to the few, within ten years all this was to change. Urban congestion began to make access to town centres increasingly difficult, and parking in front of a shop totally impossible, thus limiting Marcel Fournier's dreams of expansion.

One day, in the course of a business meeting,[23] Marcel aired his concerns to Louis Delforey and his son,[24] who were food wholesalers[25] in Lagnieu in the neighbouring département of Ain[26] and on 3rd June 1960, the three of them opened their first 650m^2 discount supermarket on the outskirts of Annecy,[27] with – for the first time in France[28] – parking for 70 cars,[29] in a newly-completed complex[30] that the property developer had already named 'Carrefour'.[31] It was an overnight success, and confirmed Fournier's wildest dreams.[32] It was a test of the business acumen which had guided Fournier in his venture.[33] Clearly shoppers were primarily interested in value for money and prepared to drive out of the town centre to the stores which would offer them low prices.

Elated by this first flush of success, on June 15th 1963 Carrefour, still in its infancy,[34] opened the first hypermarket in France – a supermarket with a sales surface of 2500m^2 and space for 400 cars – on a green-field site in Sainte-Geneviève-des Bois to the south of Paris.[35] Jacques Defforey, Denis's brother was put in charge of the management team.[36] At first no-one thought it would work,[37] and yet in its first year the hypermarket more than doubled its target takings.[38]

With the opening of a third store in Bassens near Chambéry, something else happened: a new phenomenon – that of customer loyalty – made its appearance:[39] satisfied shoppers would return time and time again to the same store. From then on, nothing could halt the march of progress or prevent Carrefour from going from strength to strength.[40]

When Marcel Fournier died in 1985, Carrefour was already operating 57 stores in France, 18 in Spain, 9 in Brazil and 2 in Argentina. Today, some twenty years later, there are some 179 stores in France and another 810 in 23 countries throughout the world trading under the Carrefour banner and upholding Carrefour standards.

Notes

1 ***Accentuating the Positive*** was a 1930s song (written by Johnny Mercer, sung by Bing Crosby), but, to use that same expression for a commercial slogan such as here would be outright plagiarism and infringement of copyright. Advertising agencies must be wary of anything that resembles a recognised expression – visit www.adslogans.com and their Hall of Fame.

2 Since these words already figure in an English dictionary, some mention has to be made of the French term in order to explain the end of the sentence. Note however that the English version of the www.carrefour.com website leaves the expression in French, probably since it was only ever used in France. Also acceptable are ***motto*** and ***slogan***; ***catchphrase* qualifies expressions associated with personalities (e.g. *'Tout à fait, Thierry', C'est votre dernier mot ?'*) while a politician aims at *sound-bites* – short, pithy expressions that the public will remember easily – Blair and Sarkozy are currently exponents of this art.

3 ***tends to [do]* = have a habit of doing (usually something negative); Try ***expresses C's professional approach to retailing***.

4 ***the whole employees* = les employés entiers, pas découpés. Note that the confusion in French minds between the uses of 'all' and 'whole' arises simply out of the failure to distinguish clearly the pronunciation of these terms: since the French ear makes little or no distinction, the structures becomes confused.

5 Obviously *finding solutions and anticipating needs* is possible; but it is vague and not positively 'public relations-oriented'. Tesco UK, for example, states that *"our team of over 250,000 people is committed to delivering an Every Little Helps shopping trip for our customers."*

6 ***it nevertheless figures in the dictionary.*** You *coin* a word or phrase; strictly speaking, a ***nonce word*** is a 'one-off' – used only on one occasion, but possible here since its only occurrence is in this usage by Carrefour.

7 English does not over-do the use of the historic present tense in the same way as French, and to translate the first three sentences as they stand - by present tenses and in three separate units - would be a very bad start. The simple past is called for throughout this recitation of the early stages in Carrefour's development. In any case, ***he is born* is quite simply not English. "il va succéder" would also be the opportunity to use the future-in-the-past ***Born in Savoy in 1914, he was to follow on from five generations before him***

8 In no way could it be called a **company* – simply a *family concern / family business.*

9 ***like five generations before him he took over the running of; followed in the footsteps of five generations of the Fournier family***. The verb *succeed* is followed by *to* if the complement is a title or a position (*Elizabeth succeeded to the throne in 1952*), but not if the complement is a person (*John succeeded Peter as export manager*) – this is the case here.

10 *downtown* is an Americanism, which can be used one of two ways – either we Europeans use it to refer to the business centre (center) of an American city, or an American uses it to refer to any city he/she chooses. In both cases, the city must be larger than Annecy!!

11 Often a company profile of this type will begin***: Carrefour traces its humble beginnings back to the family haberdashery in the centre of Annecy which***.. International names see in this approach the possibility of ordinary people identifying with them, and thus they become closer to their potential customers. ***The sort of small business, there since time immemorial and which will never change.*** The set expression "s'il en est" can be translated by ***if ever there was one***.

12 Beware of the faux-ami, since it only has an indirect link with the French meaning of "entreprise". This is a key word in career profiles, as it sums up ***initiative, drive, self-reliance, "oomph"*** everything that Fournier has in this paragraph, and what French calls "dynamisme". Mrs. Thatcher in the 80s introduced the *enterprise culture* – "l'esprit d'entreprendre".

13 By far the most likely explanation. Take care with spelling of *responsibilities.*

14 In other circumstances, the notion of "situations acquises" could be put over by *"not content to sit back on his laurels"* – it is not the case here, however, since Marcel Fournier had no personal achievements to his name at this stage in his career.

15 There is also the saying – inappropriate in this context – *faint heart never won fair lady* (qui n'ose rien, n'a rien) while *Who Dares Wins* is the motto of the British elite military unit, the SAS (Special Air Services), who might not look too kindly on it being used for a shopkeeper!

16 Inverted commas are used to point out the classic proverb. Closer to the original French: ***He had (family) responsibilities and ambition plus an awareness that by risking nothing he risked losing everything; he would get nowhere unless he took a gamble***.

17 In order of size *retail outlets* can take the names of *corner shop – department store – supermarket – superstore* (which is the closest Britain gets to the "hypermarché").

18 ***The early Fifties witnessed economic growth and the development of new technologies***

19 Note the correct spelling of *techniques* – which however is inappropriate here.

20 = *about to appear on the scene* – to translate "en attendant mieux" which under NO circumstances should be translated literally!! – ***with plenty more to come / and there were plenty more innovations to come***.

21 ***All that was needed was for consumers to be able to afford their new-found taste for luxury***. English does refer to *material comforts*, but the term remains somewhat abstract. In any case, this context is definitely referring to luxury items suddenly becoming accessible to everyone. In GB, this period is known as *the affluent society*. The 1950s mark *"the early stages of a consumer boom that brought the biggest improvement in the material standard of living in Britain since the Middle Ages."* (J.Obelkevich in *Understanding Post-war British Society*, Routledge). Prime Minister Macmillan is remembered for having told the British people during the 1959 election campaign *"You've never had it so good"*, though he claimed never to have pronounced those words. *Affluence* refers more to the behaviour associated with spending power than to the actual size of a bank balance (cf. *une clientèle aux appétits de confort tout nouveaux*).

22 ***Stack 'em high, sell 'em cheap*** – to use the byword of retailing in the Seventies. ***distribution* is only part of the ***retailing*** chain: be they corner shops or superstores, they are all ***retailers,*** i.e. they sell directly to the final consumer. ***mass marketing* is totally inappropriate – to begin with the term is out-of-date and derogatory, especially when addressing customers themselves; prefer ***bulk buying and volume sales.*** The meaning here of "grande consommation" is items that everyone buys, i.e. ***everyday items, ordinary goods, basic necessities***. **staple* is less likely here.

23 What on earth is a ***professional meeting*? Can you have an *"amateur meeting"*? Beware too of the spelling!

24 Although certain dictionaries suggest ***he opened his heart* the expression is inappropriate unless the context concerns matters of the heart, personal feelings, hopes, fears or guilt. Here it would be sufficient to say ***he shared his concern with Louis Defforey*** (*his concern* does not mean the same as *he shared THIS concern with LD = partager*) or even more simply ***he talked of …*** Pay attention to the order of the phrases to avoid misinterpretations such as ***the problem he was having with Louis Defforey* = the problem Defforey was causing him.

25 The term allows several interpretations, but in fact, several sources define the Defforeys as 'grossistes'. See, for example *"Hyper, ton univers impitoyable…"* by Paul Vaca & Paul Boulant, éditions Alternatives, 1994 or Papa Waly Diabong, Université du Littoral: « à la tête du comptoir Badin et Defforey qui approvisionne plus de 500 détaillants ruraux ».

26 ***next door in the county of Ain*** – most English county names end in *-shire* meaning 'sheriffdom' (= the jurisdiction of the sheriff) so it is only possible when talking of British place-names. In the USA, e.g. *Wells County* is the preferred structure, but again it hardly sounds right with French place-names. There is a strong case therefore for keeping the French term.

27 The text does not say this in so many words, but logically it would not be in the centre of town.

28 ***an innovation / a first / a novelty in France***

29 Note ***parking*** here has a semi-verbal function and is not to be confused with the French noun usage: ***with parking space for 70 cars; with a car park for 70 cars; with a 70-place car park, with room for 70 cars*** (but not ***a 70-room car park*!!).

30 it is somewhat illogical to state that ***the store opened its doors in a building still being built*. What is meant is that building had already started – Carrefour did not have it built. The sentence is rephrased to put equal emphasis on the chance choice of the name 'Carrefour' (which obviously must be kept in French – it would be ridiculous to rename it 'Crossroads'!)

31 Why on earth would a property developer ***nickname* a building? It is necessary to avoid terms such as ***block of flats* (which is residential) or ***office block* (inappropriate). Nor is it yet a ***shopping centre.*

32 Note too the opposite notion of *confirmed* (or *went beyond) his worst fears*.

33 ***business acumen*** = "son don pour les affaires, l'acuité." *venture* has a connotation of daring and calculated risk, as in *venture capital*, which refers to the money investors are willing to risk in buying shares in new companies.

34 ***in its early stages of growth, formative stages, first phase of development***

35 Note the structure ***TO*** the south of..; ***a green-field site*** sounds more suitable to the context than *in the middle of nowhere* (which is where you are when you are lost!)

36 ***was given managerial responsibility***

37 ***Everyone thought it was sheer madness / Folk thought they were as mad as a hatter***

38 ***its forecasts***

39 Beware of any term which suggests a strong emotion; customers do not feel *affectionate* in their dealings with a shop – loyalty is quite sufficient; shops often hand out *loyalty cards* ("cartes de fidélité"). Incidentally only a ghost makes an *apparition*, and *fans* frequent pop concerts and football stadiums, not supermlarkets!!

40 Surely "société" here refers back to "la jeune société Carrefour" rather than to the general notion of the *onward march of society*.

Barbour, the all-weather classic[1]

The streets of our towns have recently been invaded by bottle-green silhouettes. Schoolboys from well-to-do families, businessmen and men-about-town[2] now sport in all weathers the same rain-proof outdoor wear with its recognisable dull sheen[3] – the Barbour jacket.[4] A singular success[5] for an item of clothing which is the by-word of conservatism.[6]

It couldn't be anything but English[7] – from the North-East to be precise, where exactly a century ago; John Barbour, a small-time tailor[8] from Newcastle had the ingenious idea of cutting clothes for his farming customers out of oiled sailcloth.[9]

Then in 1930,[10] having thrived[11] on this one item, he replaced it with an Egyptian cotton, dyed sage green.[12] A number of styles were then designed for hunting, shooting and fishing[13] and even for the pioneers of motorcycling, who all wanted[14] a totally weatherproof[15] jacket. The Solway Zipper – the first outdoor zipped jacket – dates from this period and is still available to this day in the catalogue.[16]

Until the end of the 60s, Barbour, whose main office[17] and workshop[18] are located[19] in South Shields was known only in Britain, and even then only to members of the upper-classes[20] who would never have thought of going "shootin' or fishin'"[21] without their Spey Wading Jacket[22] or their Gamefair. The company, which supplied the Royal Household, thus obtained official recognition as *"Suppliers to Her Majesty the Queen, the Duke of Edinburgh and the Prince of Wales"*[23], and within the space of a few years, the jacket was to be seen everywhere on the streets of London.[24]

At the end of the 1980s, with the environmentally-correct *"back to basics"*[25] fashion for hard-wearing,[26] functional, sturdy clothing, the first Barbour jackets imported onto the Continent were a big hit in Italy, Germany and then in France, despite their upmarket, Sloane Ranger image.[27]

Established in 1989, the French side of the business[28] saw sales soar sevenfold within a mere four years to total sixty thousand units by 1993.[29] Barbour France, with a workforce today of 18, had a turnover of € 9m last financial year,[30] a fifth of which[31] with other items such as hats, shirts and wellington boots.[32] Oddly enough, the Beaufort, at present the world's best-selling model[33] was designed some fifteen years ago with French hunters in mind.[34] Its game pocket is much appreciated for its practicality by schoolboys.

Nowadays, Barbour & Sons exports two thirds of its production[35] and has twice won the annual Queen's Award for Export.[36] But everything is still produced in one of five workshops. Each model, made up from some thirty to forty pieces of cloth, requires fifteen thousand stitches. This manufacturing technique and the wax dressing[37] that has to be applied regularly – and whose composition is kept a closely-guarded secret – guarantee these jackets will stay totally waterproof even under the heaviest showers.[38]

Regular waxing[39] – just as for a good pair of shoes – is the only way to keep the material supple[40] – an instruction booklet and a tin of wax dressing are supplied free of charge to the customer.[41] Nevertheless, Barbour undertakes in its workshops re-proofing or re-styling, and if need be repairing, as the customer requires. One in ten of the 700 firm's employees work[42] in this after-sales department *"It has become one of our sales arguments, but we have to keep on explaining it to our retailers, who are afraid they'll only ever see their customers for repairs,[43] whereas, in reality, these customers provide living proof of the sturdiness of our jackets, which sell on average for under € 300"* the head of Barbour France explains. But fame has its drawbacks.[44] Barbour has become a household name[45] and imitations abound. But Margaret Barbour, who manages this small family firm, is adamant.[46] No-one other than Barbour has the right to use the firm's triple crown trademark.[47] In the last three months alone,[48] the French subsidiary took out 47 court actions against retailers selling[49] common-or-garden oilskin as the genuine, century-old article.

Notes

1 Although *all-time* and *all-purpose* could perhaps be used to refer to Barbour jackets, *all-weather* is what is meant here. Note that the definite article is not used in English in this structure – you can talk of *a Barbour*, but more often than not the name is used simply as an adjective followed by 'jacket' or another such term.

2 ***dandies*** – though old-fashioned, this term has the advantage of being shorter than ***well-dressed / stylishly-dressed / fashionable men-about-town***, which are all totally acceptable. Since this is not the main focus of the sentence, the choice is open.

3 Unlike the French term, the English equivalent, *raincoat,* doesn't fit into the context of all weathers. A ***mackintosh* is totally inappropriate, since it refers to a quite different article – Charles Mackintosh (1760-1843) invented *rubberized* cloth. Nor is a Barbour a *coat* – it is a *jacket*; thus a more general term is required here. *Sheen* is better than ***shine* – silk has a sheen.

4 This French use of the colon is very 'un-English'. Note how in English texts it becomes a dash ("tiret"), or is totally avoided by rephrasing.

5 ***Somewhat surprising / This comes as something of a surprise for an item of clothing...***

6 ***which is the hall-mark of good taste; which stands for everything conventional.*** Here the French meaning is closer to that of "BCBG" than of age-old habits, given that Barbour jackets were only introduced some twenty years ago. See note below on Sloane Rangers/ Home counties. In fact Barbour & Sons claim to be *"synonymous with the best of country living"* – which is not incompatible.

7 While ferries may be *cross-channel,* the term seems inappropriate to simply refer to England. Note *overseas* corresponds to "outremer": ***It couldn't come from anywhere else than from England. From the North-East***.

8 **modest* in English is a personal characteristic synonymous with *diffident / bashful / unassuming*. A **small* tailor would refer to his height. A ***little-known*** tailor is possible, while obviously ***a humble tailor*** would be excellent in this context (cf. *from these humble origins* in many company profiles).

9 ***waxed canvas originally intended for making sails.*** Do NOT confuse *cloth* (plural *cloths*) and *clothes* !!

10 *It was not until1930* suggests on the part of the writer a reproachful regret, i.e. it should have been done sooner.

11 ***prospered*** or ***his business having prospered, having made his name with this single item***

12 The verbs ***tint*, ***tinge* and ***shade* & the noun ***hue* all put over the idea of a slight colouring only, insufficient here. Colours are often problematical and cannot always be translated word for word. When they can as in *bottle green* (above) or *moss green, apple green,* this is fortunate, but as a general principle, attention must be given, and it cannot be assumed that everyone interprets colours in the same manner. Remember that fashion too plays a determining role in naming certain tones and shades; here the precise nuance is unimportant, as there is no commercial intention, but try to put over an accurate idea in tune with the product; *forest green* might also have been appropriate, but in actual fact the company uses the terms ***sage green*** & ***olive green***. See www.barbour.com.

13 **fishermen* refers to professionals – *deep-sea fishermen, inshore fishermen*, while ***anglers*** are sportsmen who fish with a rod ("pêche à la ligne"). Yet, the terms *fly fishing* and *fly fishermen* ("pêche à la mouche") do exist. At the same time, however, there is no single term for "chasseurs" – *hunting & huntsman* in the British context imply fox-hunting, and is more or less restricted to the south of England, while *shooting* refers to all forms of small game, but is more especially evocative of *grouse-shooting* in the Scottish Highlands. Fox-hunting is done on horseback, and *huntsmen* wear special scarlet coats (*hunting pink*), consequently the Barbour was not designed for them.

14 ***needed / required*** but less probably *demanded, called for*.

15 ***waterproof*** obviously, but the term chosen introduces a wider meaning – for example to protect motorcyclists from the wind. There is no single term in English for 'étanche' : all depends on what has to be kept out; *dustproof, leakproof, airtight, lightproof, light-sealed*, etc. Barbour jackets are also *stain-repellent* and *thornproof* ('résiste aux épines', ne s'y accrochent pas).

16 ***can still be found in the Barbour catalogue***. *Still .+. to this day* is a tautology (i.e. a repetition of the same idea), but it is a common one. Distinguish between the uses of *still* and *always*.

17 For such a small firm, it sounds strange to talk of *headquarters* – it is the only site. ***Registered offices* is perhaps appropriate for headed notepaper, but unlikely in this type of text.

18 ***factory,* with connotations of mass production and dirt and grime, is totally inappropriate for a hand-crafted item such as a Barbour jacket; for similar reasons ***manufacturing unit* and ***production plant* are also to be rejected. ***Settled* cannot be used with this meaning, while ***set up* stresses the initial creation; ***established* suggests a permanence – a final location – which is not suggested here by the text . The possessive *whose (workshop)* is far more elegant and effective in such contexts than ***of which.* A similar use is to be found later in the text.

19 **settled* is on the Blacklist!

20 More likely than **aristocracy* which sounds .... French or at least "foreign". Note also the structure *was only known TO some-one.*

21 This transcription reproduces the supposed pronunciation by upper-crust people, omitting the final "-ng" sound.

22 The river Spey in the North-East of Scotland, although best known for its whisky distilleries (Speyside), is also renowned for salmon fishing.

23 As can be seen on the packaging of any brand item thus distinguished. Alternatively ***Purveyors to...*** The expression is preceded by "*By Appointment*". The actual phrase used in the case of Barbour is *"By Appointment to Her Majesty the Queen, Manufacturers of waterproof and protective clothing"*.

24 The use in the opening paragraph of the passive voice *streets have been invaded* is acceptable, but the active usage ***the garment invaded the streets* conjures up animated cartoon images of empty jackets running through the streets – an *inanimate* object such as a jacket cannot actively *do* anything.

25 This was originally the Conservative government's slogan under John Major in the 1990s – meaning something totally different – but the expression has stuck and become part of everyday English.

26 ***tough, durable, long-lasting*** are possible alternatives, but insist on time alone rather than on the rough treatment that clothes sometimes undergo.

27 The expression cannot be more precise! A 1980s catchphrase referring to *"the stereotype of a young person from an upper middle-class family, especially from the Home Counties (country areas of the south of England). Sloane Rangers wear designer clothes and spend a lot of time in fashionable places such as Chelsea. People joke about them driving Range Rovers, wearing Barbour jackets and green wellies" (wellington boots – source: Longman Dict. Of English Language & Culture).*

28 ***subsidiary, branch, offshoot.*** The term *established* suggests solidity and permanency, in keeping with the image of Barbour; *spun off* implies transforming one part of an existing company into a separate unit, which is the case here.

29 What do you understand by ***distributed*? From the company's point of view, a jacket is "*sold*" as soon as it leaves the retail outlet. It is highly doubtful that they would hand them over free! This is a classic Blacklist error.

30 ***realise* is also a classic 'Blacklist' error (= se rendre compte). The financial year in Britain runs from April to end March. Company figures, financial and other, indicated in this exercise have deliberately been changed.

31 Note the structure of the expression and especially of the figure – *le* cinquième but English sees only *one* of a total of five fifths. See also next paragraph *two-thirds.*

32 probably *green wellies*! (gumboots) – see note on Sloane Rangers. If hats and not caps, then they are likely to be *deerstalkers*, i.e. the type of hat usually associated with Sherlock Holmes, but which – as the name implies – was used when stalking deer. Collectively, such items are known as ***accessories.***

33 Although the meaning of this adjective is immediately recognisable (cf. *best-seller)*, note that it may on occasions correspond to the French use of "numéro 1 / premier". A newspaper may be *the most-widely read by businessmen / the biggest circulation paper in Wales*, etc. – English makes use of a wide variety of such expressions to put over the classification of a product.

34 ***at the request of* is unlikely; ***to answer a demand among French hunters, to respond to the needs/requirements of French hunters.*** A participant in a shooting party is known as *a gun* or *a leading shot* if he/she is very accurate.

35 *exports* includes the idea of *abroad.*

36 As this award is not necessarily limited to a single company, an expression such as *was given the top exporter award* would also do.

37 The proprietary name given by Barbour is *Sylkoil.*

38 *rain-proof;* beware of a coat that is merely *shower-proof(ed)* – it will not stand up to the British climate. Note also the term *re-proofing* in footnote below. A totally different use of *proof* comes with the measurement of alcoholic spirit (= titrage en alcool). Most commercial spirits, such as whisky, gin etc., are 70° proof (40%), whereas duty-free liquor is often *over-proof* (43%). This calculation used to be based on the effect of setting alight a mixture of the spirits to be tested plus gunpowder – if it exploded, there was too much alcohol; if the degree of dilution of the spirits allowed the gunpowder to burn without exploding, it was acceptable; obviously if the spirits had been diluted too much, then the powder would not burn at all. Finally, note yet a further use of the term – *living proof* – later in the text.

39 ***upkeep;*** – but you *look after* your clothes.

40 ***is the only way to prevent /avoid the material cracking as it dries out***

41 "With regular maintenance a Barbour waxed jacket should give you many years of wear. A 'Care and After Sales Booklet' can be found in the right hand pocket of all jackets. Reproofing waxed jackets will increase the garment's lifespan and ensure it retains its waterproof qualities Before returning it to us, please ensure that no articles remain in the pockets, with particular care taken to remove potentially hazardous items such as fishing hooks or cartridges, as well as organic or intoxicating substances" (www.barbour.com).

42 Curiously either the singular or the plural (*works / work)* would be acceptable in everyday English, as 10 % means that in all 70 people (a plural number) are involved in this aspect of the firm's activity.

43 Beware of *come-back* – Customers may *come back* for repairs, but the noun *comeback* is to be avoided = "recours" (to have no comeback – n'avoir aucun recours); = "répercussions" Indeed retailers would be afraid of a comeback from customers!

44 ***there is a price to be paid for success.***

45 ***generic* = (of goods, esp. a drug) having no brand name; not protected by a registered trade mark (Concise Oxford Dictionary) – consequently, by definition, the term is inappropriate here, since the text goes on to say that everything is done to protect the name. A ***household name*** or ***household word*** = a familiar name or saying, including terms that were originally brand names, e.g. to hoover the carpet, a pyrex dish, un frigidaire.

46 she ***takes a firm line; she is implacable***.

47 Not quite exact! To be honest, Barbour has simply adopted as a trademark the three Royal Appointment insignia (see earlier footnote), and it is this that appears on the inside label of its jackets – but only since 1987. The original trademark for almost three-quarters of a century was the beacon at the entrance to South Shields harbour at the mouth of the River Tyne.

48 Keep *quarter* for financial statements, including household bills, and term for academic contexts. Elsewhere count the number of months; *'une mensualité'* becomes a *monthly / weekly / quarterly instalment* depending on the frequency.

49 ***passing off*** – to use the legal term for this type of fraud. ***vulgar* is more commonly synonymous with coarse ('grossier, ordurier').

The Smoking Habit

Teenagers have taken to smoking again.[1] A survey carried out[2] in April involving some one thousand 12-18-year-olds[3] for[4] the French Department of Social Security[5] shows that 35 % of 12-18 year olds light up,[6] at least from time to time. This figure represents a rise of 4.5 % over the previous survey[7] and is only just below that of adults,[8] of whom 36 % smoke.[9]

Despite this relapse, the overall trend has been downwards since 1987,[10] when almost half of all teenagers smoked. Other figures, moreover, confirm that smoking is less popular with youngsters than it used to be.[11] The number of regular smokers, defined as smoking at least one cigarette a day,[12] is also falling: down from 77.5 % of all young smokers last year to 74 % this year.

Youngsters start smoking later,[13] up from $12\frac{1}{2}$ years of age fourteen years ago to $14\frac{1}{2}$ today. Finally more and more young smokers want to stop smoking.[14] A little over half of them say so,[15] and almost two-thirds claim[16] to have made at least one attempt at giving it up,[17] for reasons of health in 81% of cases, kicking the habit[18] for 62 % of them and the cost of cigarettes[19] for 48 %.

And yet, at the same time, the smoker is less and less socially accepted.[20] Two thirds of the teenage respondents[21] saw the smoker as being essentially of a *"depressive"* nature,[22] while the non-smoker was perceived by three-quarters of respondents as *"full of life,"*[23] by 44 % as *"outward-looking"*,[24] and by 39 % as *"nice to know"*[25].

If this is so, how do teenagers come to take up smoking in the first place?[26] Peer group emulation,[27] obviously, but also influenced by their parents.[28] 45 % of youngsters both of whose parents smoke are themselves smokers, as against 31% of those neither of whose parents smokes.[29] Just how strict parents are about smoking plays a determining role:[30] of youngsters whose parents forbid smoking only 18 % smoke, while 90 % of those whose parents tolerate it do so.[31]

Whatever the influence of their milieu,[32] the incidence of teenage smoking increases[33] with age – as does the number of cigarettes smoked.[34] The daily intake of regular smokers goes up from 2.2 cigarettes a day amongst the 12-13 year-olds to 8.9 among the 16-17 year olds, and 10.7 for young 18-year-old adults.

The results from two other studies among GPs and hospital staffs show that 34 % of family doctors[35] smoke, although 88 % of them feel it their duty to discourage smoking,[36] and 84 % claim they systematically warn parents against the consequences of their smoking for their children's health.[37] As for hospital staffs, although they recognise they should set a good example to patients,[38] only 37 % of them see active discouragement of smoking as part of their duties.[39]

Notes

1 ***Young people have taken up smoking again, have started smoking again***. Remember throughout this text that *youth* is ambiguous in English – without a determiner (definite / indefinite article, etc), it refers to "LA jeunesse" in general, whereas *a youth, two youths* restricts the meaning to "jeune homme", usually in contexts of criminality. Consequently, in this text, reference should be to ***youngsters, young smokers, young people,*** (and even ***young girls*** since more girls smoke nowadays than boys).

2 ***realise* = se rendre compte. *A* ***survey / poll / study*** is ***carried out / conducted / undertaken***, as are *experiments* and *research* (no definite article).

3 ***amongst nearly a thousand youngsters aged 12-18.*** ***by* = the teenagers carried out the survey; ***near* means they were in the neighbourhood, but is otherwise meaningless. The survey covers those above and below the legal age of 16, otherwise it would have been possible to use the adjective *under-age (smokers)*.

4 ***on behalf of; commissioned by, at the request of***

5 Remember that *Social Security* in English terminology refers principally to unemployment benefits, etc. Until the end of the 80s, the *DHSS – Department of Health & Social Security* – combined the activities of two ministries today. In this context, it is quite clearly the *Youth Department of the Ministry of Health* which ordered the enquiry. However, there is a convention that when referring to an administration in another European Union member country, a simple translation of the nomenclature is acceptable. Thus, here *Social Security* can be accepted as correct, as would be *Ministry / Department of Health*.

6 the ***butt* is the un-smoked bit of the cigarette you throw away, while *cancer stick* and *nail in your coffin* (coffin nail) are humorous social comments that are also inappropriate in this context. A *fag* is the most easily-recognised familiar term for cigarette, but, as shown above, there is no absolute need for a noun.

7 ***compared to the previous survey.*** Note throughout the text, the various structures used to express relationships between figures and to express ages.

8 *hardly* is used in contexts to express the speaker's regret that this is the case, e.g. *I hardly had enough time to finish my translation before the end of the exam*. Here you could say this figure ***is only slightly lower than that of adults at 36 %; slightly below the 36 % of adults who smoke***. Alternatively, rephrase and talk of ***adult smokers.*** A neologism in English is *a tad* = a little, thus ***just a tad below that of adult smokers***.

9 ***who are 36 % to smoke* is a classic mistranslation of this structure: *We are 36* can ONLY refer to age; *there are 36 of us in this room* translates "nous sommes 36 ici".

10 ***there has been a (steady) downward trend.*** In Stock Market jargon, the terms *bear market* (and *bearish*) & *bull market* (and *bullish*) translate respectively 'orienté à la baisse' ou 'à la hausse'.

11 ***teenagers are less tempted to smoke than they used to be***.

12 Firstly, beware of ***consummate* which has an entirely different meaning. Then, English does not use *consume, consumer* and *consumption* as often as French uses 'consommer' and its derivatives, quite simply because the English terms do not cover the same broad notion : here *to consume cigarettes* suggests that youngsters eat, chew and swallow them! When it comes to the quantity, English would quite simply say *she gets through a packet and a half a week.*

13 ***The average age at which youngsters start smoking has gone up; youngsters nowadays are on average older when they taste their first cigarette***. A classic example of the need to first of all ask yourself what the sentence means, and then express it as simply as possible in English, otherwise.

14 ***wish they could stop smoking* implies that they want to, but realise that smoking is habit-forming and that they are unable to give it up – cp. *I wish I could but I can't*. Note (perhaps for your own personal use), the terms *casual smoker*, i.e. some-one who smokes from time to time but can stop whenever he wishes, and *social smoker* meaning someone who simply enjoys

a cigarette on a social occasion, at a party or with friends in the pub. Pay attention to the structure of the sentence – 'de plus en plus souvent' has to refer to the number of people in this situation (= *more and more smokers*), not to the repetition of their wish *(**wish more and more often*).

15 Note the plural of the verb *say*. Similarly ***a little over half of them ARE in this situation***. Although the figure in French is considered as singular, English sees a multitude of youngsters behind the concept *"half"*. In such cases, decide whether the noun to which the fraction (half, two-thirds) refers is countable or uncountable – i.e. can take a plural form or not: e.g. *half the sugar WAS poured into the mixture, two-thirds of our business COMES from overseas orders; a quarter of 18-25 year-olds ARE unemployed.*

16 *claim* indicates that the speaker does not associate himself with the affirmation – here the speaker is simply reporting what respondents in the enquiry told him. Thus *claim* has a wider range of uses than "revendiquer" by which it is often translated.

17 *one attempt at stopping smoking* is grammatically correct but difficult to say and it sounds funny; therefore either drop *smoking* from the phrase or use *kicking the habit / giving it up.*

18 Note the spelling of *dependENCY* – ***the fear of dependency*** – they are not yet ***addicted to cigarettes* ; before addiction, you can talk of *being hooked on the habit.*

19 Not ***tobacco* unless you are suggesting that they *chew tobacco*, or *roll their own (cigarettes).*

20 ***and yet, more and more, smoking gets a bad press; the social image of the smoker is getting worse***. ***degrading* is inappropriate in this context: *the image of women in washing powder adverts or car manufacturers' brochures is degrading.*

21 ***two-thirds of those questioned / interviewed / polled.*** Only the police ***interrogate* (suspects). A person who takes part in an (opinion) poll is a *respondent*.

22 ***melancholic*** refers to a person's nature; *dull* = uninteresting in social situations, while *unhappy* is merely a temporary state of mind.

23 ***lively; full of energy, full of zest; a go-ahead sort of person / a get-up-and-go character / an enterprising type***; but some-one who is *"a live-wire"* is more "fêtard" than anything else.

24 ***outgoing; sociable;*** **extrovert* is perhaps too strong, tending towards *a show-off* (= "vantard"). The opposites would be *shy, retiring*. *Strong-willed* could just be the meaning here, i.e. resisting the temptation to follow the others and smoke.

25 ***friendly, likeable, easy to get on with*** – what in English one simply calls ... *"nice"!* ***sympathetic* is a faux-ami and means showing kindness to some-one who has suffered a misfortune.

26 ***how come [teenagers start smoking ?]* belongs to informal spoken English only, and should be avoided in written styles.

27 ***peer pressure.*** A *peer group* is a circle of people of similar age, social status, educational background, etc. The term means "equal" and gives the French term "au pair". The *peers of the realm* (= pairs du royaume) were precisely that – a group of equals.

28 ***by copying their parents / by modelling themselves on their parents / Through the influence of their parents / through their parents' influence***. – **under the influence* tends to be limited to negative contexts suggesting a *bad influence* and loss of control, such as the charge of *driving while under the influence of alcohol.* Several set expressions describe the similarity from one generation to another: *Like father, like son; a chip off the old block; to follow in father's / mother's footsteps.*

29 Note particularly the structure ***both of whose parents / neither of whose*** used to translate "dont les parents". Note also the plural with *both* but singular with *neither.* It is not possible to use ***none,* which only applies to more than two. Also possible to say ***whose parents are both smokers*** – (but not ***whose both parents)* ***...from a non-smoking family background.*** Note also the faux-ami : in English if you are *adept at* something, you are an expert.

30 ***the extent to which parents condone the habit; the degree to which they are for or against smoking;*** ***repressive* is inappropriate in the context – the adjective usually employed to describe the attitude of parents is ***strict*** , e.g. *a strict upbringing.*

31 Remember the classic faux-ami : *to dispose of* is synonymous with *to get rid of.*

32 ***their background***. If you add a verb, then note the structure requires the verb to come at the end – *whatever the influence of their background may be / is.*

33 ***becomes more pronounced with age.*** *******nicotinism* is a medical term, referring to nicotine poisoning rather than simply smoking. Note how the verb *"increases"* refers to both parts of the sentence and is taken up by *"does"*; if you say ***The nicotine habit grows as they get older..*** it is impossible to say that *the number of cigarettes* ***"grows"* – ***and the same is true of the number of cigarettes lit up.*** In this context, ***from 16 years old* is not possible – the expression is not an adjective referring to a person, but an expression of time, a starting-point for the data, as in, for example, *from 1999 onwards, the Euro will come into use.*

34 ***amount* is used for uncountable nouns; ***quantity*** is also possible with countable nouns.

35 A ***General Practitioner*** (GP) is more often than not referred to as a *family doctor*, since the British system of registration – being on a doctor's *list* or *panel* – implies that a patient consults the same doctor every time (the notion of "médecin traitant"). There is no direct access to specialists, you must be referred to a hospital consultant by your GP, who arranges an appointment for you. This means long waiting-lists, although the theory is that the GP screens – i.e. filters – cases, and only those which merit the attention of a specialist take up his time.

36 ***feel duty-bound to discourage...*** It is hardly possible for a doctor to **deter* a patient from smoking, since the term implies a threat and fear. The *nuclear deterrent* is a threat to a potential aggressor, and the fear of cancer may *deter* you or *put you off* smoking. A doctor can however ***dissuade*** you ***from*** smoking (i.e. *persuade* you *not* to smoke – a direct object [you] is required). ***Prevent* as a verb is impossible in this context, while the noun *prevention* is ambiguous - the primary meaning in general English is similar to that of the verb, i.e. to (physically) force some-one not to do something, and only the adjective carries the French sense of "prévenir" – *preventive medicine.* Compare 'prevention routière' = *Road Safety Campaign.*

37 Note the *danger /impact/ consequences FOR* or *ON their children ('s health).* This effect on non-smokers is known as ***passive smoking***. Note too the use of the possessive to avoid all ambiguity; without "*their*" the sentence could mean more simply that doctors tell parents not to let their children smoke. *Expectant mothers* are also warned of the risks for *their unborn child.* However, there is no justification for the use of the possessive ***tobacco's risks* – before using the structure "-'s" to translate "de", always ask yourself the question as to whether the two elements are linked by an idea of ownership.

38 ***show a good example to patients; their behaviour in front of patients must be exemplary***

39 ***part of their function/role***

4

Grilles vierges

Texte 1 La Route Payante	
1	
2	
3	
4	
5	
6	
7	
8	
9	
10	
11	
12	
13	
14	
15	
16	
17	
18	
19	
20	

Texte 2 M & S	
1	
2	
3	
4	
5	
6	
7	
8	
9	
10	
11	
12	
13	
14	
15	
16	
17	
18	
19	
20	
21	
22	
23	
24	
25	

Texte 3 BNP	
1	
2	
3	
4	
5	
6	
7	
8	
9	
10	
11	
12	
13	
14	
15	
16	
17	
18	
19	
20	

Texte 4 Méthode Blair	
1	
2	
3	
4	
5	
6	
7	
8	
9	
10	
11	
12	
13	
14	
15	
16	
17	
18	
19	
20	
21	
22	
23	
24	
25	
26	
27	
28	
29	
30	

Texte 5 Chat Gras Garnier	
1	
2	
3	
4	
5	
6	
7	
8	
9	
10	
11	
12	
13	
14	
15	
16	
17	
18	
19	
20	
21	
22	
23	
24	
25	

Texte 6 Apache	
1	
2	
3	
4	
5	
6	
7	
8	
9	
10	
11	
12	
13	
14	
15	
16	
17	
18	
19	
20	
21	
22	
23	
24	
25	
26	
27	
28	
29	
30	

Texte 7 Prime de maternité	
1	
2	
3	
4	
5	
6	
7	
8	
9	
10	
11	
12	
13	
14	
15	
16	
17	
18	
19	
20	
21	
22	
23	
24	
25	
26	
27	
28	
29	
30	

Texte 8 Universités	
1	
2	
3	
4	
5	
6	
7	
8	
9	
10	
11	
12	
13	
14	
15	
16	
17	
18	
19	
20	
21	
22	
23	
24	
25	
26	
27	
28	
29	
30	

Texte 9 Polluant mais indispensable	
1	
2	
3	
4	
5	
6	
7	
8	
9	
10	
11	
12	
13	
14	
15	
16	
17	
18	
19	
20	

Texte 10 Abeilles chercheuses	
1	
2	
3	
4	
5	
6	
7	
8	
9	
10	
11	
12	
13	
14	
15	
16	
17	
18	
19	
20	

Texte 11 Oui pour la vie	
1	
2	
3	
4	
5	
6	
7	
8	
9	
10	
11	
12	
13	
14	
15	
16	
17	
18	
19	
20	

Texte 12 Foot en danger	
1	
2	
3	
4	
5	
6	
7	
8	
9	
10	
11	
12	
13	
14	
15	
16	
17	
18	
19	
20	
21	
22	
23	
24	
25	

Texte 13 La City	
1	
2	
3	
4	
5	
6	
7	
8	
9	
10	
11	
12	
13	
14	
15	
16	
17	
18	
19	
20	

Texte 14 Seniors créateurs	
1	
2	
3	
4	
5	
6	
7	
8	
9	
10	
11	
12	
13	
14	
15	
16	
17	
18	
19	
20	
21	
22	
23	
24	
25	

Texte 15 Réforme retraites	
1	
2	
3	
4	
5	
6	
7	
8	
9	
10	
11	
12	
13	
14	
15	
16	
17	
18	
19	
20	
21	
22	
23	
24	
25	
26	
27	
28	
29	
30	

Texte 16 La « cup of tea »	
1	
2	
3	
4	
5	
6	
7	
8	
9	
10	
11	
12	
13	
14	
15	
16	
17	
18	
19	
20	
21	
22	
23	
24	
25	

Texte 17 PC pour Pauvres	
1	
2	
3	
4	
5	
6	
7	
8	
9	
10	
11	
12	
13	
14	
15	
16	
17	
18	
19	
20	
21	
22	
23	
24	
25	
26	
27	
28	
29	
30	

Texte 18 Le Kombilohn	
1	
2	
3	
4	
5	
6	
7	
8	
9	
10	
11	
12	
13	
14	
15	
16	
17	
18	
19	
20	

Texte 19 Les SMS	
1	
2	
3	
4	
5	
6	
7	
8	
9	
10	
11	
12	
13	
14	
15	
16	
17	
18	
19	
20	
21	
22	
23	
24	
25	

Texte 20 Enfants Pauvres	
1	
2	
3	
4	
5	
6	
7	
8	
9	
10	
11	
12	
13	
14	
15	
16	
17	
18	
19	
20	

Texte 21 Taxe d'embouteillage	
1	
2	
3	
4	
5	
6	
7	
8	
9	
10	
11	
12	
13	
14	
15	
16	
17	
18	
19	
20	

Texte 22 Carrefour	
1	
2	
3	
4	
5	
6	
7	
8	
9	
10	
11	
12	
13	
14	
15	
16	
17	
18	
19	
20	
21	
22	
23	
24	
25	
26	
27	
28	
29	
30	

Texte 23 Barbour	
1	
2	
3	
4	
5	
6	
7	
8	
9	
10	
11	
12	
13	
14	
15	
16	
17	
18	
19	
20	
21	
22	
23	
24	
25	
26	
27	
28	
29	
30	
31	
32	
33	
34	
35	
36	
37	
38	
39	
40	
41	
42	
43	
44	
45	

Texte 24 Les jeunes et le tabac	
1	
2	
3	
4	
5	
6	
7	
8	
9	
10	
11	
12	
13	
14	
15	
16	
17	
18	
19	
20	
21	
22	
23	
24	
25	

Achevé d'imprimer sur les presses de l'Imprimerie BARNÉOUD
B.P. 44 - 53960 BONCHAMP-LÈS-LAVAL
Dépôt légal : juillet 2006 - N° d'imprimeur : 606098
Imprimé en France